ENGLISH MONKS
AND THE SUPPRESSION
OF THE MONASTERIES

Geoffrey Baskerville, M.A., F.R.Hist.S., was born in 1870, the son of Colonel J. Baskerville of Crowsley Park, Oxfordshire. He was educated in the Royal Navy and at Christchurch, Oxford. Geoffrey Baskerville died in 1944.

ENGLISH MONKS AND THE SUPPRESSION OF THE MONASTERIES

Geoffrey Baskerville

PHOENIX
PRESS

5 UPPER SAINT MARTIN'S LANE
LONDON
WC2H 9EA

A PHOENIX PRESS PAPERBACK

First published in Great Britain
by Jonathan Cape in 1937
This paperback edition published in 2002
by Phoenix Press,
a division of The Orion Publishing Group Ltd,
Orion House, 5 Upper St Martin's Lane,
London WC2H 9EA

A CIP catalogue record for this book is
available from the British Library.

Printed and bound in Great Britain by
Clays Ltd, St Ives plc

ISBN 1 84212 588 5

CONTENTS

PREFACE

THE four hundredth anniversary of the suppression of the English monasteries would seem a fit occasion on which to attempt a summary of the latest views on a thorny subject. This book cannot be expected to please everybody, and it makes no attempt to conciliate those who prefer sentiment to truth, or who allow their reading of historical events to be distorted by present-day controversies, whether ecclesiastical or political. In that respect it tries to live up to the dictum of Samuel Butler that 'he excels most who hits the golden mean most exactly in the middle'. It is based throughout on the contemporary documents which are described in the introduction or in the footnotes. My obligations to many writers are recorded in these. I should wish further to proffer my warmest thanks to the Reverend Doctor Salter for his kindness in reading the manuscript of the book and for much helpful advice and criticism, and to Professor Hamilton Thompson for his courtesy in lending me his transcript of those visitations of the diocese of Lincoln which are so far unprinted.

G. BASKERVILLE

Crowsley Park
Henley-on-Thames
July 1936

INTRODUCTION

Nihil bene quod non jucunde

THE period which beheld the disappearance of the religious houses in England can be described in many ways and from many points of view. It can be represented as an age of martyrs: of martyrs incinerated by conservatives in a panic, or of martyrs disembowelled by radicals in a hurry. We could stand in the market place at Carmarthen and look at an aged Augustinian prior consuming slowly away in the midst of flames 'holding up his poor stumps till a merciful bystander with a staff dashed him on the head and struck him down'. We could go to Newgate prison to see a learned Cistercian monk being degraded from his orders, follow him to Gloucester and, after watching him burning in the morning, sit down to a sumptuous lunch with the high sheriff and all the 'county people'. Or we could go to Smithfield to see one friar after another put to a like death. But the story of the sufferings of Doctor Ferrar, Doctor Hooper, Doctor Cardmaker, and other former religious of their way of thinking is best read in that old and tried book, *Foxe's Book of Martyrs*.

Again, we might accompany the Duke of Norfolk and all that counted for most in London society to Tyburn, there to see conservative martyrs hanged, cut down alive, and disembowelled. But the history of the Carthusian victims of state policy is best studied in Maurice Chauncy's *Historia Aliquot Nostri Saeculi Martyrum*, or in one or other of the numerous modern works which have been inspired by it. In days when there were no gangster films to cater for the taste of the public, burnings and disembowellings must

9

certainly have been welcome to persons who craved for excitement. Doubtless the pillory, with its constant succession of tradesmen who had overcharged, or given short weight, palled after a time, and one would tire of seeing the light ladies being dipped in the Thames. It might have been exciting to go to Paul's Cross in Queen Mary's time, along with the Lord Mayor and Sheriffs, to gaze at former monks with sheets about them, and tapers in their hands, doing penance for the crime of committing matrimony; or to see a clergyman's wife go through the city in a cart and to hurl at her decayed vegetables and rotten eggs, or even household utensils of a formidable and unseemly kind. Even to see a general servant boiled alive for poisoning her mistress would not be so exciting as the doings at the stake or the scaffold. And always after 'commotion times' one could go to London Bridge to see the heads and quarters set up and guess the names of their former owners. But we must leave the accounts of these proceedings to the city annalists, to Wriothesley, to Machyn, and to Stow.

The period might be described from the point of view of the exiles. We could follow the former religious who had imbibed new ideas to Germany or to Switzerland and listen to 'the poor sheep of Christ dispersed abroad' quarrelling about rites and ceremonies. We could hear a Carmelite[1] bawling in Frankfort that the latest book of Common Prayer was but the leavings of popish dregs, devised, in John Knox's plain words, for upholding of massing priests and all the trash of the pope's sinful service: or a Franciscan[2] objecting from Strasbourg that 'the goodly order set forth and received in England stood with God's word'. The details of these dreary controversies may be found by

---

[1] John Bale.   [2] Guy Eton.

those who are interested in them, in William Whitting-
ham's *Brief Discourse of the Troubles at Frankfort*. Or again
we could follow conservative exiles to Flanders or Spain or
Italy, watch the Carthusians reconstitute their order, or
study the quarrels between the pro-English and pro-
Spanish factions, bitter as those which were to be waged
between the Jesuits and the secular clergy at the time of the
'Wisbech Stirs'.

The careers of these martyrs and exiles have filled too
many pages, not only of the works of professional martyr-
ologists, but of those of sober historians. Since, however,
the whole number of martyrs and exiles, conservatives
and radicals, which the monasteries provided scarcely
amounted to one per cent of the former religious, it is
surely time that some notice was taken of the fate of the
ninety-nine per cent — the exact proportion of just persons
to lost sheep — who were neither martyrs nor exiles.

This book, then, is to be the story of those of the former
monks who were not willing to sacrifice their heads or
their bowels, or to risk the loss of their property, for the sake
of 'keeping of opinion'.

The history of the suppression in England has often been
treated as if it could be explained wholly from without the
religious houses themselves. Instead of giving us a picture
of the internal condition of the monasteries, many controversialists lash themselves to fury over defects of character
in Henry VIII and his officials, just as others explain
the continental reformation as if its only importance consisted in the bad language which was habitually used by
Martin Luther.

The faults of the King are plain enough. All his contemporaries and in particular the foreign ambassadors at

his court (of whom he had generally got the best) agree that he was covetous, mean, fickle, suspicious, and, above all, ungrateful. Sir Walter Raleigh, in his *History of the World*, has well summed up the last trait of Henry's character: 'To how many gave he abundant flowers from whence to gather honey and in the end of harvest burnt them in the hive.' Thomas Wolsey, Archbishop of York and Cardinal; Thomas Cromwell, Earl of Essex; Thomas Howard, Duke of Norfolk — had ever a king three such faithful servants? Yet one perished on the scaffold, and of the other two, one was, perhaps, only saved from a like fate by his own death and the other by that of the King. But was he really the 'tiger and ramping lion raging and roaring after blood' that Archdeacon Harpsfield pictured him? or even the 'picture and pattern of a merciless prince' that Raleigh described? Contrast these outbursts with what contemporary conservatives said of him. Sir Thomas Wriothesley may have had his tongue in his cheek when he told the Duchess of Milan that his King is 'a most gentle gentleman, his nature so benign and pleasant that I think till this day no man heard many angry words from his mouth'. But Bishop Gardiner was almost as fervent in admiration, as his letters written just after Henry's death show. The owners of the gift of bonhomie can do a great deal that those who do not possess that dangerous quality cannot, and if Henry was *faux bonhomme*, so much the worse for those who served him. But it is sad that this great King should be judged solely by his matrimonial misfortunes and on this account to be made a figure of fun for the benefit of film fans. Did he not, as he said himself, have a set of ill-conditioned wives? If Anne Boleyn *would* carry on with an organist and Katharine Howard with a piano-tuner (for so I suppose the player on the virginals was), and if Anne of Cleves was repulsively ugly and Katharine of Aragon battered and dingy, was that Henry's fault? And was he not more respectable with his consecutive plurality of wives than King Francis with his concurrent plurality of mistresses? And who followed more obediently St. Paul's advice 'It is better to marry than to burn', he or his daughter Mary?[1] His most faithful wife, as Lord Herbert truly said, was his parliament, and on its significant obedience he could always rely.

And if the King has been misrepresented, so have his agents; in particular Thomas Cromwell, and his chief assistants in the royal visitation of the monasteries in 1535 and subsequently, down to the final surrenders of 1539 and 1540. A sketch of the characters of these gentlemen will be essayed when we come to discuss the events which led up to the suppression. That they had their failings is obvious, but it is ridiculous to assert that they were the unsavoury persons they have been represented. They were zealous servants of the Crown in the same measure that inland revenue officers are now. Everybody grumbles at the inquisitiveness of these persons. Some of them may be ruder than others, just as Doctor Leigh had worse manners than Doctor ap Rice. That the reputation of Cromwell's agents has come to grief is chiefly due to the fact that it is difficult nowadays to understand the great part which the form of propaganda known as denigration played in the middle ages. They had numerous precedents for their reports, furnished by all classes, from pope and bishops down to household servants. The object of the government was nationalization, and if poison gas could most easily secure it why not use it?

The position can be best understood if we could visualize

---

[1] Who was originally responsible for this quip I cannot remember.

modern governments employing the same methods. A left wing government, with a capital levy in view, might appoint a commission to inquire, not only into the financial assets, but also into the morals, of the merchant princes and princesses of this country. One would be indeed optimistic in supposing that a commission of this kind, after picking up gossip from commercial rivals, disgruntled clerks, stenographers, and the like, could not submit a report to the government which would enable it to embody in a finance Act a clause to the effect that 'the possessions of such wealthy men now being spent, spoiled and wasted for increase and maintenance of sin, should be used and converted to better uses and the unthrifty commercial persons so spending the same to be compelled to reform their lives. The state therefore is authorized to have the possessions of all and singular persons which are above the clear annual value of £2000'. In like manner, a fascist government might make inquiries of the habits and customs of the potentates of trade unions and co-operative societies, and seize their possessions under colour of the report. But in neither case would the state's real object be moral reform, but financial gain.

This book does not attempt to deal with the monastic system in general. Those who want to learn about its splendid ideals and achievements must go to the admirable work of Abbot Butler[1] and those who would see how sadly in the course of centuries the religious fell short of those ideals, must read the works of Doctor Coulton and his disciples. The course of the Pilgrimage of Grace is only treated here cursorily. Those who would have further details must go, if they like partisan histories, to the glittering rhetoric of Froude's *History of England* or to the

[1] *Benedictine Monachism* (1919).

tear-stained pages of Cardinal Gasquet's *Henry the Eighth and the English Monasteries*. And if they would prefer a sober account they would do well to study carefully *The Pilgrimage of Grace 1536-7 and the Exeter Conspiracy 1538* by the Misses M. and R. Dodds (1915). The book does not profess to deal with the arrangement of the monastic buildings or with the rules of the different orders. For the former may be recommended Doctor D. H. S. Cranage's *Home of the Monk*, and for the latter, Doctor J. W. Clark's Introduction to *The Observances in use at the Augustinian Priory at Barnwell, Cambridgeshire*, which, though primarily an account of the rules of the Augustinian canons, may be said to apply in very great measure to all the religious, except the friars.

Neither does the book profess to cover all the history of the English monasteries. I have tried to confine the material to the period of fifty years or so which preceded the dissolution, only in special cases going further back. For this purpose I have used three main sources. First, that great collection, the *Calendar of the Letters and Papers of Henry the Eighth* (quoted as *L.P.*). Secondly, the only two complete sets of episcopal visitations which have come down to us — those of Norwich — printed by Doctor Jessopp,[1] and those of Lincoln, which are in print for the period 1420-1449.[2] So far as the episcopates of Bishops Atwater (1514-1521) and Longland (1521-1547) are concerned, the records are still in manuscript (quoted as *Norwich* and *Lincoln Visitations* respectively), and thirdly, to the *Letters relating to the Suppression of the Monasteries* printed by Thomas Wright[3] (quoted as Wright, *Suppression*). For earlier instances I have often used the articles (strangely mixed in quality) on the

[1] *Camden Society*, New Series, vol. XLIII (1888).
[2] *Lincoln Record Society*, vols. VII, XIV, XXI.
[3] *Camden Society*, vol. XXVI (1843).

religious houses in the different volumes of the *Victoria County History* (quoted as *V.C.H.*).

One of the difficulties of sixteenth-century history concerns the use of words and phrases which lend themselves to distortion, or to employment as ecclesiastical and political catchwords, and these I have, so far as is possible, tried to avoid. Take the expression 'the old religion' for example: does it mean that of the Jews, of the Druids, or of the early Christians? It is surely better to apply the term 'reformers' to Cardinal Pole and his colleagues on the commission, known as the '*Concilium de emendanda Ecclesia*'[1], than to the iconoclasts whom Doctor Samuel Johnson called 'the ruffians of reformation', such as John Foxe and John Knox. I have, therefore, chosen to confine myself to terms like conservative, applied to those who wished on the whole to retain the ecclesiastical *status quo*, and whose shade might vary from very pale blue, like that of the Duke of Norfolk and Bishop Gardiner, to ultramarine like that of Pole: and radical, or innovating, for those who wished for changes great or small, and whose colour ranged from pale pink to scarlet. Between these shades was a prevailing kind of grey, and it is with persons clothed in habits of that uninteresting colour that this book is mainly concerned. How did the suppression affect individual monks and canons, nuns and friars? and what happened to them when their houses were dissolved? This is the theme of the last chapter but one.

[1] *See below*, p. 289.

ENGLISH MONKS

and the

SUPPRESSION OF THE MONASTERIES

CHAPTER I

MONASTIC DUTIES AND ACTIVITIES

I

WHAT was the chief value of the monasteries to the ordinary person? It is St. Paul who suggests the answer, when he bids his Roman disciples to continue 'instant in prayer; distributing to the necessity of saints; given to hospitality'.[1] Prayers, hospitality, alms, were the duties which the medieval monasteries were bound by law to perform. How far at the time of their fall were they carrying out their legal obligations? That these obligations were legal is sufficiently illustrated by the terms of the Statute of Carlisle of 1307. The King and nobles of the realm had founded religious houses in which 'sick and feeble men might be maintained, hospitality, almsgiving and other charitable deeds might be done, and that in them prayers might be said for the souls of the said founders and their heirs'.

There can be no doubt that of the three main duties of the religious houses the prayers counted first with the ordinary layman. When the last of the monasteries were giving themselves up one after another in 1539 a Lincoln-shire correspondent of Cromwell wrote that he thought 'the abbeys are now nothing pitied, the commons perceiving more conveniences to grow from their suppression. *Saving that they lose their prayers*'.[2] A monastery was like a cathedral

---

[1] Romans XII, 12-13   [2] *L.P.*, XIV (1), 295

(I transpose the writer's words) 'a great chantry foundation in which intercession for the dead never relaxed, coupled with prayers for the good estate of the living whose names were inscribed on the books of the church'.[1] 'The offering of the prayers of the brethren,' wrote the abbot and monks of the Cistercian abbey of Roche to the prior and monks of the Carthusian priory of Axholme, 'is the sole return we can make for the kindness shown to us by your house.'[2] Prayers, first for founders and benefactors, then for all christian souls: these were the most important duties of the religious, for were they not the condition on which they held their lands? What is stated of the Augustinian priory of Michelham in Sussex that 'it is held by the service of finding thirteen canons to celebrate for the soul of the founder'[3] is true of all the monasteries.

It was because they were not fulfilling their feudal obligations in this respect that apostate monks were sought for by the police (as one would say to-day), and numerous indeed were the Chancery warrants issued by the Crown on the application of abbots for the arrest of one or more of their runaway brethren. 'Warrant to the Sheriff to arrest an apostate and vagabond monk (or canon) and deliver him to his abbot for punishment', as the phrase went, meant that the apostate was risking the welfare of the founder's soul. Other persons besides the founders could purchase the benefit of their prayers. The monks of Combe, a Cistercian abbey in Warwickshire, got from a neighbouring squire £30[4] to rebuild the cloister and glaze its windows in return for a yearly obit for himself and his wife. It was important to keep the monasteries at their full numbers, though in practice this was not often

---

[1] A. Hamilton Thompson, *The Cathedral Churches of England*, p. 195.
[2] *L.P.*, v, 226.   [3] *V.C.H. Sussex*, II, 78.
[4] Perhaps £900 nowadays. *V.C.H. Warwickshire*, II, 74.

achieved. 'I have,' wrote the Earl of Essex to Cromwell in 1532, 'two children at my own cost in the house of the canons of Bylegh of which I am founder and someone has come from King's College, Cambridge, with a placard to take them from me. I want a placard to keep them still, or the services of God cannot be maintained.'[1] The Earl was, of course, having the children educated to become canons who should devote themselves to the welfare of his soul and of those of his ancestors. When the suppression of the monasteries was at hand solicitude for the welfare of their ancestors' memory fought in the bosoms of great personages against a desire to benefit financially by the change. Some compromised with their conscience and shifted their ancestors' tombs, as the Duke of Norfolk shifted his from Thetford priory to Framlingham parish church. 'Will you,' wrote Lord Lisle's agent to his master, 'have my Lady Lisle removed from Titchfield abbey to the parish church of Titchfield?' It is to be feared that the religious did not always fulfil all their obligations towards souls. The abbess and convent of Barking, for example, once passed a resolution to the effect that anniversaries of abbesses who had died over one hundred years ago should be discontinued.[2] Surely unfair treatment for those ladies. Again, the system of rotation by which only a proportion of the religious were present at divine service seems difficult to reconcile with their obligations to founders and benefactors.[3] When Abbess Bulkeley, of Godstow, wrote in 1538 to Cromwell, 'Be assured there is neither Pope, purgatory, images nor pilgrimage, nor praying to dead saints used amongst us',[4] while at the same time protesting

---

[1] *L.P.*, v, 803.   [2] Dugdale, *Monasticon*, 1, 442.
[3] Complaints about this practice are very numerous in the Episcopal Visitations of the Lincoln diocese.
[4] *L.P.*, XIII (2), 911.

against the suppression of the house against her and her sisters' wills, she was unwittingly giving away most of her case, and the campaign undertaken by the government against the doctrine of purgatory was, as has been often pointed out, aimed directly at the religious houses. In the well-known words of Bishop Latimer 'the founding of monasteries argueth purgatory to be, so the putting down of them argueth it not to be'.

Before we go on to the next most important duty of the monasteries, that of hospitality, it may be well to touch on an aspect which has some relation to it, as well as to prayers. Nearly every monastery was in great or small measure a resort of pilgrims. 'And every one that hath forsaken houses, or brethren, or sisters, or father, or mother, or wife, or children, or lands for my sake, shall receive an hundred-fold, and shall inherit eternal life.' Such was the text which was quoted to authorize the practice, and all over England men and women resorted to famous shrines in the hope of curing spiritual or bodily ills. It was not only famous tombs like that of St. Thomas at Canterbury, images like that of our Lady of Walsingham, or objects of devotion like the Holy Blood of Hayles which attracted pilgrims. 'I live,' wrote Latimer in 1533, 'within half a mile of the Fossway and you would wonder to see how they come by flocks out of the west country to many images, but chiefly to the blood of Hayles.' There were, too, great crucifixes, like those of Bermondsey, or of Meaux, to which women came 'more out of curiosity than devotion' as the chronicler of that Cistercian house admits, or Boxley near Maidstone — 'so holy a place where so many miracles are showed' as Archbishop Warham told Wolsey. And what psychological reasons were there against them, even if the image did contain 'certain engines and old wires with old rotten sticks at the back of the same which caused the eyes to wink?' In nearly every monastery were girdles of our Lady, of St. Mary Magdalene, or of St. Bernard, to be worn by expectant mothers. Some set up as general practitioners, others as specialists. Repton Priory had a bell of St. Guthlac which cured diseases of the head, Bury St. Edmunds a skull of St. Petronilla which got rid of fevers, Arden an image of St. Bride which recovered lost, or healed sick, cows.

A great many popular, but not formally canonized, saints were also in vogue. There were pilgrimages to Simon de Montfort's foot at Alnwick Abbey, to St. Richard (Scrope) at Hampole Priory, to Thomas of Lancaster's felt hat at Pontefract, to Edward the Second (of all people in the world) at Gloucester Abbey. Quite apart from their advantages in the spheres of devotion and the healing arts, pilgrimages had great value in widening the minds of those who engaged in them; they stimulated trade and (to use a modern expression) served to keep down the local rates. When the great shrine of St. Thomas of Canterbury was put down, the licensed victuallers of the city were hard put to it to make a living. 'Please,' wrote John Hales, one of the barons of the Exchequer, to Cromwell, 'allow the city of Canterbury to have a mill, of late belonging to St. Austin's Abbey. A great part of their yearly charges used to be paid by victuallers and innholders, who made their gain out of the pilgrims which heretofore came to the said city, but do not now continue. It is like that they will not be able to pay their yearly charges without this grant.'[1] A statement which is borne out by a letter of the Mayor of Coventry to Cromwell, which shows incidentally what a huge amount of drinking accompanied the Corpus Christi

[1] *L.P.*, XIII (2), 1142, under date December 20th, 1538.

day pageants in that city.[1] Nobody can read the *Canterbury Tales* and remain under the delusion that pilgrims wanted to travel in discomfort, and if anybody can discover a shred of evidence that a single pilgrim ever made his journey to Canterbury by the so-called Pilgrims' Way along the Kentish Downs he would deserve a reward. Why should pilgrims choose a long disused prehistoric trackway, when they could go along the main roads and stay at the best hotels?[2]

The offerings of the pilgrims at the shrines which they visited naturally formed some part of the monastic income, but except, perhaps, at Walsingham, they had declined very much before the great attack on wonder-working images was opened by Cromwell, aided by Bishop Latimer, in 1538.[3] The motives of the opponents of images were not the same. To Cromwell the gold and jewels which adorned them were the chief object, to Latimer the superstition which accompanied devotion to many of them was the stumbling block. It is probable that educated opinion was on the Bishop's side. Sir Thomas Wriothesley, a conservative in religion, could talk about 'rotten bones called relics' and report that Bishop Gardiner (a vehement conservative also) 'did not dislike the doings at Canterbury'. The fact that they boggled at some of the objects of popular devotion can scarcely be wondered at. The evidence of the Prior of Cardigan about the taper which burned in that house without being consumed, and that of Doctor Price about

---

[1] *L.P.*, XIV (1), 77.
[2] Since these lines were written I have read the late Mr. C. G. Crump's article 'The Pilgrim's Way', in *History*, vol. XXI, No. 81 (June, 1936). Mr. Crump's exposure of the legend is complete and devastating. He shows how a simple conjecture on the part of a somewhat naive nineteenth-century antiquarian has been developed by one romantic writer into a historical fact, and by another into ecclesiastical propaganda.
[3] Savine, *English Monasteries*, p. 103.
[4] *L.P.*, XIII (2), 442. The 'doings' were the destruction of St. Thomas's shrine.

the image of Darvell Gatheren, which was of such power that it could stop Welshmen from going to hell,[1] are sufficient proof of this.

There was no society for the protection of ancient images in those days, and many perished all over the country. Even St. Uncumber with her beard was ejected from St. Paul's Cathedral, and could no longer receive pecks of oats to induce her to rid women of their husbands. But she was suffered to remain in Westminster Abbey, where she may still be seen, beard and all. Her image at the abbey, being almost un-get-at-able, had not attracted the attention of devotees, so it was saved, together with the relics of the Confessor, who was spared, presumably, because he was a king.

II

It is now time to leave the next world and to return to this. The second main duty which was laid in the middle ages on the clergy, both regular and secular, was that of hospitality. What precisely the word means it is very difficult to say. A questionnaire[2] which Archbishop Parker sent to the bishops in 1561 contains this item in respect of the beneficed (but not of the unbeneficed) clergy: 'Is he hospitable?' When Cromwell's agents made a visitation of Wales in 1536 they seem to have 'detected' many of the clergy of incontinence and to have made a general clearance of the female housekeepers of parsonages. The clergy of the diocese of Bangor wrote to protest and to ask 'that some way may be found for us that we may maintain such poor hospitality as we have done hitherto by the provision of such women as we have customarily kept in our houses,

[1] Wright, *Suppression,* pp. 190, 191.
[2] The answers to which are now in the library of Corpus Christi College, Cambridge.

for if we must put them away according to the late injunctions we must give up hospitality to the utter undoing of such servants and families as we daily keep, to the great loss of the poor people who are by us relieved. We shall be driven to seek our living at alehouses and taverns, for we have no mansions on our benefices. No gentlemen or substantial honest men will lodge us in their houses for fear of inconvenience and knowing our frailty, and they begin to refuse us our accustomed tithes and duties.'[1] Both parsonages and monasteries were looked upon as inns or boarding houses. 'The [Dominican] Friars here,' wrote Sir William Fitzwilliam to Cromwell from Guildford, 'is but a little house and will be sorely pestered at the King's being here. I recommend you to lodge at the parsonage of St. Nicholas, which is near the court.'[2]

Naturally travellers preferred staying at monasteries to facing the horrors of a medieval inn where, as a friar, expounding the King's title of supreme head in Glastonbury Abbey in 1536, said, 'men's conversation was only swearing and talking bawdry'.[3] The cooking and accommodation in monasteries were far superior to those that could be got in inns, the bread was whiter, the beer of better quality, the feather beds in the guest chambers softer, the sanitary arrangements far in advance of the time. It was as important to monasteries to attract wealthy and influential guests as it is to hotel companies to-day. The demeanour of the head porter of an hotel is of considerable importance to the welfare or otherwise of the establishment. So with monasteries. The porter at Croyland gave the house a bad name with travellers because of his rudeness to them, 'often when pilgrims come to the monastery and ask the way to Walsingham he laughs

<hr>

[1] *L.P.*, x, 215.   [2] *L.P.*, XII (2), 415.   [3] *L.P.*, x, 318.

at them and directs them wrongly out of sheer malice'.[1] Again, just as a good manager makes or mars the fortune of a modern hotel so did the cellarer or sub-cellarer make or mar the fortunes of a monastery, and only those religious who were 'temperate in their answers, courteous to strangers, and of polished manners' were appointed to those offices. Rich patrons would naturally refuse to patronize or recommend a place where they had suffered from discourtesy. In the last days of the great abbey of Evesham the convent, after asking the King to turn it into an educational establishment, proceeded to urge that as there were few inns in the town the abbey is able to receive and lodge noblemen resorting thither.[2] The great guest halls, situated either above the western side of the cloister or as separate buildings, must have been the scenes of great gaiety. The gentry who were lodging in monastic houses were not going to spend dull evenings if they could help it, and it was up to the monks to provide them with entertainment; just as hotels and restaurants nowadays furnish cabaret shows to amuse their guests, so did the monks provide theatrical companies, minstrels and comedians. In Finchale Priory there was a 'players' chamber', in which actors were lodged or entertainments given. The accounts of many houses show how much money was spent in hiring troupes of mimes to entertain guests.[3] A great comedian must have been a windfall for an abbey. 'I have espied,' wrote one of Cromwell's agents, 'a young fool at Croyland, much more pleasant than ever Sexten[4] was; not past fifteen, who is every day new to the hearer. Though I am made of such heavy matter that I have small delecta-

[1] At the Bishop of Lincoln's visitation of 1518. Atwater MSS., fol. 47.
[2] *L.P.*, XIII (2), 866.
[3] See *L.P.*, VIII, 865, for the large amount the small priory of Dunmow spent on players.
[4] Sexten was the King's chief fool.

tion in fools he is the best I have heard. He is very fit for the court and will afford the King much pleasure. Do send for him to the Abbot of Croyland'.[1]

Although the accommodation provided was ostensibly free, there can be no doubt that an equivalent was looked for and that the monks expected to gain rather than lose by the transaction. 'We thought,' wrote Jocelin of Brakeland, 'that the King (John) came to make offering of some great matter, but all he offered was one silken cloth, which his servants had borrowed from our sacrist, and to this day have not paid for. He availed himself of the hospitality of St. Edmund, which was attended with enormous expense, and upon his departure bestowed nothing at all either of honour or profit upon the saint, save thirteen pence sterling, which he offered at mass on the day of his departure.' That was not the kind of guest that was wanted.

The constant influx of a heterogeneous crowd of lay persons must have had a sadly disintegrating effect on the religious life. For if the buffoons had access to the guest-house was there not a danger that they would invade the refectory? Indeed, episcopal injunctions show that they sometimes did. It must remain a moot point whether the guests were or were not useful to the religious. In view of the fact that during the last century before the suppression many houses were following the example of Glastonbury and St. Albans in building inns for travellers, the probabilities are that the burden of hospitality was getting too irksome. Nevertheless, it remained a legal obligation on the monasteries to the end, and not only on them but on their successors. Under the Act of 1536 grantees of monastic buildings were obliged to keep 'an honest continual house and household in the same site or precinct'.

[1] *L.P.*, x, 181.

Thus a great many of the domestic buildings of religious houses were preserved and adapted to secular uses. After the surrender of Furness Abbey, Sir John Lamplieu, the royal agent, was ordered 'to keep household' on the site of the late monastery, and if compelled to remove by sickness he is to leave a substantial person resident with four able men. He is to tell the tenants that they are better used than they were by the monks.[1] And when Bishop Latimer, just after the dissolution of Winchcombe Abbey, begged that its demesnes should be given to his friend Squire Tracey it is on the ground that the squire is given to 'good hospitality.'[2] The fall of the monasteries did not probably affect the south so much as the north in respect of their uses as inns. But the fact that the Pilgrimage of Grace centred round the three abbeys of Jervaulx, Salley and Whalley showed how justified was Robert Aske's claim for their value in that respect in the wild district between Yorkshire and Lancashire. The royal commissioners of 1536 made similar claims for many of the southern houses. To take Hampshire alone, Quarr and Netley were singled out for their use to travellers by sea; while the prior of Christ Church urged that there was no other place of refuge for honest men within eight or nine and sometimes sixteen or eighteen miles. Arguments of this kind were reinforced by men who either had no sympathy with, or who had lost what they had in, the religious life; as is seen by Bishop Latimer's pleading for the priory of Great Malvern, by Bishop Barlow for Nostell, or by Sir William Parr, a prominent innovator in religion, for Pipewell Abbey. There can be no doubt but that the disappearance of the monasteries was a cause of great inconvenience to many travellers, rich and poor.

[1] *L.P.*, XII (2), 1216.　　　　[2] *L.P.*, XIV (1), 84.

III

The third of the main duties of religious houses, that of almsgiving, provides a problem equally difficult with that of hospitality. What exactly were the monasteries expected to do in this connection? When that eminent prelate, William of Wykeham, Bishop of Winchester, made a personal visitation of the small priory of Selborne in 1387 he furnished the answer to this much disputed question. The canons were ordered, under pain of the greater excommunication, not to say divine wrath, to distribute to the poor according to the will of the founders and benefactors of the priory; the fragments left from meals were also to be given to the poor; and so were the canons' old clothes.[1] 'Compulsory monastic alms consisted chiefly of common and open doles on holidays and commemoration days', says Savine.[2] 'Of the many forms assumed by monastic charity, the evidence of the sixteenth century attaches most importance to the common doles.' Thus in the large Premonstratensian abbey of Cockersand in Lancashire there were at the suppression five poor aged impotent men whom the foundation charter required to be kept at the abbey. Two other poor men were provided with food and board daily for charity, while two persons were living in the house by purchase as corrodians.[3] It is, in fact, often difficult to distinguish between inmates of this kind. Some, perhaps the greater number, were not in receipt of alms at all, but had bought an annuity from the monastery. The twelve old men at Furness who 'had their living by purchase' were of this class,[4] and these people

[1] *Charters of Selborne Priory* (Hampshire Record Society), p. 103.
[2] *English Monasteries*, pp. 240 and 265.
[3] *V.C.H. Lancs*, II. 157.   [4] *L.P.*, XII (2), 205.

continued to receive their incomes after the dissolution. Of the food doles we may quote the rules at the Yorkshire house of St. Agatha's by Richmond, where an endowment of fifteen shillings a year provided one poor person a day with food and two poor people with a meal on the anniversary of the death of the founder.[1] There was in the monastery of St. Nicholas, Exeter, 'a certain house, called the "Poor Men's Parlour" to which place there repaired daily seven poor men before dinner-time, and to every one of them was delivered on the flesh days a two-penny loaf, a pottle of ale and a piece of flesh, and on the Fridays likewise at afternoon, as soon as dinner was done, all such poor as were tenants came, and every of them should have also a two-penny loaf, a pottle of ale, a piece of fish and a penny in money . . . and likewise at the after dinner, there came to the said parlour all other poor folk which were either tenants to the said monastery, or dwelling within their fee, called "St. Nicholas' fee" and they should have meat and drink sufficient, and upon every day called St. Nicholas' day there was provision made of bread, and then there was delivered to every poor body one loaf, and likewise upon every Good Friday there was used a general alms, which was one penny in money to every poor body coming.'[2]

This extract shows how the Selborne injunction worked in practice. The dependents of the monastery attend to get what falls from the monks' table, and on founder's day a few more persons participate. But there was no *organized* system of relief, such as some controversialists have imagined. Savine has calculated that not more than three per cent of monastic income was spent on charity, while episcopal visitations show over and over again that much of the food

---

[1] *V.C.H. Yorks*, III, 247.　　[2] Oliver, *Monasticon dioecesis Exoniensis*, p. 116.

which should have gone to the poor went, in fact, to the monks' relations and friends, or to their packs of hounds. 'The sub-prior (of Westacre) does not give the fragments to the poor but to his own friends, especially to Mrs. Waseney and another lady'.[1] That both kinds of charity were apt to foster the growth of vagabondage seems certain. The term 'abbey lubbers' which appears in the vagrancy law of Edward the Sixth was a common one in the middle ages. It may mean sturdy beggars, or else the useless dependents and servants of monasteries, against whom the bishops were always inveighing. There is a great conflict of evidence as to the effect of the dissolution on vagabondage. Contemporaries went so far as to state that it disappeared as a result; and statements to the contrary are those of persons writing a couple of generations later. That the problem was a very serious one is shown by the Act of 1531, which recounts that the number of vagabonds is daily augmented and increased and orders a whipping for those who begged without a licence. The problem of the really deserving poor was being gradually worked out in the middle ages. And it was not till the late sixteenth century that it received its solution. The foundation of numerous almshouses, hospitals and guilds in the course of the fifteenth century is one aspect of it. But there was no co-ordination any more than there was of monastic charity, which was in any case somewhat of the lady bountiful order. Much monastic charity was dispensed, but only of the compulsory dole kind and the system 'did nearly as much to increase beggars as to relieve them'.[2]

---

[1] *Norwich visitations*, p. 250.
[2] The problem of medieval forms of charity is best treated in Miss E. M. Leonard's *History of English Poor Relief* (1900).

IV

Prayer, almsgiving and hospitality were, then, the chief duties of the monasteries. But there were many other ways in which they were of use to the public. 'Also,' said Aske in his examination in the Tower of London, 'were all gentlemen much succoured in their needs, with many their young sons there assisted . . . and also their evidences and money left to the use of infants in abbeys hands — always sure there.'[1] In an age of the stocking-at-the-foot-of-the-bed finance, when specie, plate and jewels were the tangible evidence of wealth, the religious houses were of the greatest possible convenience to capitalists. That 'troublesome and busy' man, Doctor Robert Holdsworth, for many years vicar of Halifax, kept all his money in bags under the stairs of his vicarage. What wonder that one morning he was found murdered by burglars and that all his savings had vanished? Their high walls made the monasteries far safer repositories, and vast sums were consigned to them by people of all classes. In Westminster Abbey reposed the royal treasury, in St. Mary's Abbey, York, the money to pay the garrisons on the Scottish border. When Doctor Rayne, Bishop Longland's chancellor, had been brutally murdered by the Lincolnshire rebels in the course of the rising of 1536, his executors found that he had left an exceedingly comfortable bank balance.[2] A bag of gold and £130 in money was deposited in the Cistercian abbey of Pipewell in Northamptonshire, while the Augustinian priory of Newenham in Bedfordshire had belonging to him three bags of gold, two of silver and other money amounting to £268. These two houses had, therefore, in their charge,

---

[1] L.P., XII (1), 901.   [2] L.P., XI, 1407.

treasure, the property of one individual, to the value of what nowadays would amount to some £12,000.

When, in 1524, Sir John Husee bought for £800 from the King the wardship and marriage of the late Lord Monteagle's son, he placed £300 of the sum in the hands of the abbot of Whalley for the King's use.[1] In the old days the Templars had been the chief bankers in England, and now the London religious houses seem to have taken their place. The Bishop of Bangor, for example, made the London Carthusians his bankers. When Aske claimed that the monasteries succoured gentlemen in their needs he meant that they gave 'temporary accommodation' of a financial kind. Is it to be supposed that they failed to charge even bank interest? The title deeds were their security. It was often very difficult for the depositors to get them back again.[2]

It may well be imagined, however, that there were dangers inherent in the system and that the vast sums lying idle in the monasteries often excited evil passions. Gangsters were anything but unknown in the middle ages, and even the most exalted personages were apt to be found in their ranks. In the struggle between King Edward II and the barons, the Earl of Hereford and other chiefs of the Opposition learned that the King's favourites, the Despensers, had a large bank balance in Stoneleigh Abbey. Without more ado they broke into the abbey and carried away £1000 in money and charters, bonds, gold and silver, jewels and plate to the value of £1000 more. Some £60,000 in our money was lost to the Government.[3] Unfortunately for the religious life burglars of this kind were only too often helped by inside information, and there

[1] L.P., IV, 13.
[2] See 'Monastic Chancery Proceedings' (*Yorkshire Archaeological Society's Record Series*), vol. LXXXVIII (1934). for many instances of this.
[3] V.C.H. Warwick, II. 80.

are many instances of monks participating in the raids. The famous robbery of the King's treasury at Westminster Abbey in 1303, to which many of the monks were certainly privy, is a case in point, while in 1536 the Winchester monks seem to have made a clean sweep of the jewels of their church.[1] Abbot Salisbury of Valle Crucis seems to have been a forerunner of motor bandits, and in May 1535 was caught robbing an Oxfordshire gentleman on the highway. He was also an expert forger and spent long years in the Tower of London after he was detected.[2] After Abbot Addingham of Swineshead had left Spalding Priory it was found that no less than £500 was missing and the Spalding monks suspected that he had taken it.[3]

Besides forgery these hoards led to a great deal of necromancy and kindred superstitions. In the fourteenth century an abbot of Missenden was sentenced to be hanged drawn and quartered for coining,[4] and in the period immediately before the suppression we find a great many similar instances. 'We have found,' wrote Lord Ferrers to Cromwell in 1532, 'a monk of Strata Florida making false coins in his chamber in the abbey and now have him in Carmarthen jail.'[5] A monk of St. Benet's, Norfolk, was anxious to get a dispensation, but how was he to get the money for it? He bethought himself of a friend of his who knew the art of digging, and a number of evil spirits, with Oberon at their head, were called up to help him to find the necessary funds, though whether with success or no does not appear.[6] Over and over again we find religious persons calling in necromancers or 'calculators' to discover treasure, while the practice of alchemy was by no means unknown to them.

[1] *L.P.*, x, 472 and 480. [2] *L.P.*, VIII, 789 and 1001.
[3] *L.P.*, v, 1576. [4] *V.C.H. Bucks*, I, 371.
[5] *L.P.*, v, 1120. [6] *L.P.*, IV, 5096.

V

Great claims have been made for the monasteries as educational establishments. How far were they justified? It is significant that Aske makes no such claim, except, incidentally, in respect of nunneries. If some perfervid controversialists were to be believed, medieval education was under the control of the monks. If so the great teaching orders would have to be antedated by centuries. In sober fact the monks did practically no teaching. It was not their job, but that of professional ushers, just as it is to-day.

There were three classes of persons who were in one way or another helped in their studies in the monasteries. First, the rich boys who were being brought up under the aegis of the abbot, secondly the poor boys who were housed in the almonry, and thirdly the younger monks and canons. It was the custom in the middle ages for a nobleman or gentleman to send his sons to be brought up in the household of some great ecclesiastical or lay personage, and the scions of the great houses were expected to do personal service to their patrons. One of the haughtiest men in England, Lord Hussey, was not ashamed to write to the low-born Cromwell 'my kinsman, son of Sir John Thimbleby, wants to enter your service. He shoots well, puts a bar well, *and waits well at a board*. He has been with me seven years';[1] all of which sounds as if a footman's references were in question. The young gentlemen who were placed under the care of abbots were evidently somewhat in the position of the 'noblemen' who, a hundred years ago, sat with the canons at the high table in the hall of Christ Church, Oxford, except that in medieval times they would perhaps

[1] *L.P.*, x, 206.

have helped with the waiting. That the abbots took a personal interest in them cannot be doubted. Lady Lisle sent her son James Basset to Reading. 'I have,' wrote the abbot of Reading to Lord Lisle, 'set your young gentleman with William Edwards, my under-steward, that he may be well seen to by a woman for his dressing, for he is too young to shift for himself. He is the most towardly child in learning that I have known.'[1] James's brother, George, was at Hyde Abbey by Winchester; and a correspondent of his mother was able to report that the boy is very well and profiting by his learning, and that the new prior says he shall be treated by him as well as he ever was by the old.[2] Young gentlemen of this kind were called '*commensales*' of the abbot's table; they were taught by schoolmasters specially hired for the purpose. It was the usher of Master Carey, Master Morice and Master Hervey at Woburn who appears to have had no small share in bringing the abbot to his tragic end.[3]

It is not to be supposed that abbeys paid ushers or boarded young gentlemen for nothing. 'The house of Hyde looketh for every penny,' wrote a Hampshire clergyman to Lady Lisle, 'we are in debt to it twenty shillings (say £30).'[4] Lady Lisle wrote hastily to order that the prior of Hyde should be paid for the keep of her son, and the abbess of Nunnaminster for her daughter. That school bills of this kind were often in arrear is shown by a complaint of the priory of Westacre in Norfolk in 1494. 'There are many boys, sons of gentlemen, in the house, but the prior can't get the money to pay for their board and tuition.'[5] In days when Eton and Winchester were still confined to poor and destitute boys it was obviously a great advantage to the nobility and gentry to send their sons to great houses,

---

[1] *L.P.*, VII, 1451.   [2] *L.P.*, X, 1148.
[3] *L.P.*, XIII (1), 981.   [4] *L.P.*, XI, 12.
[5] *Norwich Visitations*, p. 50.

whether lay or ecclesiastical, and the suppression must have been a heavy blow to the upper classes for that reason.

Towards the end of the middle ages the larger monasteries, partly by reason of the growing devotion to Our Lady, began to house 'choristers to sing the anthems in her honour in the Lady Chapel', in the almonry by the great gate of the monastery.[1] In well regulated houses these boys must have had considerable opportunities for acquiring education of more than one kind. At Glastonbury, for example, an organist and choirmaster was engaged to teach six children to sing prick song.[2] The numbers varied very much, though twelve may be taken as the normal figure, and this was not very often attained. In 1520 it was reported that though the prior and convent of Norwich were formerly accustomed to 'exhibit' fourteen boys in the almonry there were then only eight,[3] and even the great Augustinian priory of Thornton could not produce more than two in 1440. They were under the charge of the almoner or sub-almoner and were taught the rudiments of learning by a secular master for a term of five years at the most, for 'this period suffices for becoming proficient in grammar'.[4] It has been reckoned that at the time of the suppression there were some fifteen hundred charity boys of this kind 'who would not otherwise have enjoyed the benefit of the grammar schools'.[5] The fall of the monasteries must, therefore, have carried with it the disappearance of most of this class of boy. Two poor boys in Nocton Priory, were given three shillings (about £5) a piece at the suppression of that small house,[6] so that some consideration must have been given to them, and a considerable number

---

[1] A. F. Leach, *Educational Charters*, p. xxxi ff.
[2] *L.P.*, VII, 1056.   [3] *Norwich Visitation*, p. 192.
[4] Leach, op. cit., p. 296.   [5] Leach, op. cit., p. xxxii.
[6] *V.C.H. Lincs*, II, 169.

would have been incorporated in the choir schools of the cathedrals, whether old (like Canterbury) or new (like Westminster).

VI

Finally there is the question of the education of the religious themselves. This was regulated by the Statutes of Pope Benedict the Twelfth.[1] All houses which could afford it were to provide a master to teach the monks elementary sciences, viz. grammar, logic and philosophy. If there was a monk fit for the purpose he was to undertake the task; if not (as in practice was generally the case) a secular master was to be engaged. After making due allowance for the fact that medieval boys grew up more quickly than they do nowadays, many of the religious were ludicrously youthful. The increasing difficulty of keeping up their numbers forced heads of houses to get monks professed well below the canonical age. The abbot of Peterborough, as the Bishop of Lincoln found in 1519, shaved very young and ignorant monks, mere boys.[2] It is unluckily only too true that many houses did not fulfil their obligations to these youths. And there are constant complaints in bishops' visitations of neglect to provide them with teachers. 'The ignorance of the religious in the small religious houses,' wrote Doctor Gwent, Dean of the Arches, to Cromwell, 'is incredible. They can't construe their own rules.'[3] 'There are fifteen brethren here,' wrote the abbot of the large Cistercian house of Warden in Bedfordshire, 'and, except three of them, none understand nor know their rule, nor the statutes of their religion.'[4] The abbot of Hayles told

[1] Leach, op. cit., p. 288.
[2] Visitations of Bishop Atwater, fol. 143.   [3] *L.P.*, IX, 25.
[4] Wright, *Suppression*, p. 54.

Cromwell that none of his monks was learned enough to expound the scriptures to others and that he would have to get down an Oxford don to do so.[1] At St. Benet's, Norfolk, in 1532 four of the monks were reported to be so ignorant that they could scarcely read or sing.[2]

The obligation to send students to the universities was clearly laid down in Benedict the Twelfth's statutes. All Benedictine houses having eight monks or more were to send five per cent, that is one monk out of twenty, to Oxford or Cambridge 'to acquire the fruit of greater learning'. But this salutary rule was honoured in the breach rather than in the observance. Nearly every episcopal visitation shows cases of neglect to send up the full number, sometimes indeed any at all. The 1519 visitation of the great abbey of Peterborough shows that it was a mere chance whether it had any scholars at the university or no. Indeed, the abbot was accused of disliking seeing students studying and of encouraging them to be negligent. Why, he evidently thought, should he spend the equivalent of £200 to £300 a year on a monk who might learn nothing and run up any amount of debts? Indeed, cases are found where the friends of a monk or canon despairing of getting help from the convent subscribed to send him to Cambridge. The monks who did go to a university seem to have been apt to get swelled heads, and to look down on their colleagues who were not so lucky as to have an academic degree. Dom Richard Norwich and Dom (Thomas) Morton of Norwich 'scholars, despise the other monks, are intolerably puffed up. They sow discord in the house and are in debt at the University'.[3] Their academic arrogance must have been somewhat like that of the Cambridge don who, after

[1] *L.P.*, VII, Appendix 35.   [2] *Norwich Visitations*, p. 281.
[3] *Norwich Visitations*, p. 264.

having been presented to Napoleon, observed of the Emperor that 'you could tell he was not a University man'.

The total number of monks who had had a University education was very small. It may be doubted if there were as many as a hundred monks and regular canons at Oxford University at any given time, and at Cambridge the number was always smaller;[1] while the great monasteries of Rewley and Oseney in the suburbs of Oxford, and that of Barnwell just outside Cambridge, seem to have contributed little or nothing to learning. Oseney 'though best in discipline of the Oxfordshire houses and with twenty-six canons in 1445 had no school and no learned canon'.[2]

'To the Benedictines is largely due the survival of the Latin classics; indeed it would be difficult to overrate their services as guardians of books in the darkest age of Europe.' Such is the judgment of one of the greatest classical scholars of modern times.[3] And what should we know of Anglo-Saxon history without the aid of Bede, or of the play of political forces in the reign of Henry the Third without that of Matthew Paris? In the century before the suppression, however, what services were the monasteries giving to learning? Their great libraries were everywhere intact, but how far were they used? A bibliomaniac once said to a friend that he had so many books that he did not know what to do with them. 'Why not read them?' was the cynical answer. It is to be feared that the monks were in similar case. 'Formerly,' wrote Doctor Gascoigne, writing in the reign of Henry the Sixth, 'learned books and valuable historical works were written in monasteries, but nowadays the religious allow their books to rot or to get lost; nothing can induce them to write new ones.'[4] Had the mon-

[1] Leach, op. cit., p. lxxxiii.   [2] V.C.H. Oxon, II, 91.
[3] Professor Jebb in Cambridge Modern History, I, p. 534.
[4] Loci e libro Veritatum, edited by J. E. T. Rogers, p. 73.

asteries been preserved there might, of course, have been eventually a literary revival of the kind which was to make the French congregation of St. Maur so famous. But there was nothing to warrant such an expectation in the early sixteenth century. That the suppression involved wholesale destruction of books and manuscripts is a commonplace, while those which survived were to run further danger at the hands of the fanatical visitors of Edward VI, with their obscene objections to pictures of saints. Luckily for scholarship their reign was short and was never in any case so destructive as was that of the Huguenots in France, of which it has been said that the one regret of scholars is that the Massacre of St. Bartholomew did not occur thirty years earlier.

That the suppression also involved great loss to music, with the disappearance of organ and choir schools, and to painting and the arts generally is obvious. But the claim that the religious themselves contributed much to these in the period just before the suppression must be given up. Architects designed and masons built churches just as they do nowadays; and for the monks as well as for other people. And so to a great extent in respect of painting, vestments and the like. When Prior More of Worcester wanted a new cope, did he get his monks to make it? of course not.[1] He knew of an ecclesiastical emporium in London which specialized in vestments and he paid William Dyce, 'Vestment maker of London' for the 'orphreys to a cope of cloth of gold £7 . . . the making of the cope with the lining . . . ten shillings; the orphreys to the other cope, the chasuble and two tunicks £14. Item, paid to Thomas Stilgo, for gilding and painting of the images of John and our Lady

[1] He was prior from 1518 to 1535. His *Journal*, printed by the Worcestershire Historical Society, is full of details of this kind.

in the midst of the altar in St. Cecilia's Chapel 28 shillings and four pence. Item, the gilding of all the other images with the curtains £10 7s.' Thomas Stilgo was a Worcester tradesman, presumably a painter and decorator of repute. He was certainly no monk. When the prior wanted a copy of the whole works of St. Augustine he sent to a book shop in London for them. John Cranks, goldsmith of London, made him two new parcel gilt goblets. It was to Richard Gerves, mercer of London, that he sent for a new Brussels carpet. In fact, just as he bought his groceries in London and his wine at Bristol (from his own brother, the wine merchant) so it was with *objets d'art*. He knew better than to trust the making of them to unskilled monks. He would still less have entrusted any repairs, the designing of new barns or cottages on the estates to them. Why should he? It was not their job, but that of carpenters, builders, architects. 'The case against the monastic architect,' says a recent writer, 'seems overwhelming,' and anybody who is still, directly or indirectly under the influence of Montalembert, may well study the pages of Mr. Swartwout's *Monastic Craftsman* and he will be, or ought to be (for no evidence, however plain, seems to affect sentimentalists) convinced by its exposure of this legend. A perusal of the diary of Prior More, to which allusion has been made, should complete the disillusionment.

That a good deal of decorative work was done by many of the religious at this period cannot be doubted. But it was probably of an amateur kind like the excessively nasty sweets which are confected by nuns nowadays. The often-quoted letter of George Gifford, one of the commissioners for the suppression of the small midland houses, to Cromwell about the canons of Ulverscroft Priory where 'there is not one religious person there but can and doth use either embroidering, writing books with very fair hand, making their own garments, carving, painting or engraving'[1] would lead one to suppose that the time of the inmates was wholly occupied in pursuing these decorative arts. But the writer was not wholly disinterested in the matter. He wanted the lands of the priory for his brother. Twenty years after the surrender the former sub-prior gave a very different account of the activities of his former colleagues. The prior and canons, he told a commission of inquiry, kept their own pack of hounds and their own hawks. They hunted the fallow and roe deer in Charnwood Forest and Bradgate Park and hawked partridges and pheasants and kept a huntsman of their own. They also had free fishing. All the canons save three, said a former servant of the priory, were common hunters.[2] They were not going to spend their time knitting when they could ride to hounds.

[1] Wright, *Suppression*, p. 137. Where Wolstroppe should read Ulverscroft.
[2] Nicholls, *History of Leicestershire*, III, 1091.

CHAPTER II

LAY INTERFERENCE IN MONASTIC AFFAIRS

I

THE services of the monasteries to the laity, in addition to their employment as inns and banks, were very great. They offered careers for the sons of the country gentry as land agents, farmers, surveyors and so forth, fat pickings for lawyers, and profits for tradesmen. The number of lay people of all classes who had claims to interfere in the internal affairs of the monasteries was very large. Founders and high stewards, members of county families, lawyers and townspeople, corrodians or other annuitants,[1] all with their divergent interests and pretensions, were an abiding source of trouble to the religious. 'His official position,' says Savine, 'enabled a squire to become well acquainted with the monastic estates and to feel at home within the monastic walls: and this was one of the causes which contributed to the success of the dissolution. When the monastic estates came into the market, the squires knew not only to whom they should address themselves, but knew also what particular estates to ask for: thus they easily selected the most profitable portion for themselves.'[2]

The founders or patrons of a monastery transmitted a large number of rights of interference to their descendants, and all the way down to the dissolution they exercised a profound influence on the internal affairs of the houses of which they were patrons. Nor could those rights die out,

[1] See below, Chapter II, p. 65.   [2] *English Monasteries*, p. 259.

for they could pass to other families by grant from the Crown, or by sale. The most powerful of all the founders was the Crown, for not only were nearly all the oldest abbeys of the foundation of kings, but numerous others had fallen to it in the course of centuries, whether by marriage or inheritance, or by attainder and confiscation. Only a few years before the general suppression all those of the Duke of Buckingham's foundation fell to the King as the result of the duke's attainder in 1521. Great nobles might have the patronage of many houses, a country gentleman of no more than one, but their rights, from king to squire, were identical. The relations of the founder to the house of his foundation are well described by John of Gaunt, Duke of Lancaster, in 1373: 'I am bound,' he wrote, 'as advocate (i.e. patron) of the house of holy religion of the nuns of Nuneaton to give succour and help to the said nuns, and their goods and chattels, that they may serve God in peace and quiet according to their foundation and the rule of their religion.' Protection, however, entailed right of interference and the Duke went on to say that the nunnery was in a shocking state; 'in order that they may be in charity to perform divine service and to pray for my ancestors' he had handed over the whole administration 'of our said house' to guardians and surveyors in the persons of the abbot of Leicester and three gentlemen.[1] A century and a half later, in the autumn of 1533, the King, as Duke of Lancaster, was appealed to by one of the neighbouring gentry to interfere in this same house in the same way and for the same reason. 'No good rule is kept there either to God or the world, one of the nuns is now with child. Please move the King, as founder, to have a new prioress.'[2]

[1] Register of John of Gaunt (*Camden Society*, Third Series, vol. XX), I, p. 143.
[2] *L.P.*, VI, 1184. See also *Calendar of Papal Registers*, XII, p. 135, for the shocking state of this priory in 1461.

The founders were useful to the houses of their foundation in many ways. They could use their influence at court to enable the religious to circumvent the mortmain laws and to acquire further lands. They could get the business of their house expedited in the royal courts, or in the courts of the bishop, the archbishop or the pope. 'Please,' wrote Thomas, Earl of Lancaster, to Pope Clement the Fifth, 'expedite the business which the Abbot and Convent of Barlings (which is of my foundation and that of my ancestors) have in your court.'[1] If it was a question of suppressing a house they could hold up the business altogether, or obtain more favourable terms for it. So the Earl of Northumberland, early in 1536, saved the small Sussex priory of Shulbred from the Bishop of Chichester, who had intended to suppress it. The prior had been accused of pulling down the frater, and much of the church, and the bishop had got him out. Then the earl, as founder, stepped in and had him put back.[2] The same Lord Northumberland interfered very decisively in a property dispute between the Yorkshire monastery of Healaugh Park 'of my foundation' and a neighbouring squire.[3] The latter could scarcely have failed to perceive the threats which underlay the earl's letters to him and he gave way. The founders were constantly stepping in to safeguard the financial interests of monasteries in their patronage. An Earl of Arundel once forced a prior of Castleacre to take an oath not to cut down woods or manumit serfs without his leave, and although this oath was subsequently declared null and void in the papal court, it shows to what lengths patrons of monasteries were prepared to go.[4] Even if the monks had wished to

[1] 'Collectanea Anglo-Premonstratensia' (*Camden Society*, Third Series, vol. x), I, p. 30.
[2] 'Plumpton Correspondence' (*Camden Society*, First Series, vol. IV), p. 226.
[3] *L.P.*, IX, 533.   [4] *V.C.H. Norfolk*, II, 357.

be easy landlords, the patron in his own financial interests saw to it that they were not.

In the struggles between the English houses of the Cluniac and other orders with foreign heads the patrons took up the cause of the former and often refused, in their capacity of founders, to accept the nomination of the oversea abbots. In the conflicts between great abbeys and their subordinate houses the patrons usually took the part of the latter and, in order to exercise their own influence, forwarded their desire for independence. Sir Robert Tateshall, patron of Wymondham priory, defied the Abbot of St. Albans and kept his representatives out of the priory with armed forces. But he failed, for the abbey of St. Albans was of royal foundation, and in a contest between the Crown and a country gentleman there was not much doubt as to who would win.[1]

A return for all these services was naturally expected by the patrons. The founders had the first claim on the prayers of houses in their patronage. The prayers of the Cistercian monks of Ford were thought to have preserved the Courtenays, their founders, in the midst of many and great dangers. When an Earl of Oxford died in 1509 his executors had to arrange for the saying of 2000 masses in the houses of which he was the founder.[2] After the death of a founder, his successor was solemnly installed in the abbey church with all the ceremonies which were due to a bishop. 'Be it known', said the Abbot and Convent of St. Agatha's, 'that we have received John, Lord Scrope of Bolton, as very true and undoubted founder of our said monastery with procession and such other ceremonies as our predecessors have received his noble ancestors, granting to him and his heirs not only to be partitioner of our prayers and suffrages

---

[1] *V.C.H. Norfolk*, II, 338.   [2] See his will in *Archaeologia*, LXVI, 310.

and other devout and meritorious acts and good deeds, but all other customs, duties, pleasures and all that doth appertain and belong to the just title and right of a founder.'[1]

When Edmund Reade, Esquire, of Boarstall, Bucks, was installed in their church as founder of the Austin Friars of Oxford in 1456, the ceremony was attended not only by the Provincial of the Order, but by the Prior of St. Frideswide's, the Warden of New College, the Proctors of the University and the Mayor of Oxford, while he and his son were given rooms in the house, part of a garden and free board whenever they visited or resided in Oxford.[2] In every religious house there was a founder's lodging, often of very considerable size, in which he and his family resided for long periods: and when the first statute of Westminster of 1275 sought to protect monasteries from enforced hospitality it excepted the founders. A great noble like the Earl of Oxford could move from one house to another of his foundation, getting free board and lodging through most of the eastern counties. How far the ladies of the family were admitted seems uncertain. The Archbishop of York allowed the patron's wife to stop one night and one night only at Newburgh Priory.[3] On the other hand the Duke of Suffolk and his wife, Queen Mary, sister to Henry the Eighth and dowager of France, seem to have spent weeks at a time in the great Augustinian house of Butley, near Ipswich. The Queen used to have picnic suppers in the canons' gardens during the hot weather.[4] Not only their imposing lodgings or houses, but everything in the monastery served to impress the monks with the importance to them of their founder. Over the great gate of Kirkham Priory, Yorkshire, the arms of successive founders may still

[1] *V.C.H. Yorks*, III, 248.   [2] *Capgrave's Chronicle* (Rolls Series), p. 329.
[3] *V.C.H. Yorks*, III, 228.
[4] J. N. L. Myres, 'Butley Priory', *Archaeological Journal*, 1934, p. 205.

be seen. Inside the church they had the right of burial in the choir. So King John is buried before the High Altar of Worcester Cathedral and King Edward II before that of Gloucester. At Tewkesbury the tombs of the Clares are ranged round the High Altar of that abbey and the figures in the glass high above it are portraits of the founders and not pictures of saints. Their arms were on the seals and even on the vestments. At Lanercost in Cumberland the arms of the Scropes were embroidered on a cope, and at Warter in Yorkshire an inventory shows 'one suit of blue silk called the water bowges (the arms of the founders, the Roos family), a cope for a priest, also vestments for priest, deacon and sub-deacon and also copes of the foresaid water bowges'.[1] Even the monks' names in religion might be those of the founders, or reputed founders, of an abbey.[2]

The founders expected the religious to do literary work for them, especially in the matter of providing them with long (and often faked) genealogies. That very disgruntled Oxford don, Doctor Thomas Gascoigne (who hated monks like poison) attacked the religious of his time for their neglect of their duty in this respect. The founders, in their own interests, ought to force the monks to write, or else say to them 'Depart from me, ye cursed'.[3] Not only were the founders' families 'written up', but they had a good chance of becoming, at any rate local, saints. Lord Wake of Liddell, for example, was very successful in curing persons of fever at Haltemprice, a house of Augustinian canons founded by him near Hull. Even a ruffian like King Offa got perilously near being regarded as a saint by the monks of St. Albans.

[1] *Historical Manuscripts Commission Reports on Duke of Rutland's MSS.*, I, p. 28.
[2] Thus at Glastonbury in a visitation of 1526 are found monks who bear names of Saints connected by history or legend with the abbey, and also some who took the names of Anglo-Saxon kings who had been benefactors to it.
[3] *Loci e libro Veritatum*, p. 73.

II

The founders were not always, however, profitable to a monastery. They were often a great expense to it. The great Cluniac priory of Thetford was reported in 1279 as being crippled by the residence there of the advocate (the Earl of Norfolk's brother) who cost the house more than the whole prior and convent. Their attitude towards the religious was often very insolent. They would talk about 'my prior' or 'my abbot' as country squires used to talk about 'my parson'. That very haughty northern noble, Lord Dacre, referred to the Abbot of Newminster as 'my monk', while he interfered actively in the affairs of his priory of Lanercost in Cumberland. 'As I am your founder,' he wrote to the convent, 'and bound in conscience to see to your welfare and give unto you my faithful counsel, please go to the chapter house and elect a sub-prior to look after the internal affairs of the house. What about Canon Richard Halton? I know that he has shown some obstinacy, but by the help of the Holy Ghost he is virtuously reduced of his own good mind and my singular pleasure, content and consolation. In my opinion you would do well to elect him. I am founder and, as far as in me is, assent to his election. You had, therefore, better elect him without any obstinacy or grudge as you intend to please me.'[1] There was not much doubt about the meaning of this letter and, considering that the priory was almost at the gates of Lord Dacre's castle at Naworth, it is scarcely to be supposed that the canons withstood their founder's wishes.

A founder could demand a visitation if he was dissatisfied with the state of affairs in a monastery of which he was

[1] *L.P.*, IV, 128.

patron. 'The Earl of March,' wrote Bishop Spofford of Hereford to the canons of Chirbury in 1423, 'complains, as patron and founder, that his priory is in a state of collapse. My duty forces me to get the present prior out and have another elected. After consultation with him you have delegated the matter to me, and I shall proceed to appoint a new prior.'[1] The Duke of Gloucester in 1372, on an appeal from the neighbouring gentry, got out a weak abbot of the great Cistercian abbey of Meaux, near Hull. The new abbot had to resort to armed force to protect himself against his own monks.[2]

'I desire,' wrote King Edward II to the Archbishop of Canterbury, 'to send Alexander Stonwyk, monk of Christ Church, to some other place' (i.e. monastery), 'because he has misused his office and alienated its property to his relations. As I desire to preserve the quiet of that church on account of the devotion to it of my progenitors, its founders, I have ordered the prior and convent to assist you in the matter. You are to certify your proceedings to me before the next parliament.' So that even individual members of a monastery had the founder's eye on them.[3]

When a vacancy occurred by reason of the death or resignation of the head of a monastery, the convent was obliged to ask the patron for leave to elect a new head, and only when it had received his licence could they proceed to an election.[4] 'I hear,' wrote the Duke of Norfolk to Cromwell in 1538, 'that the prior of the house of Newburgh, being of my foundation, is lately departed this world: and

---

[1] Register of Bishop Spofford (*Canterbury and York Society*), under date August 20th, 1423.
[2] *V.C.H. Yorks*, III, 148.
[3] *Calendar of Close Rolls, Edward II*, under date November 2nd, 1315.
[4] For a good account of proceedings of this kind see *Archaeologia*, vol. XL, which gives the complete correspondence between the nuns of Canonslegh, Devonshire, and their patron, the Earl of Warwick, after their Abbess's death in 1470.

albeit of many years heretofore it hath not been seen contrary but the religious persons of the same in such like
cases have ever first repaired unto me and my ancestors for
our consent as patron of the same, and thereupon to the
Archbishop of York for their confirmation.' The Duke
went on to suggest that in existing circumstances it would
be better if he and Cromwell got the appointment of the
new prior to be delegated 'to us two, to the intent that we
both conjointly together may so order the matter as to us
shall be thought convenient.'[1] Not many signs of freedom
of election here! Not only could and did the founders
'work' the election, but they could be very formidable
enemies to the religious if their wishes were ignored. Lord
Berkeley, who was founder of the Premonstratensian abbey
of Croxton in Leicestershire, took the extreme course of
occupying the abbey the day before the election in 1534
and telling the abbot elect that unless he will pay £500
(=£10,000 to £15,000) another abbot would be elected at the
patron's pleasure.[2] Still worse, as might have been expected,
was the fate of the religious in houses where ladies were
foundresses, and so the monks of Earl's Colne in Essex once
found.[3] The Bishop of London in 1395 had managed to
get rid of an unsatisfactory prior and to appoint another in
his place. Unfortunately for the new prior his predecessor
was a particular favourite of the Countess of Oxford, the
patroness. Directly she heard of the proceedings she flew
into a violent rage, collected a party of armed men, broke
into the priory by night and carried off the intruding prior,
clad only in his pyjamas (or whatever answered to them in
those days), shut him up in her private jail and only released him after he had sworn by the Host to trouble her no

---

[1] *L.P.*, XIII (1), 743.   [2] *L.P.*, VII, Appendix 17.
[3] *V.C.H. Essex*, II, 103, 104.

further. The lady won her case, notwithstanding all that the ecclesiastical authorities could do.[1] A century and a half later, that terrible old lady, the dowager Marchioness of Dorset, after driving an abbot out of Newenham, a Devonshire abbey in her patronage, had settled down at Tilty, in Essex, another Cistercian house. So unpleasant did she make herself that three abbots resigned one after another after a very short tenure of office. One fled to Ireland,[2] and another to his old home in Bedfordshire, where twenty years later we find him settled down as a married man.[3] After all his sufferings at the hands of the other sex he must surely have said, with Doctor Johnson, that his marriage was a triumph of hope over experience.

Abbots and priors who made themselves displeasing to the patron could often be worried into resignation. The Marquis of Exeter, patron, by grant of Henry the Eighth, of the large Cistercian house of Buckland, Devonshire, had made up his mind that Abbot Whyte had exceeded his usefulness and set to work to procure his resignation. 'I don't want to resign,' wrote the abbot piteously to him, 'I can do everything except ride and that can be done by servants. Let me continue in my office and not resign, as you wish. Above all don't give office when I die to Sir Toker, who has been recommended, because of his untoward conversation and intolerable charges.'[4] It is evident, however, that the patron had determined to promote 'Sir Toker', for not only did the abbot resign, but it was John Tucker who succeeded to his post in 1528, and who surrendered the abbey ten years later, after making ample provision for himself and

[1] V.C.H. Essex, II, 103.
[2] L.P., VIII, 728. Lady Dorset had a lengthy correspondence with Cromwell on the affairs of this abbey.
[3] Abbot Emery was brother of the last Abbot of Warden in Bedfordshire. He resigned Tilty in 1533, and went to live at Warden. In 1554 he was reported to be living at Bedford and married. P.R.O. Exchequer, 101, 76/26.
[4] L.P., VI, 1376.

most of his relations. The King had granted Lord Exeter the patronage of another priory, that of Tywardreth, a small Benedictine house in Cornwall. Here poor old Prior Collins was getting into his dotage. Nearly every day his servant used to go down to Lostwithiel to fetch liquor, which the prior consumed in his study until he got softly drunk:[1] but he would not resign. The Cardinal, the Bishop of Exeter and the patron put their heads together and decided to force him to do so. The Cardinal wrote him a most polite letter, dwelling on his former merits and good administration; but going on to suggest that at his age a change would be well, and ending by saying that he should be assured of a 'convenient and honest pension' in order that he might 'live restfully and at ease in this your great age'. A few days later Lord Exeter wrote, anything but politely, saying in almost so many words that the prior will be deprived of his pension unless he gives way. Since these pensions were usually assigned by the patron the prior was put into a great fright. He was still more alarmed to get a letter from a monk of Tavistock, Dom Robert Hamlyn, enlarging on the danger to the pension. He suspected only too well that Dom Hamlyn wished to succeed him and was scarcely deceived by another and most hypocritical letter, in which Dom Hamlyn suggested that the priory should be resigned to him and that the prior would be happier in leisured retirement. 'Commonly they that have a competent living live more merrier than they that have much more.' Soon afterwards there appeared at the priory 'a gentleman called Fortescue and one Benett which be servants to my Lord Marquis of Exeter and showed me'

---

[1] More than half a century later the grocer's assistant who had served the shop which supplied the priory with wine gave evidence that Prior Collins's butler used to come to fetch the bottles and that everybody said that the Prior was often drunk. *Exchequer Depositions*, 31 Elizabeth, Hilary 24. I owe this reference to Mr. A. L. Rowse.

(wrote the prior to the sub-dean of Exeter) 'that my lord and master willed and instantly desired me to resign my poor room of the priorship to my brother Hamlyn, monk of Tavistock, and how, by so doing, my lord would be my especial good lord, and if I would not do so, that there should such things be laid to me that I should leave it whether I would or no'. A plain answer was demanded and met with a refusal. 'They said I should hear other things before long and so departed.' He must have heard 'other things' shortly, for he was no longer prior at the suppression of his house: but he was not succeeded by 'Dom Hamlyn' who was successful — doubtless by similar intrigues — in getting the rich abbey of Athelney in Somerset.[1]

This kind of thing was going on all over the country, and scores of such cases could be quoted to show how powerful nobles could treat 'their' abbots. Quite apart from questions of influence, considerable financial advantages accrued to the patrons of monasteries. The dowager Duchess of Norfolk, for example, was getting £40 (say £1,000) a year out of Thetford Priory in 1470. Consequently, when any religious house was suppressed the patron had to be compensated, both spiritually and financially. When, in 1524, Sir John Longville granted the small Benedictine priory of Bradwell in Buckinghamshire to Wolsey he did it *jure hereditario fundator* so long as the Cardinal found a chaplain to sing mass for him and his ancestors at Bradwell, or at the college to be founded by Wolsey at Oxford. In all the early suppressions the welfare of Christian souls was thus provided for. In the last years of the monasteries this welfare was overlooked. Not only was purgatory abolished by law, but many patrons, under the influence of

[1] This amusing correspondence will be found in full in Oliver, *Monasticon dioecesis Exoniensis*, pp. 45 to 47.

Frith's *Disputation of Purgatory*, had begun to doubt its existence. 'I am,' wrote Lord Wentworth to Cromwell in 1538, 'founder of the Ipswich Franciscans. The order is not a stock planted by the Heavenly Father, but a hypocritical weed planted by that sturdy Nimrod, the Bishop of Rome.' 'The inhabitants of Ipswich,' he said, 'look upon the house as a nest of idle drones.'[1] Since Lord Wentworth had just persuaded the friars to sell him their property, it was obviously to his interest to put things in this way.

The Act of 1536, under whose provisions the lesser monasteries were dissolved, professed to save the rights of 'founders, patrons or donors of any abbeys, priories, etc.' in respect of rights, fees, leases, etc. But this proviso does not seem to have helped them much. Many of them ingenuously supposed that, since their ancestors had given lands to houses of their foundation, those lands would go back to their successors after the suppression. 'Please', wrote that poverty-stricken and well-nigh bankrupt peer, Lord Audeley, to Cromwell, 'be means to me to the King for some of the abbeys in consideration of my losses and that by their hypocrisy they have got out of my ancestors most of my patrimony.'[2] Sir William Goring got the canons of Hardham, Sussex, to surrender that priory to him, as patron. He soon found that he had to pay for it, and that the Act of 1536 was one of nationalization, with few regards for the claims of individuals. Even men so high in the King's favour as the Duke of Norfolk were aware of this. 'I intend,' he wrote to Cromwell, 'within two or three days to ride to Norwich and take the surrender [of the Grey Friars] to the King's use, for I would not give example to other founders to take surrender to their own use.'[3] Founders must, however, have been given some preference when the Crown

[1] *L.P.*, XIII (1), 651.　　[2] *L.P.*, XIII (2), 140.　　[3] *L.P.*, XIII (2), 365.

leased or sold the lands, for a very large number of them are, in point of fact, found in possession. Thus the Earl of Oxford got Castle Hedingham, next door to his own castle, and Earl's Colne, where his ancestors were buried; while his neighbour, Lord Fitzwalter, was equally lucky in respect of his foundation of Dunmow. Indeed, they felt themselves aggrieved if they were not given the first offer. 'When I was in London,' wrote Sir William Parr,[1] 'I told you I had moved the King for the preferment of Jervaulx, whereof I am founder, in case it were suppressed. Being founder, failure in the suit would be a great reproach.'[2]

III

Scarcely less influential in the monasteries were the high stewards. The office was in some ways a sinecure. It was usually held by some great personage who could forward a monastery's influence at court and elsewhere. The Earl of Shrewsbury, for example, was steward of no fewer than eleven houses and drew in fees what would nowadays amount to £1200 to £1500 a year. The eagerness with which grasping politicians like Wolsey and Cromwell sought for the office, or had it thrust on them by the religious, shows what opportunities it must have furnished. The high stewards were useful to the religious in many ways. The canons of Oseney, for example, begged Cromwell, in his capacity of steward, that their new abbot might be chosen from among their ranks. 'The office is only worth forty shillings (say £60), but it will place twenty-five or thirty men at your command for the King's service,' wrote the abbess of Godstow to Cromwell. Sir Thomas Dennis, the

[1] Of Kendal. He is to be distinguished from Sir William Parr of Horton, Northants, whom we shall meet again (Chapter VII) in connection with Pipewell Abbey.   [2] *L.P.*, XII (I), 1298.

recorder of Exeter, used his influence sucessfully in getting a prioress appointed to Polslo who would be acceptable to the nuns. The Prioress of Nuneaton called in Lord Dorset to protect her against her rebellious tenants. Like the founders, they interfered extensively in the internal affairs of the abbeys and treated the monks with equal disdain. When Sir Edward Baynton, the friend and correspondent of Bishop Latimer, was interesting himself in the choice of a new abbot of Malmesbury, of which he was high steward, he did not trouble to go to the abbey in person. The prior and some of the monks were forced to ride all the way to his country house at Bromham, twenty miles or so away, in order to interview him, and he vigorously supported one party in the abbey against another.[1] 'There is a monk in Lenton Abbey,' wrote Sir John Willoughby to Cromwell, 'called Dan Hamlet Penkrich, who has run three times forth from his religion, but has always been reconciled and recognized his faults *before me*, *as steward of his house*, and his father in religion.'[2] When the Prior of Gisburn wanted advice as to how to treat what he called his 'irreligious brethren' he resorted for advice to the steward, Sir John Bulmer, while Sir Thomas Willoughby, as steward of Malling Abbey, instituted an inquiry into the treatment of the old abbess by her successor.

It is natural that there should sometimes be disagreements between the patron and the high steward. When the Cistercian abbey of Hilton (or Hulton) in Staffordshire was vacant in 1534 the patron, the Earl of Shrewsbury, wrote to Cromwell to say that he had been informed that most of the brethren would give their votes to their colleague, William Chalner, 'who is said to be of good learning and wisdom'. On the following day the steward, Sir Philip

---

[1] *L.P.*, v, 322.   [2] *L.P.*, XII (1), 1537.

Draycott, also wrote to Cromwell. His version was very different. 'I am told that one Chalner of Hilton (of which I am steward) will make suit to be made master. He is supported by his brother, the Abbot of Croxden, Lord Shrewsbury and the Bishop. But instead of being a good man, as he will be reported, he is very vicious and exceedingly drunken.'[1] Cromwell seems to have accepted Sir Philip's version, who, being on the spot, was obviously in the best position to know the facts. At any rate the drunken Chalner was not made abbot. A steward could be a very expensive ally, as the monks of Christ Church, Canterbury, found to their cost. When the Duke of Buckingham lodged in that monastery in 1504 he had with him 124 servants and 240 horses. It was not, however, only great nobles who were high stewards. Eminent lawyers often held the office. Sir Roger Cholmeley, the Recorder of London, was steward of the Cistercian abbey of Stratford Langthorne in Essex, and it was to him that the monks reported that their abbot had developed scruples about accepting the King as supreme head of the Church in 1535. 'If you think it contrary to the law show it to the Visitors.'[2] Sir Thomas Dennis, Recorder of Exeter, had more than one stewardship. So had Sir Christopher Hales, the attorney-general. It is hardly necessary to add that when the dissolution came these great lawyers took care to protect their own interests. 'The monastic lands acquired by Sir Christopher were chiefly lands of the Kentish monasteries of which he held the stewardship, St. Augustine's, Canterbury, and Christ Church, Canterbury.'[3]

The receivers who collected the rents and the auditors who made up the accounts of the monasteries were also of

---

[1] L.P., VII, 1094 and 1096.   [2] L.P., VIII, 297.
[3] Savine, *English Monasteries*, p. 257.

the country gentry class. A man might be auditor of one monastery and receiver of a second. The younger sons of the gentry had a fine opportunity for advancing their careers by taking service under an abbot or prior. Every religious house had a crowd of persons of the squire class, wearing its livery, administering its estates, presiding over its manorial courts, acting as stewards, bailiffs, gentlemen farmers, etc. The records of episcopal visitations often contain complaints of the insolence of the 'servants' to the religious, but it has to be remembered that most of these 'servants' were of higher social standing than the monks, upon whom they tended to look down. 'Wages of servants who are gentlemen' is a frequent entry in monastic accounts, and account for a large proportion of the monastic expenses. It may, indeed, be said that the share which the religious themselves had in the management of their own estates was but small. When the Earl of Sussex, during the later months of the Pilgrimage of Grace, wanted to get evidence against the Abbot of Whalley, he reported that it was difficult to do so because of the large number of the abbot's feed men. A whole crowd of gentlemen had clothing, board and lodging free in every religious house. It was obviously vital to the interests of all these individuals that a monastery should be well governed and run on sound financial lines, and whenever a vacancy occurred, it was of the first importance to them that an abbot fit for his job 'in the opinion of the gentry thereabouts' should be elected. 'Certain gentlemen of Surrey,' wrote Sir William Paulet to Cardinal Wolsey in 1529, 'make great labour to you to make a young man to be abbot of Chertsey. I beg your Grace will be careful in the election.'[1] In other words 'we don't want a doting old man who will let his monks do

---

[1] *L.P.*, IV, 6438.

as they like, or let himself be run by his relations, to our financial detriment and that of the monastery'.

They did not want a saint, for saints are rarely much good at accounts. Rather they wanted a good business man, and one who would put down poaching. Many difficulties naturally arose from the fact that 'all the gentry thereabouts' did not want the same man. In 1525 there was a vacancy in the great Augustinian priory of St. Augustine's, Bristol. 'We have,' wrote Wolsey's agent, 'had great trouble over this election. The dissensions of the canons grew to a dangerous pitch and the laity were not less audacious. We scarcely dared to enter the chapter for fear of the assemblage, retainers of noblemen, etc.'[1] The peace of a whole countryside could be endangered by the mutual jealousies of local chiefs. In the long struggle as to who should be the new abbot of Muchelney, Somerset, after the resignation of Abbot Sherborne in 1532, the rival factions were headed by a country gentleman, Sir Nicholas Wadham, and an eminent lawyer, Sir Henry Thornton, the former in league with disorderly monks, the latter desirous of a young and vigorous abbot. 'If I fail,' wrote Sir Henry plainly, 'my credit will fail also.'[2] In the neighbouring county of Devon, about the same time, a fierce conflict was going on between two rival groups of gentry over an election at Hartland, where the old and useless abbot had been deprived through the machinations of Sir William Courtenay and put back by force by Sir Thomas Arundell, the patron of the monastery. 'You never saw such a fool as the late abbot,' wrote Sir William to Cromwell,[3] while Sir Thomas's son asserted that nobody could be more fit for his job and that all was well with the abbey. About the same time Sir Gregory Conyers and Sir Francis Bigod were acting in

[1] *L.P.*, IV, 1544.　[2] *L.P.*, V, 1614.　[3] *L.P.*, VII, Appendix 37. See below, p. 188.

very similar fashion in the great abbey of Whitby. It is
evident that desperate struggles of this kind were being
waged by rival potentates all over the country.

It was not only during a vacancy that the gentry interfered. They were always on the watch for spendthrift or
sensual abbots, for if the abbot wasted the property of a
house there was all the less profit for them. They allied
themselves with disgruntled monks, from whom nearly
all the accusations against the abbot eventually came.
Shortly before its suppression there was great dissatisfac-
tion in the large Cistercian house of Bruerne, Oxfordshire.
Abbot Macy had bought his post from Cardinal Wolsey
and then had to recoup himself out of the revenues of the
abbey. Besides this he had expensive tastes, and numerous
relations and (according to his monks) lady friends to
support. The consequence was a rebellion. One of the
monks went off to London to pawn the abbey plate in
order to raise funds to get the abbot out. The neighbouring
gentry supported the rebels and prevailed on the Duke of
Suffolk, the King's brother-in-law, to force a visitation on
the heads of the Cistercian Order in England. Two abbots
came down to Bruerne and compelled the abbot to resign,
and a more prudent one took his place.[1]

Lawyers, both lay and ecclesiastical, had, as has been
pointed out, vast interests in the monasteries. Nearly all
the rich livings in the gift of the monasteries were given
to ecclesiastical lawyers as a kind of retainer, and it is
astonishing how many they managed to hold at the same
time. Nowadays we should regard them as pluralists of
the most abandoned type. Since the monks were mainly
of middle class origin it is natural that tradespeople had a

---

[1] This report, of which there is a copy in the episcopal registry at Lincoln
among the Longland MSS., has not, so far, been printed. See below, p. 106.

good deal of influence in a monastery. Prior Codd of the Augustinian house of Pentney in Norfolk had the good luck at the time of the suppression of his priory to be brother to the then Mayor of Norwich. In consequence we find him quickly provided with the mastership of St. Giles' Hospital, which was in the gift of the Corporation. In the furious disturbances which marked the last years of the priory of Launceston in Cornwall, the Mayor was brother to one of the canons and vigorously supported the brethren against the new prior. The financial difficulties of the abbeys also caused them to have extensive dealings with goldsmiths and jewellers, not to say pawnbrokers, in London and elsewhere, and that a great deal of their plate was almost permanently pledged there can be no doubt.

It cannot be pretended that the monks were particularly popular in the towns which had grown up round the abbeys, as the desperate struggles, often ending in blood-shed, between them and the townspeople in places like St. Albans and Bury St. Edmunds show. Like the country gentry, townspeople would send complaints up to London against a religious house. 'Satellites of Satan' annoyed the canons of Repton. 'Certain men of Nottingham' hostile to the priory of Lenton probably brought about the fall of that house and the execution of Prior Heath in 1537. The rights which the parishioners had in many of the monastic churches were another fruitful cause of quarrel, the for-tunate results of which can be seen to this day. If the parishioners had not been so tenacious of their rights, a great many fine buildings which still exist in part would have gone the way of the rest: we should, for example, have lost Dunstable, Shrewsbury, Bolton and Wymond-ham: over the naves of which churches the parishioners had rights which could not be ignored at the dissolution.

The disciplinary and financial stability of the monasteries were also apt to be threatened by the existence of the pensioners or annuitants, known under different names, but chiefly as corrodians. These persons were of more than one class. First, there were pensioners which both the Crown and private patrons were entitled to plant on the religious houses. Nowadays retired generals and admirals, civil servants and the like, draw their pensions and live where they will. In the Middle Ages it was far less expensive to send them to a monastery there to receive maintenance, food, clothing, shoe leather, firewood and a chamber within the enclosure of the abbey for their residence. Each monastery was bound to keep one or two of these old gentlemen. They must have been a great nuisance. One has only to listen to their successors in the smoking rooms of Pall Mall clubs to understand what their conversation must have been like. The kings of France eventually found the system so unsatisfactory that they established the 'Invalides' in Paris to take its place.

Then there were people who performed services of divers kinds for the monasteries, from professional men like lawyers, physicians, schoolmasters, organists, down to plumbers and hen-wives. Shortly before the suppression of Ford Abbey, Dorset, the abbot granted to William Tyler, Master of Arts, an annuity of £3 6s. 8d. (=£25), a broad-cloth gown of 4 yards at five shillings a yard (appallingly dear!), and a furnished chamber in the monastery. In return he was to teach grammar to the boys of the house and also to expound Scripture to the brethren in the refectory. Finally, there were people who bought annuities as a provision against their old age. Another example from Ford Abbey will show the nature of these bargains. Mr. and Mrs. Michell were to have yearly eight marks

(£150 nowadays), a house and garden, bread and ale, from the monastery bakehouse and brewhouse (far better than they could have got at an inn) and a pottage of fish or flesh 'as much as two of the monks of the monasterie receive'.[1]

All these persons must have been the occasion of disputes and quarrels. It was sometimes sought to guard against this by forbidding the religious to associate with those holding corrodies or to play games with them. But the system went on unimpaired to the dissolution. This did not as a rule injure the holders of the corrodies, for the Court of Augmentations confirmed the bargains and only disallowed them in particularly flagrant cases. The system was no doubt of great value to many people, but it had its disadvantages, and many abbeys were crippled financially by the reckless granting of corrodies, while they were also apt to lead to quarrels between the abbot and the monks, by reason of the tendency of the former to grant them to his relations and friends without the consent of the convent.

It goes without saying that the ladies did not fail to have their say in the appointment of abbots or priors, or in interfering in the internal affairs of monasteries. If they were patrons of the house such interference was not only a pleasure, but a duty. But even so they did not always confine themselves to strictly legal methods, as the above-mentioned doings of the Countess of Oxford at Earl's Colne show only too clearly. They were apt to treat all clergymen, whether regular or secular, with great indignity. When the Dean of Westbury in Gloucestershire found Lady Berkeley and her guests playing 'the unlawful game of tennis' one morning during the hours of divine service, he tried to stop them. The lady was naturally furious: she

[1] Oliver, *Monasticon dioecesis Exoniensis*, pp. 340 and 341.

used terrible language to the poor Dean and brought an
action against him for trespassing on her lawn.[1] Lady
Worsley quarrelled with the parson of her parish, Thomas
Bradshaw, the vicar of Godshill, in the Isle of Wight.
'If,' said she, 'I can't drive him out of the Island by trouble
and vexation I will cause a villain to murder him privily,
and if the villain is hanged it will only mean the loss of a
knave worth some three halfpence.' Sir James Worsley
wrote to Cromwell to say that the vicar had tried to poison
his wife. Lady Worsley, on her part, visited a woman whom
she wished to use as a witness, and said, 'If you don't tell
the truth I will have you sent to London to be racked. You
go on pilgrimage to our Lady's Grace at Southampton and
buy some powders with which we will poison the vicar'.
Such conduct could not be tolerated, and the King wrote
to the lady to order her to stop her nonsense and to leave
the vicar alone. She appears, however, to have got her
way in some sense, since he was deprived some five or six
years later.[2]

There was a great deal of the same kind of thing going
on in the monasteries. Lady Mary Carey (née Boleyn) was
a great busybody. This lady had procured the election of
Prior Stonywell to Tynemouth priory, a favour which
resulted in a grant to her of an annuity of one hundred
marks. Two thousand a year was a pretty stiff price for
the convent to pay: and in April, 1537, Prior Blakeney,
Stonywell's successor, wrote to Cromwell, 'the lady can
now demand no such annuity, as she can do no great good
for me and my house'.[3] In other words she had now no
influence, since her sister, Anne the Queen, had by now
lost her head. Anne herself was constantly interfering in
the affairs of religious houses both before and after her

[1] *L.P.*, XI, 1041.   [2] *L.P.*, IV, 5293; V, 117; VI, 289.   [3] *L.P.*, XII (1), 822.

marriage, and it was one of her manœuvres of this kind which led almost directly to the fall of Cardinal Wolsey.[1] The lady had determined to get her sister-in-law, Eleanor Carey, a nun of Wilton, elected as abbess of that rich and fashionable house. The Cardinal, to whom the nuns had delegated the choice of a new abbess, wished to appoint the Prioress, Isabel Jordan: and his Commissary, by the simple method of imprisoning the nuns who objected, got the convent to elect her. The King was furious, not so much because the Prioress was 'spotted with incontinence' and had had in her young days two illegitimate children, as because 'he had promised it to certain friends of Dame Eleanor Carey'; in other words to his new love, Anne. Unluckily, Dame Eleanor had no better reputation than the Prioress, and in the end it was the Cardinal's nominee who won. But Anne never forgave him. An investigation of the activities of great ladies in affairs of this kind would well be worth the while of a student gifted with a cynical disposition.

IV

We have still to deal with the arch interferer in the economy of the religious houses and that was the Crown. First, as has been already shown, in its capacity of founder of the greater number of the oldest and richest monasteries, while the Crown lawyers were constantly engaged in making claims to the patronage of other abbeys, for the fees during vacancies amounted to very large sums. To protect the financial interest of houses of their foundation, kings over and over again took the administration out of the hands of the monks or put them into those of royal

[1] The long correspondence about this election will be found in *L.P.*, IV.

officials. 'Trusty and well beloved in God we greet you well and forasmuch as we have commanded the abbots of St. Alban's, Abingdon, Colchester and Chertsey to visit and inquire in our monastery of Westminster and to reform all things there . . . we will and straitly charge you that you . . . meekly obey the said visitation without any contradiction as ye will do us pleasure.' It is not King Henry VIII who thus talks about 'his monastery', but his grandfather, King Edward IV, who is addressing 'his' abbot and convent.[1] 'Their' abbots were used by kings for all manner of purposes, most of which would have pained and astonished St. Benedict or St. Bernard to a high degree. The greater abbots who sat in Parliament were obliged to serve on committees of all kinds, as triers of petitions and so forth. In the country they sat on the magistrates' bench, were commissioners of the peace, collectors of subsidies granted by the clergy to the Crown, took the fealty of other abbots to the Crown, surveyed the royal castles and forests; indeed, on occasion acted as super gamekeepers. Their efficiency in this respect could earn them promotion. When the rich abbey of Beaulieu was vacant in 1533, Sir William Fitzwilliam pushed the claims of the Abbot of Waverley on the ground that he had been a good keeper of the King's game. 'The abbey of Bindon is now void,' wrote Henry's bastard son, the Duke of Richmond, to Cromwell in 1534. 'It adjoins lands of mine in Purbeck and the convent will look after my deer. Please give the monks licence to elect their own abbot.'[2] Hardly the way to advance true religion in Bindon Abbey! It has been already pointed out that apostate monks and nuns were sought for by the police on the ground that the founders of a monastery were losing the prayers which its inmates were legally bound to

[1] *English Historical Review*, vol. XXXVII (1922), p. 88.   [2] *L.P.*, VII, 821

furnish. On the other hand the Crown lawyers were not going to lose the King's rights and their fees in the matter of wardship and marriage. Lady Katharine de la Pole was being brought up in the Suffolk nunnery of Bruisyard. She was the daughter and heiress of the Earl of Suffolk and the lawyers were apprehensive. 'We hear,' wrote King Henry V to the abbess, 'that you propose to make her a nun, which will be to our prejudice and her disinheriting. You are ordered to stop her being professed either in your abbey or anywhere else.'[1]

Long before the sixteenth century the elections of abbots and priors of houses of royal foundation were to all intents and purposes in the hands of the King, that is to say of his chief minister. Wolsey and Cromwell followed the example of many others before them in taking bribes from candidates for promotion, a matter of comparative ease since the convents by this time almost invariably 'compromitted' the election to the Crown. 'Mind,' wrote Bishop Foxe of Winchester, 'that you delay the *congé d'élire* at Bristol: make the canons come up to London and then you can order them as you please.' It was not often necessary for the religious to go to that trouble. 'We have elected John Bradley as abbot,' wrote the convent of Milton, Dorset, to Wolsey, 'in accordance with your letters.' 'Letters' of this kind were not to be disregarded. The only stipulation that the monks ever seemed to make was that the Crown should appoint one of their own number and not a stranger. But even so they never seem to have refused to elect the royal nominee any more than the Chapter of Wells in 1526, 'on receipt of the Cardinal's letters', refused to elect one Thomas Wynter as Dean at the next vacancy. The

[1] H. A. Napier, *History of Swyncombe and Ewelme*, p. 319, from Close Roll, 10 Henry V.

vacancy occurred in the following year, and the new Dean was Thomas Wynter. Now Thomas Wynter happened to be the Cardinal's son — a boy in his teens. Could a simpler and more profitable way of disposing of one's bastards be imagined?

CHAPTER III

ECCLESIASTICAL INTERFERENCE IN MONASTIC AFFAIRS

I

IT is now time to turn from the feudal aspect of monasteries, for that was what lay interference in their internal affairs meant, to ecclesiastical and, therefore, more normal forms of intervention. To the bishop of the diocese, or, during vacancies of a see, the archbishop of the province, was entrusted the task of looking after the discipline of the religious houses. But his powers, extensive enough in theory, were much limited in practice. He could be superseded by a papal legate, like Cardinal Wolsey, or, after the breach with Rome, by a royal visitor, like Thomas Cromwell. His disciplinary measures might be upset on appeal to Canterbury or to Rome, and the weakness of his position was still further aggravated by the fact that a great number of the religious were not answerable to his disciplinary powers. He could not visit Cluniac, Carthusian or Cistercian monks, Premonstratensian or Gilbertine canons, or any friars soever. His power was limited to Benedictine monks and nuns, Cistercian nuns and Augustinian canons and not even to all of them, for the greatest of the Benedictine houses were exempt also. Over and over again, too, he was obliged to call in the aid of higher powers in order to get his wishes obeyed. 'I can't get the Prior of Spalding to resign,' wrote the Bishop of Lincoln to Wolsey, 'though all legal means have been tried.'[1] In this case the bishop had

[1] *L.P.*, IV, 4708.

been trying to get an easy-going head to retire and put in a prior who would put the fear of God into the monks, who had heard that the Prior of Tynemouth[1] was to be their new head 'and they much fear that man'.[2] At the same time the Bishop of Norwich was writing to the Cardinal, 'The Prior of Cokesford has brought his house to ruin. Please inquire of Sir Roger Townshend' — the leading lay-man of the district — 'and put another prior in.'[3] The impugned abbots and priors naturally wished to get their revenge, and they on their part would appeal to the Crown to save them from the bishop.

'The Bishop of Lincoln,' wrote the Abbot of Leicester to Cromwell in 1533: 'plagues my house with visitations and has maintained three or four canons put in office by him whom I have removed because they are unprofitable and put in others.'[4] This abbey was, as the visitation of 1518 shows, in a shocking state of indiscipline and the bishops evidently thought that a new head was imperatively needed. But they took over fifteen years to gain their end. Some abbots and priors had bought from Rome (or, after 1533, from Canterbury) the right of wearing the mitre. Their desire for this form of head-gear, known to the Puritans as a 'forked cap', arose partly from what is called in the American language 'swank' and cost a pretty penny. Prior More of Worcester spent what would nowadays amount to £1000 to £1500 on a new one for himself, as may appear by his account with John Crancks, goldsmith of London, yet he was never a bishop.[5] The bishops were apt to look with suspicion on pretentions of this kind; and no wonder. 'I can't be made to resign,' wrote John Smart, Abbot of Wigmore, to Cromwell in 1528, 'because I am a

---

[1] This was John Stonywell, later Abbot of Pershore.   [2] *L.P.*, IV, 4708.
[3] *L.P.*, IV, 4808.   [4] *L.P.*, VI, 1496.
[5] Journal of Prior More (*Worcestershire Historical Society*), I, 167.

bishop and my abbey is in perpetual *commendam*.'[1] This strange abbot was, by reason of his bishopric of Pavada *in partibus*, able to snap his fingers, not only at the Bishop of Hereford, but also at the Cardinal, now tottering to his fall. He threw the diocese of Llandaff into confusion by ordaining on his own responsibility a thousand priests in seven years at the rate of sixty a time. Bishop Foxe of Hereford made a desperate attempt to get rid of him in 1536, and his injunctions show that he believed all the charges which the canons had brought against their abbot.[2] But he was still in office when the abbey surrendered in 1538. Not only did he receive the huge pension of £80 (about £2000 a year) but he was subsequently employed by the Bishop of Lichfield as his assistant. A number of abbots and priors were acting in this way before the suppression, and Pope Clement VII's bull of 1529 seems to have contemplated an extension of this practice, so to provide the bishops with episcopal assistance at little or no cost to themselves.

Visitations were carried out at intervals of roughly three years. They might be performed by the bishop in person, or by an official acting for him. Bishops employed at court, or who held high office under the Crown, naturally had to resort to the latter method. Bishop Longland of Lincoln, for instance, rarely intervened except on receipt of a report of a particularly scandalous nature furnished him by his chancellor, whereas his 'predecessor, Bishop Atwater, carried out most of his visitations in person. A time-table of a very strenuous kind was made out by the secretary, for the bishop often managed to get through a visitation of a religious house and of a whole deanery of secular clergy in the course of a single day. He spent the night, if he had no country house of his own in the district,

---

[1] *L.P.*, IV, 5121.   [2] *L.P.*, XII (1), 743.

at one of the monasteries he was inspecting and at its
expense, or he was entertained by one of the local clergy
or gentry.[1]

How far did the bishop know beforehand the state of
the monasteries which he was to visit? It is to be presumed
that he knew a great deal. He had, of course, the record
of the previous visitation to guide him. In addition, he
could always count on being furnished with information
either from country gentry and townspeople who had an
interest in the welfare of the religious houses of their
neighbourhood or from disgruntled monks or canons.
In fact, the country gentry and discontented religious were
often hand in glove and joined together in presenting
complaints to the bishop against an abbot or prior, just
as parishioners did and do against their incumbent. The
misdeeds of Bishop Smart, Abbot of Wigmore, for instance,
were denounced by a local magnate, Thomas Croft (son of
Sir Edward Croft, an important member of the Council of
Wales) on information given by one of the canons. Bishop
Foxe of Winchester had a report from the canons of Merton
in 1509 that their prior had been keeping women and
stealing jewels, and he had to issue an order that no canon
should be punished for writing to him.[2] The Bishop of
Lincoln seems to have kept a regular party among the
canons of Leicester, the members of which furnished him
with gossip about the abbot, and who looked to the bishop
for preferment. Hugh Oliver, prior of this abbey, was
continually running off to London or to the bishop on this
errand, trying to work the resignation of the abbot in the
hope of succeeding him.[3]

[1] See the arrangements for the Visitation of the diocese of Norwich by Bishop
Nicke in 1514; Jessopp, *Norwich Visitations*, pp. 65-71.
[2] See the Bishop's injunctions in Heales's *Records of Merton Priory*, pp. 318-21.
[3] He failed, but he soon got the priory of Huntingdon instead.

II

The bishop, coming to a religious house for the purpose of visitation, was accompanied by his legal advisers, generally the archdeacon, the official of his consistory court, the commissary general and a public notary 'by apostolic and imperial authority' to write down an account of the proceedings (all expecting their fees). The party arrived at the great west door of the abbey (or priory) church, was received with a solemn procession by the abbot and convent, and was conducted to the high altar among the pealing of bells and the playing of the organ. Prayers were said and the benediction given and then the whole assemblage migrated to the chapter house to listen to a sermon, preached sometimes by a religious, sometimes by a learned secular clergyman. Judging by the texts on which they were based, the sermons must often have caused much searching of heart. 'I have found my sheep which was lost' was a text most appropriate for Wymondham Abbey, in which there were far too many lost sheep in the visitation of 1520. 'I went down into the garden of nuts to see the fruits of the valley' was the text at Westacre, a house in sad decay and little likely to produce fruit of any kind. When the reforming Prior Oliver preached at the Bishop of Lincoln's visitation of Leicester in 1525 from the text 'This is pure religion and undefiled before God'[1] he was not describing the existing state of the abbey: hounds swarmed everywhere, fouling church, cloister, chapter house; canons got out of the house before sunrise to hunt or to frequent suspect houses in the town. A lot of ignorant, lazy and chattering novices, older canons entertaining and

[1] Lincoln Visitations of Bishop Longland, fol. 22.

drinking with friends in their rooms. All these facts came out at the visitation, although the abbot had beforehand told the brethren to reveal nothing. The prior must thoroughly have enjoyed holding forth from his text. Sometimes, on the other hand, the texts indicated a favourable state of affairs. Nothing could have been more satisfactory than the report of the Bishop of Norwich on the nuns of Thetford in 1514, who seem truly to have lived up to the text chosen for them, 'Mary hath chosen the better part'.[1]

After the sermon, all laymen and other unauthorized persons having been ejected, the bishop proceeded to the business of the day. The abbot (or prior) produced a certificate containing the names of the religious who were, or ought to have been, present, and the bishop, having explained the object of the visitation, proceeded, either in person or by his officials, to examine the religious, one by one, beginning with the head of the house and ending with the novices. This examination was always made *secrete et singillatim*, and the abuse which has been poured on the royal visitors by naive sentimentalists is based on ignorance of the fact that in this, as in other matters, the visitors were following rules which the bishops had always used.

Some visitations took a very short time. 'The certificate having been produced, there appeared all the monks (or canons or nuns) and after they had been duly examined and nothing having been disclosed either by the prior or by any of the monks, the visitor dissolved his visitation and dismissed those who had been visited in peace. One such happy house was the small Augustinian priory of Bromehill in Norfolk. When Prior Barlow was examined by the Bishop of Norwich in 1526 he testified handsomely to the

---

[1] *Norwich Visitations*, p. 90.

excellent state of his house, the morals and behaviour of his colleagues, the canons, and generally that all was perfect. Little could he foresee that he was destined to be a bishop and the father-in-law of other bishops, or that so much ink would be wasted on him by the inhabitants of the controversial underworld.'[1]

The bishop and his officials did not always accept reports of this favourable nature, for there was often something behind them. The bishop came and went, the abbot (or prior) was in permanent residence, and it was therefore often dangerous for his subordinates to say anything at all. At his visitation of the priory of Kirkby Bellars, Leicestershire, in 1519 the Bishop of Lincoln found that the prior was accustomed to threaten the canons who disclosed anything to the bishop and hated and ill-treated them in future if they did so. 'I told the bishop at his last visitation,' said a canon of Caldwell, Bedfordshire, in 1525, 'that the prior's adherents bring women to him with whom he commits adultery. He has imprisoned me for letting this out.'[2]

The Prior of Chacombe, again, always rebuked his canons for disclosures made. This abuse had, of course, gone on for centuries. So long ago as 1275 the Prior of Bolton in Craven had ordered his canons *by virtue of their obedience* to agree with each other on what they said at the visitation. There was also, as has been pointed out, more than once, a natural prejudice against sneaks, and for that reason the bishop had often to fall back on outside information, such as that of the neighbouring country gentry. He often got a commission appointed from their ranks, as

---

[1] *Norwich Visitations*, p. 241. For the career of William Barlow, Bishop of St. Asaph 1536, St. David's 1536-48, Bath and Wells 1548-54 and Chichester 1559-68, see *Dictionary of National Biography*.
[2] *Lincoln Visitations*, Longland MSS., fol. 46.

the Bishop of Lichfield did in 1497, for the purpose of inquiring into the excesses of the monks of Upholland in Lancashire.[1]

Visitors, then, might find houses where discipline was kept and all was in order. They might find houses where the inmates dared not complain for fear of consequences, in which case other sources of information had to be tapped. They might find houses in disorder of various degrees, in which case their disciplinary powers had to be brought into play.

In all cases the head of the house, abbot or prior, was examined first. Then the officers of the monastery, prior, cellarer and so forth. The notary took down the evidence, the name of each individual being placed in the margin against his complaints or commendations. Let us take first the nature of the complaints which were made by the various individuals and ranks in a religious house.

The abbot (or prior) produced the accounts of the house for the past year, so that the visitor might be informed of its financial state, and also an inventory of its jewels and plate, that the visitor might know if any of them had been sold or pawned, a very necessary subject of inquiry. The abbot would then proceed to give his opinion on the merits or otherwise of his subordinates. The usual cause of complaint was that of disobedience. 'My brethren,' said the Prior of Hickling to the Bishop of Norwich in 1526, 'are incorrigible, rebellious and disobedient, and refuse to submit to my correction.'[2] The bishop in this case accepted the prior's version of things (the canons had made bitter complaints of bad cooking and the depredations of the prior's relations) and gave him extensive powers of correcting his unruly canons, especially in the matter of gadding

---

[1] *V.C.H. Lancs*, II., III.   [2] *Norwich Visitations*, p. 212.

about the country. 'Two of my canons,' said the Abbot of Bourne to the Bishop of Lincoln's commissary in 1525, 'sleep in their own rooms instead of in the dormitory, where they and others drink, jest and tattle from morning till night.' The Prior of Woodbridge, Suffolk, made a similar complaint to the Bishop of Norwich. 'Two of my canons frequent the town without my leave . . . one of whom gets drunk and won't get up for mattins.' The Abbot of Humberstone, in 1525, lamented that his monks go into the town without his leave and spend the day playing tennis (*ludent ad tennisios*).[1] Seven years before he had been complaining that they make a habit of staying out all night. Prior Baker of Launceston, Cornwall, resigned in 1532 in despair because he could not induce his brethren to observe the rules of their religion. This is the last thing which the canons appear to have wished to do, and they tried to get a very vicious colleague elected. They failed, but they had their revenge on their new head. Prior Shere told the Bishop of Exeter, in answer to their complaints against him, that when he had punished them for running into debt in the town and had affixed a notice to that effect to the church door, three of the canons tore it down and he had to imprison them to avoid being slain by them.[2]

A reforming head had a terrible time when once a house had got out of hand. Heads of houses who tried to restore discipline after a weak or vicious regime were often faced with the hostility of the partisans of the deprived or resigned head. Such was the fate of the last Prior of Walsingham, Doctor Richard Vowell. His very unseemly predecessor, Prior Lowthe, to whose malpractices we shall come in due course, had been forced to resign in 1514. But he had immediately got himself elected — presumably by bribery

[1] *Lincoln Visitations*, Longland MS., fol. 3. [2] *L.P.*, v, 837.

of the cardinal or some other highly placed personage — prior of the almost equally important house of Augustinian canons at Westacre, less than twenty miles away. When the Bishop of Chalcedon, the Bishop of Norwich's suffragan, visited Walsingham six years later he found the priory rent in twain by two contending factions, one supporting the prior in possession, the other representing the adherents of the former prior. Nothing, said Prior Vowell, would induce the canons to obey him and the leader of the opposition, Canon John Aylsham, said flatly that nothing would induce him to do so. The Bishop of Chalcedon took the prior's part and severely punished the rebels, as punishment went: a week's sitting in the lowest place in choir, fasting on bread and beer on the following Friday, and saying the Lord's Prayer five times all together before the high altar. The report of the visitation shows that the prior had sent in a formal statement of complaints against the rebel canons, which he had evidently forwarded to the bishop before the visitation.[1]

After the head of the house had ventilated his grievances the officers next in rank had their turn. Their complaints might be directed against their superiors or against those below them. 'The prior,' said the sub-prior of Hickling, Norfolk, in 1526, 'is a tyrant and gives no leave to his brethren to go outside the precincts for the sake of exercise. I won't stay in the place any longer.' In fact, just as the prior had been examined about all his subordinates, so the sub-prior was examined both about the prior and about the rest of the brethren. Here, for example, are typical complaints of the Prior of Wymondham against both abbot and monks of his house. 'The abbot,' said he at the visitation of 1514,[2] 'keeps the offices of cellarer and

---

[1] *Norwich Visitations*, p. 170.   [2] Ibid., pp. 95-101.

sacrist in his own hands and on that account the monks have nothing fit to eat or drink.' Then he turned on his colleagues: 'I have to report that the chamberlain of the abbey, Dom James Bloom, has suspicious relations with Mrs. Collins and other women who haunt his chamber; that the sacrist Dom Richard Cambridge does not believe in the resurrection at the last day, that my brethren won't study, and just because I tried to correct them they blaspheme my name everywhere inside the monastery and out. What, too, about Dom John Hengham's relations with Mrs. Hubbard, Dom John Cambridge stealing a cookery book or Dom Thomas Ixworth breaking open a coffer?' When the monks' turn to talk about the prior came they naturally took the opportunity to turn the tables on him. It would seem that if he encountered opposition he drew a sword on his opponents almost as quickly as a modern gangster would produce a sawn-off shot gun. The evidence of the other officers was next taken; the cellarer, whose business it was to look after the food supply of the monastery. His complaints were generally directed against the squandering of victuals. 'I can't give the food which ought to go to the poor,' said the cellarer of St. Benet Holme, 'because of the number of dogs in the monastery which devour it all.' The passion for hunting which afflicted many monasteries was evidently very prevalent here, for the third prior immediately after mattins, would rush off, summer and winter, to hunt. The monks' complaints against the cellarer were, on the other hand, chiefly directed against the mismanagement of the culinary arrangements and sometimes against his diversion of stores to his relatives and friends. And so we might take the complaints of all the officers in turn — the sacrist about the size of the vestments, the outrider about the want of repairs to the farm buildings, the pitanciarius for not paying the pittances (or extra allowances of food, etc.) to the monks.

The complaints of the rank and file of the monks were of all kinds. Sometimes they were verbal, sometimes they would produce a long written statement of grievances. Complaints about food and drink were frequent. 'We are only given drink fit for peasants and the prior and his servants put down all the best liquor.' Naturally there was considerable tension between the seniors and juniors. The older monks had often to complain about the sauciness of the younger brethren, who poked fun at them and merely laughed when they were sentenced to correction. They were apt, too, to laugh at old-fashioned ways. 'They simply won't observe ceremonies,' complained one of the officers of Norwich Priory. 'They do nothing but play dice and cards here,' said another of the officers of this monastery. Sometimes the complaints concerned the monks or canons who were up at the university, either that the rule was not carried out, or that the monk students wasted their time at college and did nothing but run up debts. That no provision was made for the instruction of novices was a frequent grievance, so was the insolence of the servants. It could not have been very pleasant for the canons of Holy Trinity, Ipswich, to be told by a servant of the house, 'If you dare to meddle with me I will give you a clout that you won't recover from for a twelvemonth', or for those of Walsingham to be called fools by the servants when they were asked to set forth food and drink when the canons' relations and friends came to see them.

III

The internal difficulties of the monasteries are, however, most clearly to be seen in the grievances which the monks vented to the bishop against their head. There were nearly, always two parties in a house and in passing judgment on its discipline it is always necessary to examine very closely the relations in which the witnesses stood to the abbot. Those who favoured him naturally said that all was well under his rule; those who opposed him, that nothing could be worse. Sentimentalist writers are apt to lay exclusive stress on the evidence of the abbot's partisans, while scavengers seize upon that of the grumblers. However, it is well to see what the average monk did complain about to the bishop. Many of the grievances are on small points where a tactless superior would be likely to cause offence. 'The abbot,' testified the monks of Peterborough at the visitation of Bishop Atwater of Lincoln in 1519 'vilipends us before strangers and juniors.' Sometimes he failed to pay the *peculium* — the pocket money which was the perquisite of the monks. Sometimes he held many offices in his hands. 'Our abbot,' complained the monks of Croyland to Bishop Atwater, 'has in his hands the offices of cellarer and receiver and cuts down our food.' 'We know nothing about the financial state of the house because the abbot renders no account' is a constant source of grievance. So is the practice of appointing officers without the consent of the convent. The monks of Ramsey in 1519 asserted that the abbot had made a drunken babbling monk prior against their will.

The right of the monks to share in the administration of the property of the house was ignored over and over again

by the abbot. He would bestow rich livings in the gift of
the house at his own discretion. Using his seal of office, he
would grant leases or annuities to his friends or relatives,
and many houses were sadly crippled on this account.
He would pawn jewels and plate at his own discretion. His
friends and relations were apt to come and plant themselves in the monastery itself and this caused further
complications. 'The abbot's sister,' complained the monks
of Eynsham to Bishop Atwater, 'dwells in the precincts
and is very burdensome to the monastery.' She and several
of her relations are said to be kept at its expense. Hangers
on of this kind often egged the abbot on to heavy expenses
in entertaining guests. 'The abbot,' said the canons of
Leicester, 'is very burdensome to the monastery because
of his extravagance in feasts and banquets.'

When the dissensions between abbot and convent were
very serious the charges against the former naturally
became graver and more reckless. The canons of Leicester
revenged themselves on Abbot Sadyngton for his stern
rule (he had tried to stop them from hunting) by accusing
him of dabbling in alchemy and magic and of more than
one lapse from virtue. The fact is that a great many heads
of houses gave a handle to their discontented subordinates
by keeping unwise company.

As a result of complaints in visitation, bishops often
enjoined that the abbot or prior should not talk to any
woman except in the presence of two monks or canons.
But it was very difficult to carry this into effect, and there
can be no doubt but that women often exercised a most
unwholesome influence on the discipline and peace of
many a monastery. What could the canons of Nostell —
the greatest Augustinian house in Yorkshire — have
thought when an aged prior could not be got to resign 'by

reason of a woman that kept him',[1] or the monks of Eye of Mrs. Veere, who dwelt with the prior, kept the keys of his room, served at his table and slept in the room next to his?[2] or those of Pershore of Mrs. Westerfield who 'by reason of her unlawful familiarity with the abbot' had charge of his keys and was able to dispose of a large part of the abbey plate to her own advantage?[3] About the same time Mrs. Taylor caused a rebellion in the great abbey of Malmesbury because of her habit of going about the town picking up gossip about the monks and repeating it to the abbot.[4] Just before the Bishop of Norwich visited Walsingham in 1514[5] Prior Lowthe addressed the canons in the chapter house and said, 'You can complain as much as you like, but you will never be the better for it. If I thought that the bishop should be against me, I should work things so that he can't hurt me. And when he is gone I shall rule and ask no leave of *him*'. The reason for this outburst was apparent enough when the bishop began his inquiries. There was in the town a house kept by a Mrs. Smith, to which the canons of the prior's faction used to resort to eat and drink till eleven o'clock at night. Mrs. Smith had the keys of most of the stores in the priory: she bought fish for it in the markets, while her husband was its caterer. It was at the monastery's expense that she went on a pilgrimage to Canterbury, to what spiritual edification it would be difficult to imagine. 'Why,' said the bishop to Canon Rase at the visitation, 'is the prior so spiteful to you?' 'Because,' said the canon, 'I called Mrs. Smith a whore. Afterwards he made me apologize to her publicly in the chapter house.' How was the bishop to deal with charges of this kind? In the case of Prior Lowthe the Bishop

---

[1] *L.P.*, XIII., 409.   [2] *Norwich Visitations*, p. 184.   [3] *L.P.*, VI, 298.
[4] *L.P.*, IV, 3678, and see below, p. 93.   [5] *Norwich Visitations*, pp. 113-23.

of Norwich was able to induce him to resign, but not to reform. For at the visitation of 1520 he was reported by the canons of his new charge at Westacre to be very sensual and extravagant.[1] Mrs. Smith had, perhaps, followed him? or he had found a substitute for her.

It was very rare, however, for an unfit head to be got rid of as easily as this. The Bishop of Lincoln's commissary, Doctor Jackman, made a visitation of the large Augustinian house of Missenden in Buckinghamshire on October 10th, 1530,[2] at which the abbot and thirteen canons appeared, whose evidence and disclosures (*dicta et detectiones*) follow. The abbot and the eight professed canons gave their version of the state of the house. A very few said that all was well, but they were those against whom the most serious charges were made. The result was that Doctor Jackman gave a series of injunctions. A comparison of these with the evidence given effectually disposes of the notion that these commands were only common form, since the punishments awarded in particular cases directly refer to charges made against individuals as recorded in the *detecta*. It would seem, however, that they were not obeyed, for a few months later, namely on June 19th, 1531, the Bishop appeared in person at the abbey.[3] He must in the meantime have been furnished with additional particulars, because when the abbot appeared before him he had to 'answer to certain articles'. 'Were you or were you not familiar with Mrs. Bishop before her marriage? Is Canon Roger Palmer your go-between?' and so on. It is evident from the abbot's answers that further charges had been preferred against him in the interval between the commissary's and the bishop's visitation. The name of

[1] *Norwich Visitations*, p. 165.
[2] *Lincoln Visitations*, Longland MSS., fol. 94.
[3] Ibid., fol. 77.

Mrs. Bishop, for instance, appears for the first time. This lady had, according to the evidence of one of the canons, been brought from High Wycombe to Missenden by the abbot, who confessed that his reputation had suffered for years because of her. One of the canons, wearing a doublet and jerkin with a sword by his side, was also often in her company, having thoughtfully provided himself with a set of false keys so as to be able to escape from the monastery without difficulty. They both confessed to the charge. A week later the bishop issued a second set of injunctions, a good deal stricter than those of Doctor Jackman, and written in English instead of Latin, in order that the most ignorant canon should have no excuse for misunderstanding their purport. 'Forasmuch that as well in our late ordinary visitation, as in our special visitation also executed in our person divers things appeared and were detected worthy of reformation and punishment.' The abbot was suspended and the canon against whom the worst charges were made was to be 'gated' and given no office in future: while Mrs. Bishop's friend was forbidden to wear 'any garded or welted hose or stuffed codpiece or jerkyn or any other short or costly garments': his kirtle was to be long enough to go down to his ankles. Not a very severe punishment, even if it was ever imposed. Abbot Fox might be suspended, but he died in office a short time later. The two scoundrelly canons not only received pensions at the dissolution of the abbey, but ended their days as country parsons of neighbouring parishes, one as vicar of the Lee, the other as curate-in-charge of Choulesbury. The fact was that the bishops, whatever their theoretical powers might be, were quite helpless in dealing with religious houses which had sunk as low as this one had.

Nor were the visitors of exempt orders and houses much

more successful in this matter. Not very much is known of their activities, since the records of the visitations in the period immediately before the general suppression have mostly disappeared. The most extensive set of records which we have, that of the visitations of the order of Premonstratensian canons by Bishop Redman, Abbot of Shap, do not carry us beyond the year 1500.[1] The report of the general visitation of the Cistercians, which was undertaken by two Cistercian abbots in 1535, the year in which Doctors Leigh and Layton set out on their visitation, does not seem to be extant. Two earlier, and very discouraging, reports on Cistercian houses, Thame and Bruerne, survive, while of the exempt Benedictine monasteries there is an important case at Malmesbury in 1527. A great deal of trouble had been caused all through the Middle Ages by the fact that, apart from the Benedictines and the wholly English order of Gilbertine canons, the heads of the exempt orders resided in the domains of the King of France, and a long struggle, beginning as early as the thirteenth century, ensued between them and the Crown, anxious to stop money going to the subjects of the chief enemy of England. The only safe way for the monks and canons of these exempt establishments was to get them naturalized as purely English houses. When the large priory of St. Neots in Huntingdonshire procured from Henry IV authority to become independent of Bec in Normandy, it could only do so by promising that henceforth all the priors should be Englishmen and that none but English monks should be received into the convent. This process went on all through the fifteenth century and by the early sixteenth it was nearly complete. The Cluniac

[1] Printed in *Collectanea Anglo-Premonstratensia.* (*Camden Society*, Third Series, vols. X and XII).

houses were by now all naturalized. In 1512 the Abbot of Welbeck was given authority to hold the General Chapter of the Premonstratensians in England whose houses were freed from the jurisdiction of the Abbot of Prémontré in France.[1] The Abbot of Welbeck was also to be one of the royal chaplains, and, as a letter of Bishop Maxey in 1535 shows,[2] supervisor of all the elections of abbots of houses of his order — a post of very great emolument indeed. Under these circumstances it was not likely that the English Premonstratensians would make much resistance to royal wishes. Nor indeed did they. In 1532 the Cistercians were similarly severed from their connections oversea, and a royal commission was issued to the Abbots of Fountains, Woburn, Byland, Tower Hill and Neath to visit all houses of their order, both of men and women, in place of the Abbot of Chailly, 'since it is not thought convenient to admit him, a stranger and an inhabitant of France'.[3] Something of the same kind must have happened to the Carthusians, since it was the two priors of Sheen and Witham who were appointed by the Crown to be visitors of their order in 1537.[4]

The visitations were nominally triennial, but it may be doubted if they were, in fact, held so frequently. It is certainly suspicious that the patrons of the monasteries were continually calling for visitations, or invoking the assistance of the Crown to procure one.

In 1525, Bishop Longland of Lincoln had his attention directed to the affairs of the great Oxfordshire abbey of Thame.[5] He could not visit it in person, since it was exempt. Luckily for him, he was patron of the abbey

---

[1] *L.P.*, I, 1365. [2] Wright, *Suppression*, p. 83. [3] *L.P.*, v, 978, Grant 6.
[4] *L.P.*, XII (2), 601.
[5] This correspondence is printed in full in *English Historical Review*, vol. III, p. 704 ff.

(which was of the foundation of the Bishops of Lincoln) and so could put pressure on the Abbot of Waverley, whom Wolsey had made visitor of the Cistercians in England, to make a visitation. Early in 1526 the visitor came to Thame to examine the abbot and monks on the charges which the bishop had brought against them. 'You,' he said to Abbot Warren, 'are charged, not only with personal immorality, but with outrageous extravagance. You keep such a large staff of useless servants and entertain so many guests that the abbey is in extreme poverty and decay and its buildings in ruin. You allow your monks to give feasts at restaurants in the town and spend their time at archery parties. Both you and they are so ignorant that you don't even know the rules of the Order. You,' said the visitor to the prior, 'don't try to keep the monks in order. And what were you doing on your last visit to London, with the key of the chest in which the common seal of the monastery is kept? And you, Dom Chinnor, what sort of houses do you haunt in Thame, and wasn't your behaviour at Oxford so bad that you were indicted at the last assizes?'

The abbot and the monks denied nearly all the charges, and the visitor reported to the bishop that he had held the visitation and given injunctions. The bishop was furious. 'I never,' wrote he to the Abbot of Waverley, 'heard such ridiculous and frivolous answers as those of the Abbot of Thame. He simply tries to evade the issue. Why you don't even mention the more serious charges. Now just let me take his answers one by one. He admits that women get in. Women! and in a Cistercian monastery of all places! He admits that he allows his monks to go to public games and to give feasts. And how, pray, do they pay for these out of their stipends? As for your injunctions you do no more than repeat the rules of the Order and don't touch the complaints at all. If you don't pay some attention to them I shall seek a remedy elsewhere. And, mind you, if you won't do your obvious duty and get in a better lot of monks I shall apply the possessions of the monastery to some use more acceptable to God.' Three years later the bishop wrote to Wolsey, 'The abbot is dead. There is nobody fit to succeed him and the house is deeply in debt'. All his efforts had been in vain. The Abbot of Waverley had thought more of the independence of his order than of the welfare of Thame Abbey.

In 1533 a number of monks of Rievaulx wrote to the patron, the Earl of Rutland, to complain about the behaviour of Abbot Kirkby. 'May I,' wrote the Earl to Cromwell, 'have the King's letters to get a commission to examine and do justice on the Abbot of Rievaulx?'[1] The Commission was duly issued. 'Proceed at once', wrote Cromwell to the Abbots of Fountains and Byland, 'to the election of a new Abbot of Rievaulx according to the King's letters.' Doctor Thomas Leigh, the royal visitor of 1535, was able to report that an election to 'my Lord's mind and yours' is imminent. The visiting abbots played the part which was expected of them. To make sure of their ground they examined the monks separately in a secret chamber, and not in the chapter house, and they evidently got evidence of the kind the patron wanted, for they were able to announce that, having had the abbot before them, they had forced a pension of £44 on him. The patron's wishes were fulfilled.

In 1527 the Abbot of St. Peter's, Gloucester, *reformator* by commission from the Abbot of Westminster, president of the Black Monks of England, held a visitation of the exempt

---

[1] *L.P.*, VI, 546. See below, p. 164.

abbey of Malmesbury, where there had been a rebellion of the most serious kind.[1] There were fierce recriminations in the chapter house. The abbot accused no fewer than sixteen monks of rebellion: while they answered, 'What about Mrs. Taylor?' But they did not on her account get rid of their abbot who was still in office at the time of his death six years later.

It is quite obvious that no injunctions, however severe, on the part of visitors had any lasting effect. When Bishop Redman visited the Kentish abbey of St. Radegund's he was told by the canons of the strange behaviour of their abbot, who seems to have had considerable fame in the neighbourhood as a retailer of doubtful stories. Although the buildings of the monastery were almost in ruin, Abbot Newton made no attempt to raise money for repairs, but spent his Sundays in the local public house, where his language and anecdotes were of a hair-raising description. One hesitates, however, to place great faith in the visitor's statement that they tired his hearers, unless, of course, his reputation was that of a club bore. But although the visitor told him to mend his ways, no attempt seems to have been made to get rid of him.[2] In 1494 Bishop Redman visited the Lancashire abbey of Cockersand, where Canon Thomas Pulton's relations with more than one woman were so notorious that he was unable to defend himself.[3] But the punishment inflicted on him, mild though it seems, was soon remitted by the visitor on the petition of the abbot and other canons. Nor did Canon Pulton's lapse interfere with his promotion, for at the next visitation, only three years later, he was in charge of the discipline of the abbey as sub-prior. Again, in 1494, Canon John

[1] *L.P.*, IV, 3678, and see above, p. 86.
[2] *Collectanea Anglo-Premonstratensia*, III, 104.
[3] Ibid., III, 121 and 125.

Bebe of Dale abbey in Derbyshire confessed to having been the father of a child.[1] But that unfortunate event did not stop him from becoming abbot of Dale, from holding his post till the surrender, or from being granted a large pension.

When Wolsey became legate he was in a position to override all these exempt jurisdictions. But the cardinal was not able to effect anything notable in the way of reformation. It must, in most cases, have been almost impossible to see where the truth lay. In 1524 a visitation of the great Cluniac monastery of Wenlock in Shropshire was undertaken, evidently as a result of a petition of the monks to the patron (the Crown) against the prior.[2] They represented that his wasteful administration had brought the priory into debt to an extent which would nowadays amount to over £20,000. He on his part maintained that the whole trouble was due to an unlawful confederacy among the monks because he had restrained them from their old unlawful liberties and blocked up the back doors of the cloisters and monastery so that they could not get out at their pleasure. Their demeanour, he asserted, put him in fear of his life. He was, in fact, deprived 'for execrable living' as his enemies asserted. He got a large pension, with which he was not satisfied. It was, indeed, almost as injurious for a religious house to get a bad head deprived as it was to keep him. Prior Gosnell spent his last years in badgering the king to get him restored and in stirring up trouble for his successor. Tiresome old men like this had much to do with the Pilgrimage of Grace, as we shall see in due course. Bishops and other visitors did their best, but in practice they effected very little. When the Act of Suppression of 1536

---

[1] *Collectanea Anglo-Premonstratensia*, II, 182.   [2] *L.P.*, IV, 954.

spoke of the failure of visitations 'by space of two hundred years and more' it stated no more than the truth. Two years later a committee of cardinals and others in Italy was making the same accusation in almost the same words. The scandals of exemptions and remissions of punishment for cash was clearly indicated by them as *the* curse of the day.[1]

[1] See below, p. 289.

CHAPTER IV

PRECEDENTS FOR SUPPRESSION
1308—1534

I

THE strength of an established institution is very great, and unless external pressure of a violent kind is applied it will continue to function, however ominous may be its internal weakness. During the two centuries which preceded their dissolution, external pressure was being exercised on the monasteries in ever growing measure. We are no longer in the twelfth century when great personages, with a view to safeguarding their interests in the next world, were founding religious houses one after another.

After the thirteenth century hardly any religious houses were founded except a few for Carthusians[1] — an order which retained its primitive fervour far longer than any of its rivals — but the funds which were set aside for their endowment did not, as a rule, represent 'new money', but came from the proceeds of the disendowment of the alien priories. The rebuilding of parish churches, and the erection of colleges, schools and almshouses took the place of the monasteries as objects of fashionable devotion.

A movement towards the suppression of the monasteries can be discerned all through the fourteenth and fifteenth centuries. It took two forms. First, of cutting the connection between the English houses and their foreign heads,

---

[1] Of the nine houses of this order in England only two (Witham and Hinton, in Somerset) were founded before the fourteenth century.

followed by the gradual seizure of the property of alien priories by the Crown. Secondly, by the elimination, under various pretexts, of small and decayed English houses. The sense of nationality which set in during the thirteenth century made Englishmen increasingly disinclined to watch their money go out of the country to foreigners. The Statute of Carlisle of 1307 forbade religious persons in monasteries within the king's jurisdiction from sending money to their superiors abroad, a statute which was but a forerunner of the Annates Act of 1532, which extended the disendowment of foreigners to the pope.

Almost at the same time the pope himself was assenting to the suppression of the great order of the Templars. Their houses in England were seized into the king's hands, and though most of the property went to the rival order of the Hospitallers, it was only after a long time that the latter were able to recover it from the barons who had laid hands on it, while the Crown, the nobles and the lawyers made large profits out of the affair. Edward III and Henry V took advantage of the French wars to 'seize into the king's hands' all the possessions which foreign, i.e. French, monasteries held on this side of the sea; and in 1414 those possessions were finally confiscated by Act of Parliament. 'Henry V breakfasted and Henry VIII dined' on church property. Most, though by no means all, of the proceeds were used for charitable or educational purposes, though often not for a long time. New College, Oxford, for example, did not get possession of Newington Longeville in Buckinghamshire (of which the Norman abbey of Longeville Gifford had been deprived) for nearly thirty years after this Act.[1] There was no wholesale

[1] Salter, 'Newington Longeville Charters' (*Oxfordshire Record Society*, vol. III, p. xl). The introduction to this volume gives an admirable account of the vicissitudes to which the alien priories were exposed.

destruction of buildings because there were, as a rule, none to destroy. Commonly the property or 'cell' was occupied by one or two monks acting as representatives of the foreign owners: and all they had to do after the suppression was to retire to their mother houses oversea. When the establishment was comparatively large it might become a 'cell' of an English house. This happened to Deerhurst in Gloucestershire, which was given to Tewkesbury abbey, the monastic church of Deerhurst and most of the buildings remaining intact, as indeed they do to this day. Otherwise the buildings were just allowed to go to decay. On the eastern slopes of the Black Mountains on the borders of Herefordshire and Wales, there was a small Gramontine house called Craswall, the remains of which can still be seen. 'The buildings were apparently left standing to fall gradually into ruin or to be used as a quarry.' A foretaste of what was to happen in the sixteenth century on a larger scale.

The main difference between the earlier and later suppression was, as has been mentioned already, that most of the confiscated property was preserved for pious or educational uses. The great Carthusian house of Sheen and the Brigittine house of Sion, founded by Henry V, represented the monastic acquisitions. Colleges of Oxford and Cambridge, and the great collegiate chapel of St. George at Windsor represented the chief gains of the secular clergy. The interests of the souls of the founders' ancestors were also safeguarded. When Newington Longeville was given to New College it was on condition that the warden and fellows should 'in future pray more heartily for the said King', while the warden and fellows of All Souls were (and presumably are) similarly bound to pray for the souls of those who fell at Agincourt.

The foreign houses had, of course, their special difficulties and the French wars made their fate inevitable. But there was also going on another process which involved the fall of a large number of the smaller English houses. This process might lead to the absorption of a small house in a greater, as Flitcham was absorbed by Walsingham. But, and especially after the middle of the fifteenth century, the tendency was to convert their property to educational or other eleemosynary purposes. Some of these small houses collapsed out of poverty and loss of numbers. When Bishop Smith of Lincoln procured the suppression of the small house of Augustinian canons at Cold Norton in Oxfordshire there were no canons left. The property reverted to the Crown; the bishop bought it and gave it to Brasenose College, Oxford, of which he was visitor. In cases of this kind the first thing the king or bishop had to do was to get such of the monks or nuns as remained off the premises, after which they could treat the house as a 'waste place', a commission of inquiry having first sat to report on the state of things in the threatened house. It is useful to study the reports of some of these 'inquisitions', for they show that the commissioners of Henry VIII only copied the methods of their predecessors and above all in the matter of denigration. This was a weapon which was employed ruthlessly against the Templars, some of the charges against whom can be taken no more seriously than that which a contemporary Archbishop of Canterbury levelled against his suffragan, the Bishop of Lichfield, of not only interviewing the devil, but of practising obsequiousness in its most extreme form to that potentate.

When Bishop Alcock of Ely thought that a new college in Cambridge was needed he did not see why he should spend his own money on one. His eye fell on the nunnery of St. Radegund, just outside the town. There would, in this case, be no difficulty with the patron, for he himself held that office. All he had to do was to get a bull from the pope and a licence from the king. What he told them may be gathered from the terms of King Henry VII's licence of June 12th, 1497,[1] 'to expel the prioress and nuns from the convent of St. Radegund, Cambridge . . . which has become reduced to poverty and decay by reason *of the dissolute conduct and incontinence of the prioress and nuns on account of their vicinity to the University of Cambridge*, so that they cannot maintain divine service or hospitality or other works of mercy and pity according to their foundation, or support themselves, which are two in number, one of whom is professed elsewhere and the other an infant, and to found a college in its stead of one master, six fellows and a certain number of scholars to be instructed in grammar, to pray and celebrate divine service daily for the King, Queen, etc. . . . the college to be put into possession of the said priory and its lands and former possessions to be held in frank almoign'. How an absentee nun and an infant could bring any discredit on their house seems difficult to understand. So does the bishop's assertion that it was its neighbourhood to the university which had brought about the decay of the nunnery. But he was a Cambridge man himself and presumably had grounds for his statement. The result was the foundation of Jesus College, of which the nuns' church forms the chapel. Sad to relate, the records of the Bishop of Lincoln's visitation of similar establishments in the neighbourhood of Oxford give no better impression of the reputation of that university. The haunting of Godstow by Oxford scholars was a source of continual complaint. Even Studley, ten miles away, was not safe from them, and, in 1445, the bishop had to confide

[1] *Calendar of Patent Rolls of Henry VII*, p. 72.

the confessions of its nuns to the local vicar, 'because it is not seemly that scholars of Oxford should come to the nunnery'.[1]

A few years later Bishop Fisher of Rochester, acting as executor for the king's grandmother, Margaret Countess of Richmond, and anxious to safeguard the interests of her new and struggling foundation, St. John's College, Cambridge, directed his gaze on two nunneries, whose revenues would, he thought, be better employed in his old university. He picked out one in his own diocese, the other in that of Salisbury, and he and the Archdeacon of Rochester, Doctor Metcalfe (who was also, strangely enough, Master of St. John's) set to work to dissolve Higham and Bromhall. Like Bishop Alcock, they procured papal bulls,[2] and royal licences for the purpose. These documents could not naturally be quite in the same form as those employed by the Bishop of Ely. Bishop Fisher could not pretend that members of Cambridge University had corrupted Higham, so he fell back on another excuse, and a sufficiently odd one. He asserted that the nunnery was situated in a remote spot and was haunted by lascivious persons, especially clergymen. This charge he proceeded to substantiate. First he sent a clergyman called Doctor Richard Sharpe to inquire into the state of things at Higham. This emissary reported that there had once been sixteen nuns at the house, now never more than three or four: that these nuns were vehemently noted for incontinence: that many of them had been corrupted by a clergyman and that choir worship, almsgiving and hospitality had diminished.

To prove his statement he produced the bishop's register

[1] *V.C.H. Oxon*, II, p. 78.
[2] The bulls are dated September 28th, 1524; *L.P.*, IV, 686. The account of the dissolution of Higham is printed from documents in St. John's College, Cambridge, in Baker's *History of St. John's College*, I, 89 ff.

with its record of the correction by the bishop of two of the nuns on account of their incontinence and adultery with a clergyman called Edward Sterope. He produced also a document which showed that the three remaining nuns had resigned all title and claim in the monastery into the hands of the bishop of their own free will, and not compelled by force or dread. Soon afterwards the bishop had before him several witnesses to testify to the misdeeds of which the nuns had been accused. 'Twelve years ago,' said John James, 'I was in the service of the Prioress and knew all about the goings on. The Prioress herself told me about the behaviour of two of the nuns with the Vicar. After the Bishop had visited the house and I knew what he had found out, I went to see Dame Elizabeth Penny. I found her sitting and weeping and I said, "Alas, madam, how happened this with you?" She said, "I should have been a great deal happier if none of this had ever come out". Then followed other witnesses to the same effect, including a midwife from Cobham, who asserted that she had brought up Dame Elizabeth's little boy until his death. Finally we have the decree of suppression. The lands and revenues, together with all the documents connected with the priory, went to St. John's, Cambridge, and so remain. The bishop and the master had had their way. One of the nuns was sent off to a nunnery in Cambridgeshire, while the peccant Elizabeth Penny went to St. Sepulchre's, Canterbury, where she must have found a colleague who was shortly to make a stir in England in the person of Elizabeth Barton, the famous Nun of Kent. Very similar were the proceedings of the bishop and archdeacon at Bromhall. Evidently with the connivance of the Bishop of Salisbury they got the prioress to resign on pension: the two remaining nuns left the house, which reverted to the Crown. The

King wrote to the Bishop of Salisbury to thank him for suppressing the house 'on account of the enormities there used', while the agent of the Master of St. John's wrote: 'I shall see to it that either by dimission or incorporation in other places the nuns never come near the house of Bromhall again.'[1]

These two cases have been treated at some length to show how even a prospective saint and martyr could act when he wanted his own way. The bishop's behaviour was no worse, but was certainly no better than that of the King's visitors a few years later. Doctor Leigh and Doctor Layton had plenty of precedents to go upon, and it was not only Cardinal Wolsey who furnished them.

II

It was, however, the cardinal who made suppression systematic instead of spasmodic. Hardly had he become legate *a latere* in 1518 than he procured a bull authorizing him to reform the monasteries, as Cardinal Richelieu was to do a century later. Six years afterwards another bull empowered him to suppress not only the great priory of St. Frideswide's, Oxford, but also additional monasteries to the value of 3000 ducats. The King gave his formal licence to the bulls and authorized the suppression of no fewer than twenty-one monasteries, whose revenues were to go towards the endowment of the cardinal's colleges at Oxford and Ipswich. Wolsey was more successful in suppressing monasteries than in reforming them: but since he was unable to reform himself this is perhaps natural.

[1] For the suppression of Bromhall see *L.P.*, III, 1863 and 2080, and *Berks and Bucks Archeological Society Transactions,* Vol. XXVII (1922).

Reform was, however, in the air, and only a few years before Cardinal Ximenes had obtained similiar powers in Spain. He had effected a drastic reform of the religious houses and had dispatched the more unseemly of the monks and friars to Morocco, whether with a view to convert the Moors to Christianity or in the hope of avoiding pensions for them does not appear. It has been said of the Pilgrim Fathers that when they landed in America they fell first on their knees and then on the aborigines: but in the case of the Spanish monks it is far more likely that the aborigines got in first and fell on them.

In England the religious had a great fright, and nothing can be more pathetic than the appeal of the Benedictines to Cardinal Wolsey. 'If the reformation is conducted with too much authority,' they urged, 'there will not be enough monks to inhabit the monasteries. At the present time, now the world is drawing to its end, very few desire to live an austere life.'[1] All exemptions having gone by the board, the cardinal-legate was able to visit *all* monks, canons and nuns. The friars themselves did not escape, not even the Observant Franciscans, of whom the pope himself was afraid, 'desperate beasts past shame' as he called them. The results of the visitations do not seem to have been very great: but they must have been useful in preparing the way for the next step, the suppression of the houses upon which the cardinal had an eye.

It is usually supposed that the religious houses suppressed by Wolsey were very small ones. This is not altogether true. Some, indeed, were quite large. The Cluniac priory of Daventry had ten monks, the Premonstratensian abbey of Bayham eleven canons, and the Augustinian priories of Lesnes, Kent, and St. Frideswide's, Oxford,

[1] *L.P.*, IV, 953.

eleven and fifteen canons respectively. It does not seem very clear why the cardinal marked out these particular houses for suppression. Some of the smaller were, no doubt, near their end in any case by reason of poverty and decay. A few, like Littlemore, were hopelessly demoralized. But there was nothing in the past history of most of them to warrant their suppression on financial or any other grounds. At Bayham, the late fifteenth-century visitations of the Premonstratensian Bishop Redman had not revealed anything seriously wrong. At Daventry, in 1520, the Bishop of Lincoln's commissary had only to blame the monks for their hunting proclivities and to try to get back to the house a monk who had been four years in apostasy. The cardinal was not, however, to be deterred. It was one of the articles of accusation brought against him by the conservative party, when his fall from power was at hand, that he 'shamefully slandered many good religious houses, and good virtuous men dwelling in them, but also suppressed by reason thereof above thirty houses of religion: and where by authority of his bull, he should not suppress any house that had more men of religion in number above six or seven, he hath suppressed divers houses that had above the numbers: and thereupon hath caused divers offices to be found by verdict, untruly, that the religious persons so suppressed had voluntarily forsaken their said houses, which was untrue: and so hath caused open perjury to be committed, to the high displeasure of Almighty God'.

That there was a great deal of justification for these accusations there can hardly be a doubt. When the cardinal issued a commission to the Bishop of Chichester and others to 'enquire into certain scandals' alleged against the abbot and canons of Bayham, he probably got the report he wanted, but was it an 'untrue verdict'? Did the Prior of Daventry really resign his office into the hands of the Bishop of Lincoln of his own free will? Did the monks refuse to elect another prior? Why did they in a body depart from the house and leave it deserted, so that Wolsey could seize it as a waste place? All these statements are found in the report of the inquiry of March 1525. But with what justification? and if Abbot Gale of Bayham was a cause of scandal, why did the cardinal send him as abbot to another house of his order?[1] Partly, one may suppose, to avoid having to pay him the pension which would otherwise have been due to him. As to the monks, canons or nuns, they were given the choice of being shifted to other houses or of going into the world with a sum down of £1[2] and their wages to date. Then the cardinal, like the King later on, seems to have chosen their new abode for them, and their new house was forced to receive them under pain of his displeasure.[3]

Another of the charges against the cardinal concerned impositions of all kinds which he levied upon the religious houses, and especially the bribes he took for his favour in making of abbots and priors. When the Cistercian abbey of Bruerne was visited in 1532 the prior testified that Abbot Macy 'at his first coming into the said monastery gave unto the Reverend Father in God, Thomas, late Cardinal of England, 250 marks of money [about £5,000 to-day] and 280 oaks of the greatest and best of all the woods of the monastery (which were afterwards carried to Oxford to the building of his college) for his promotion to the abbotship of Bruerne.'[4] All over the country this kind of thing went

[1] Lavendon in Buckinghamshire.
[2] Probably equal to about £30 nowadays.
[3] When the Bishop of Norwich visited the nunnery of Thetford in 1526 one of the nuns is called 'monialis professa in Wike': i.e. Wix, a small nunnery in Essex, which the Cardinal had suppressed. Jessopp, *Norwich Visitations*, p. 243.
[4] Longland MSS. at Lincoln. I have to thank Doctor Salter for a sight of his transcript of this Visitation. See above, p. 63.

on and the result is seen in the numerous rebellions which broke out in monasteries against the heads thrust on them by the cardinal. His proceedings caused widespread alarm. He was accused, but probably wrongly, of ignoring the rights of the patrons. The naturally conservative temperament of Englishmen manifested itself at Tonbridge, where the inhabitants wished to keep their house of canons rather than get a public school in exchange.[1] At Bayham, riotous persons 'disguised and unknown with painted faces and visors put back the canons' and promised them that whensoever they rang the bell, that they would come with a great power and defend them, just as the monks of Salley were to be put back in Yorkshire during the Pilgrimage of Grace.

He was accused also of getting money out of many houses whose heads were afraid that unless they paid up he would turn his eyes their way and procure further suppressions. That he no doubt intended to do and on a still larger scale. No better proof of this can be found than in the bulls which he got from the pope shortly before his fall, one of which empowered him to inquire into the expediency of suppressing certain monasteries and making them cathedrals, and another for the suppression of monasteries having fewer than twelve monks and uniting them to other houses. The 'bulls to be requested on the King's behalf' in 1529 were still more significant in this direction.

But the cardinal's fall came and the matter was shelved for seven years, only to come up again in a far more dangerous form in 1536. The buildings of the suppressed houses suffered the usual fate of suppressed houses. Two years after its fall nothing was standing of the church of Daventry priory but the walls.[2] The cardinal had sold the

[1] But they got it and the priory went.   [2] *L.P.*, IV, 2217.

bells and lead just as his master was to do before very long.

But if lands and churches went, the agents whom he had employed in the suppression remained. They are said to have come to bad ends. This was scarcely true of Doctor Stephen Gardiner or Doctor Rowland Lee (unless becoming diocesan bishops indicates a bad end) and only applies to the most unpopular of them all, John Allen, who, as Archbishop of Dublin, was murdered by some of his flock, apparently under the impression that he was a black-and-tan. The most dangerous and ruthless of them was a layman. He, too, was destined to a bad end, but only after he had climbed to as high a position in the state as ever his master had done. He was no other than Thomas Cromwell, some time — that is a few days — Earl of Essex.

III

The immediate results of the fall of Wolsey on the monasteries were small. Several of the abbots who had been deprived by him managed to get restored to their places, while others who had been threatened with deprivation breathed again. 'My Lord of Vale Royal,' wrote a London clergyman to Doctor Bonner in May 1530, 'is in possession again and some of his brethren in Chester Castle, not all to their pleasure. In like manner the Abbot of Chester, some time now condam[1] — I trust he shall be in his house.' That is to say, the cardinal's friends were displaced in many of their monasteries and his enemies took their places. In the years which intervened between the fall of Wolsey in

---

[1] i.e. *quondam*. Abbot Birkenshaw had been forced out and the Prior of Wallingford put in to save the cardinal from paying a pension to him.

1529 and the Act for the suppression of the smaller monasteries in 1536, the religious houses remained almost wholly undisturbed. But not quite wholly. The Observant Franciscans, as a result of their devotion to Katharine of Aragon, were suppressed in 1534. Their churches were handed over to their conventual rivals, while they themselves were distributed among the conventual houses. Two years before, the large London house of Augustinian canons at Aldgate came by its end. This, as Miss Jeffries Davis points out, was the real turning point. 'Papal sanction was no longer possible, and it soon became evident that the property was not to be devoted to any pious or charitable use. The complete secularization of a monastery, with all its possessions, was contemplated for the first time; the revolution had definitely begun.'[1] Thirty years before, the prior of this house was spending so much of its money on Mrs. Hodges that the Bishop of London tried to deprive him. The attempt failed, and the only result of the prolonged litigation was that the house became bankrupt and this gave an excuse to the King to have a valuation of its property made, and on February 24th, 1532, the prior and the eighteen canons signed a deed giving him their monastery and all its possessions.

'The Cardinal's dissolutions,' says Fuller, 'made all the forest of religious foundations to shake; justly proving the King would finish to cut the oaks, seeing the Cardinal had begun to cut the underwood.' It may, however, be doubted if anybody, whether layman or ecclesiastic, had at the time of Wolsey's fall any idea of what was in store for the religious houses. Notwithstanding the suppression of Holy Trinity, Aldgate, everything seemed to point another way. A conservative administration under Sir Thomas More took the

---

[1] *Transactions of Royal Historical Society*, Fourth Series, vol. IV (1925).

place of the cardinal, whose radical tendencies had frightened all the propertied classes. The lands of the suppressed houses which were not retained by the Crown, were sold or leased to individuals, or given to other religious houses by way of exchange. The school at Ipswich perished and all that remains of it to-day is a piece of wall with a gateway in it. The college at Oxford was in dire straits, but, with its name changed from Cardinal's College to the King's College in Oxford, it was eventually completed by the King, to the disappointment of the old anti-education gang, which was everywhere in transports. 'The monks and canons,' wrote that distinguished scholar, Richard Croke, to Cromwell in 1534, 'and all other ignorant religious are delighted at the stay of works at the King's College.'

The exciting events of the six or seven years which followed Wolsey's fall, made little or no difference to any but a tiny minority of the religious. They soon had, it is true, to get dispensations — abbots to wear the mitre, monks to take livings and so forth — from Canterbury instead of from Rome, but as the charges, high though they might still be, were far lower than they were, this change was doubtless looked upon with equanimity. The attitude of the religious generally during the affair of the King's divorce illustrates this indifference to political happenings very clearly. The annulment of the marriage of Henry the Eighth with Katharine of Aragon, originally mooted in 1514[1] and taken up again in 1528, furnished just as much occasion for gossip in monastic refectories and parlours as it did in taverns and alehouses. Had Prince Arthur both wedded and bedded Katharine or had he not? There may be something in the chronicler Hall's statement that the common people had talked of doubts since the first day of

---

[1] See A. F. Pollard, *Wolsey*, p. 19.

the marriage, while it was to be one of the royal party's chief arguments that divine displeasure at the marriage was shown by the deaths of all Katharine's children save one daughter.

The general bewilderment was increased, also, by the fact that the matrimonial and semi-matrimonial affairs of most of the great personages who were involved in the business were tangled to an amazing degree. Two of the King's brothers-in-law had been divorced, while another had married his deceased wife's sister. Pope Clement himself was a bastard; at least nobody has so far discovered the surname, much less the marriage lines, of his mother, Fioretta. Of the two cardinals who tried the case, the English one had a son who was a clergyman and a daughter who was a nun, while the Italian brought his son with him to England and got him included in the birthday honours; at any rate he was knighted at the next tournament.[1] The forces which respectively opposed and supported the King were of an equally bewildering kind. Against Henry, the pope, in dread of the emperor; yet who could offer the King two wives at the same time,[2] an expedient which had already occurred to the patriarchs of the Old Testament, and which was afterwards to be suggested by Latitudinarian bishops to Charles the Second and by Rosicrucian divines to Frederick William the Second of Prussia, as a solution for the very similar difficulties under which those monarchs laboured. Both classical and scriptural arguments seemed to favour the dispensation which allowed the marriage. Had not Andromache married her deceased brother's husband? Was not Moses' father married to his aunt — not to omit the leading case of Tamar's successive

[1] Hall, *Henry VIII*, Ed. Whibley, II, 149.
[2] Pollard, *Henry VIII*, p. 207.

marriages to three brothers? And who could be more opposed to the King than Martin Luther, 'a friar of Germany' who was just then making such a noise in the world, and who was furious with Henry for putting on the stage a play which mocked at the marriage of the friar in question to his nun wife? For, or at any rate not against, the King, was an equally strange medley of divergent interests ranging from the King of France (for was not Anne Boleyn of the French faction?), the Archbishops of Canterbury and York, the Prior of the head Charterhouse, and the dons of home and foreign (even papal) universities, to Italian friars (duly rewarded for their opinions), and satirists like the formidable Pietro Aretino, who was later said to have died of a fit of laughter brought on by an improper story told to him by his sisters.

What wonder, then, that in these bewildering circumstances the majority of the inmates of the monasteries took the same complaisant view as that which was taken by most Englishmen, or that the great petition of 1530,[1] which bade the pope give way to the King's desire (not omitting a broad hint of withdrawal of obedience in case of refusal), was signed by twenty-two abbots, including those of Glastonbury, Colchester and Reading? The Spanish ambassador Chapuys has a long and picturesque account of the pressure which, as he alleges, was brought to bear on the signatories to this document. But, considering that they included all the most powerful and influential personages in the kingdom, with the Archbishops of Canterbury and York and the Dukes of Norfolk and Suffolk at their head, it can scarcely be believed that pressure was necessary. Even in convocation the Bishops of Rochester and Llandaff (a Spaniard), the abbot of Winchcombe, and a couple of

---

[1] Printed in Lord Herbert's *History of Henry the Eighth.*

doctors of divinity (all, except perhaps the abbot, bound to Katharine by ties of service) seem to have been alone in openly opposing the divorce.

Had the King set his eyes on a lady of royal rank his difficulties, both internal and external, would probably have been far smaller than they were to be. The Duchess of Alençon, the French king's sister, appears to have been quite willing to take poor faded Katharine's place, and to have been much disgruntled when she perceived the true object of Henry's desires. If only Miss Anne Boleyn had been as easy of access as Miss Elizabeth Blount, the Duke of Richmond's mother! But she 'was very cunning in her chastity: no plucking of green fruit of her till marriage had ripened it'. Her comparatively low station in life made her obnoxious to many of the old aristocracy, and the pride, not to say insolence, which resulted from her elevation to the throne made her generally hated. All the women were against her, as even the radically-minded chronicler Hall admits, and the bold black eyes which were her chief recommendation to the King, only earned her epithets of the coarsest kind. Once when the Abbot of Bury was sitting with his fellow justices of the peace on the magistrates' bench, a woman was brought up and sentenced for calling the Queen a 'goggle-eyed whore'. Chapuys, for once, seems to have been telling the whole truth when he says that she was hated by everybody.

That, however, did not prevent her from being generally recognized as Queen. At her coronation on June 1st, 1533, the monks of Westminster, all in rich copes, and many bishops and abbots in copes and mitres, received her in Westminster Hall; at the banquet which followed, bishops and abbots sat at table in their parliament robes.[1] When

[1] Hall, II, 237.

the King and Queen were on progress the Abbot and Convent of Gloucester received them in state at the west door of the abbey church with crosses, copes and cushions.[1] Abbots ended their letters 'God save Queen Anne', and when the Abbess of Bruisyard said in her letter to Cromwell that she prays for the Queen and Princess, she was referring to Anne and her daughter Elizabeth, and not to Katharine and her daughter Mary. The pope might declare the marriage null and a friar might declare that Elizabeth was baptized 'in hot water . . . but not hot enough'; but no fewer than four abbots assisted at the christening ceremony in the church of the Franciscan friars at Greenwich.

All through the year 1533 men's minds were occupied by the strange affair of the so-called Nun of Kent; but as it personally affected only a tiny minority of the religious it can be dismissed in a few words. Elizabeth Barton was by instinct a revivalist preacher, and if Doctor Samuel Johnson had been her contemporary he would doubtless have applied to her the criticism which he passed on a female preacher of his day. 'Sir, a woman's preaching is like a dog's walking on his hinder legs. It is not done well: but you are surprised to find it done at all.' Many of her correspondents were people who were suffering from what Carlyle calls 'spiritual bellyaches' and who would nowadays, according to their respective ecclesiastical tendencies, find a new saint or found a new sect. Of this type were the Carthusian Prior of Sheen and the Cluniac Prior of Horton. Their harmless correspondence with the nun was quoted against them, but they got into no further trouble; the one ended his life as a bishop,[2] and apparently a married one at

---

[1] 'Records of Corporation of Gloucester'. *Report of Historical Manuscripts Commission*, Report XII, Appendix XI, p. 444.
[2] Henry Man, Dean of Chester, 1541-6. Bishop of Man, 1546, died 1556. According to Machyn's *Diary*, p. 116, he was married.

that, and the other[1] as an archdeacon and heavily-
endowed country parson. That very silly woman, the
Marchioness of Exeter, though she was Princess Elizabeth's
godmother, was another visitor to the nun. She *did* get
into temporary trouble, as her whining letter to the King
shows.[2] Henry can scarcely have believed that she went to
a nun to ask advice as to how to rear her children. Many
of the nun's revelations[3] were of a harmless and even
salutary kind. She had, according to her own account,
performed the difficult tasks of getting Cardinal Wolsey
into heaven and of stopping unwilling religious from flee-
ing from their convents. Others were merely silly. But
when political wire-pullers got her to shift her prophecies
to events at court things began to be dangerous for her and
for them. Prophecies were dangerous things to meddle with,
as the Duke of Buckingham, at the instigation of a monk,
had found a few years before; as poor Mabel Brigg found
during the Pilgrimage of Grace, when she endeavoured to
bewitch the Duke of Norfolk by her 'fast', or in Queen
Mary's time when the bird set forth illegal religious doctrines from a hole in the wall. It is no wonder then that she
and her chief advisers, Doctor Bocking and Doctor Dering,
monks of Canterbury, and Doctors Risby and Rich,
Observants of Greenwich, found themselves first exhibited
on a platform in London, and then on a scaffold at Tyburn;
or that the Abbot of Hyde — 'a monk made bishop to
support the lady's party' — should speak of her so contemp-
tuously in his sermon at Paul's Cross. Even at Canterbury
she was not generally believed in: a monk of St. Augustine's
referred to her 'marvellous hypocrisy', while the Prior and
Convent of Christchurch, as well as the Warden and friars

[1] Richard Brysley, Archdeacon of Lewes, 1551, died 1558.
[2] *L.P.*, VI, 1464.
[3] There is a full list of them in Wright, *Suppression*, pp. 14-18.

of the Greenwich monastery, hastened in abject terms to dissociate themselves from their erring colleagues. The Government, however, had received a shock, as their manifesto issued about this time showed. It seemed that ever since the fortunate marriage the country had enjoyed fair weather and good crops.

IV

We are at the beginning of the tragedy of Fisher and More, though the latter at any rate had no belief in what he called 'the wicked woman of Canterbury'. The affairs of the Nun of Kent had few repercussions in the monasteries generally, or affected the attendance of the parliamentary abbots in the House of Lords. But the religious were soon to be put into close contact with current affairs, and this time there was no escape for any of them. The Succession Act of 1534 enacted that all adult subjects of the Crown were to swear to accept the children of Henry and Anne as lawful heirs to the Crown, and all through the summer of 1534 the royal commissioners were administering the oath of abjuration of the Bishop of Rome's authority in England.

Bishop Gardiner, in a letter to Cromwell, shows how the commission worked. 'After receiving the commission for taking oaths according to the act of his Grace's succession I used such diligence that upon the Monday following, which was yesterday, there not only assembled here at Winchester' (the commissioners, etc.), 'but there appeared in the Great Hall of the Castle, Lord Audley, a good number of gentlemen, all abbots, priors, wardens of friars, and the governor of the Friars Observants at Southampton, in the absence of the warden, with all the curates of the other churches and chapels within the shire, the Isle of Wight only exempt, which did all take the oath very obediently ... and at the same time the abbots, priors and curates did, as I had ordered them, present unto us bills of all houses of the religious and servants in their houses.'[1] This, then, was the procedure which was followed in all the dioceses of England and Wales. The royal commissioners administered the oath to the clergy assembled by deaneries and to the religious assembled in their chapter houses, and the amount of success they had may be measured by the paucity of the refusals. We have not, it is true, the complete list of the acknowledgments of the religious, but that the inmates of the houses which are missing from extant lists did take the oath, can scarcely be denied, otherwise they and we would have heard of it.

A great deal of attention has rightly been paid to the fate of those who did refuse to take the oath. Doubtless there were some who, like Friar Forest, 'took the oath with the outward man, but his inward man never consented thereto'. But most people must have been quite indifferent as to the name of the Queen Consort of the moment. 'Few,' says Hall, 'refused except John Fisher, Thomas More and Nicholas Wilson.' [The last-named recalcitrant procured his pardon and to atone for his obstinacy undertook to win over his cousin, Prior Wilson of Mountgrace.] 'The other twayne stood against all the realm in their opinion.' The Abbot of Westminster advised More to change his conscience as so many others were doing. 'I am content,' said a Hertfordshire clergyman, 'to accept the King's supremacy now that the Abbot of St. Albans has notified to me that the pope's power is abolished in England.' More himself has given a sarcastic account of a conservative leader's relief at the

---

[1] *Letters of Stephen Gardiner*, Ed. Muller, p. 56.

favourable result of his examination at Lambeth and of the speed with which he rushed to the bar to get a drink.

Hall, like all partisans, has, of course, belittled the opposition to the royal wishes. So far as the religious were concerned, however, there were not more than three centres of resistance: the London Carthusians, the Brigittine brethren and nuns of Sion, and the Greenwich Observants. Of these the third provided a few exiles; the second, one martyr; the first, several. The discipline of the Carthusians was still unrelaxed and the chief complaint of the disgruntled among them was its 'rugorosity'. They were so full of scruples that they would not answer the royal commissioners' inquiries about the assessment of their property, and they were much addicted to revelations, some of which seem to have been almost as puerile as those of the Nun of Kent herself. But the savage vengeance which was taken on the three Carthusian priors and on the three London monks probably did at least as much harm to the King's reputation in Europe as that on Fisher and More themselves, and the Government apologists could with difficulty explain it away. It is Thomas Starkey who, writing to the future Cardinal Pole, puts the King's case most clearly: 'The whole nation agreed to renounce the Pope's supremacy, including these three priors and Reynolds, but they have returned to their old obedience ... by their blind superstitious knowledge so blinded and sturdy that they could neither see the truth in the cause, nor give convenient obedience. I know this, because I interviewed Reynolds myself. It seems that they sought their own deaths, of which no man can be justly accused.'[1]

The plain man's view was probably that of Hall, who relates how stiffly and stubbornly they (the three London

---

[1] *L.P.*, VIII, 801.

Carthusians Exmew, Middlemore and Newdigate) bore themselves 'and neither blushed nor . . . at their treason, and therefore as they deserved, they received'.

It must not be supposed, however, that even among the Carthusians all were of one mind. There were several who supported the royal cause. Some of these were apostates, like Andrew Bord who ran about Europe working for the King, or like Nicholas Rawlins of London who wrote to Cromwell to express his desire for a dispensation from his religion. There were many, too, who were willing to go with the times, and Cromwell had correspondents both among the Carthusians and the Observants who kept him informed of the existing state of opinion in their respective houses.

CHAPTER V

THE ROYAL VISITATION OF THE MONASTERIES 1535

I

THE campaign for the dissolution of the smaller monasteries, begun in the fifteenth century and carried many steps further by Wolsey, was now to have another extension, but on a far more ruthless scale. Apart from the suppressions which have already been described there had hitherto been no disturbance of the religious in any way. The breach with Rome had affected only a tiny minority of them, half a dozen had been executed; while a couple of dozen or so had withdrawn oversea or to Scotland.

But the King's new Secretary, Thomas Cromwell, had, according to the Spanish ambassador, Chapuys, boasted that he would make his master more wealthy than all the princes of Christendom. And where could he find easier prey than the monasteries, with the internal condition of which he, as the Cardinal's former agent, was probably better acquainted than anybody in England with the possible exception of his former colleagues, the Bishops of Winchester and Lichfield? When he was made the King's Vicar-General in January 1535, he had the same authority as Wolsey in his capacity of legate. But his position was far the stronger of the two, since he had at his disposal the coercive powers of the Crown, which were, naturally, far more efficient than those of the Pope. Obviously his first task was to find out what exactly were the resources of the Church, with particular reference to the monasteries, and as there had been no valuation of any kind for over 200 years it was necessary to undertake a new one forthwith. Moreover, since the pope had been deprived in the previous year of the revenues he had derived from England in the shape of annates first fruits and Peter's Pence, the Crown was naturally anxious to know exactly what fresh sources of revenue it could count upon. A Sussex friar might try to frighten people by reminding them of the malign effects of an interdict upon the corn and fruit crops. But we are no longer in the days of King John, and Pope Paul III could do little more to the English government than Bunyan's giant pope did to the pilgrims, 'grinning at them as they go by and biting his nails because he cannot get at them'.

The result of the inquiry is embodied in that vast collection known as the *Valor ecclesiasticus*, which, compiled by the commissioners under the greatest possible difficulties and in a wonderfully short time, is yet an astonishingly accurate and comprehensive statement of the Church's revenues. After it had been completed the Government really knew where it was in that matter and the screw soon began to be put on; the clergy were to find that papal whips had given place to royal scorpions. A great deal of the clerical discontent which found expression in the Pilgrimage of Grace and similar movements was due, as has been pointed out, to the substitution of efficent royal collectors of revenue for inefficient papal ones.

Quite apart from financial questions, however, the royal Vicar-General was determined to investigate the internal condition of the monasteries. To this end a royal order of January 1535, commissioned the abbots of Stanley and Ford to visit the greater number of the Cistercian houses in England, but whether it was ever carried out seems uncertain. At any rate no record of its proceedings has survived.

Nor were the records of the visitations of Cromwell himself and of his agents anything but imperfect, and a great deal of misconception about them has naturally been the result. It is important, however, to notice how strong their position was. Like Wolsey and his agents they were able to override all exemptions. The Abbot of Welbeck, who, since 1512, had been general visitor of the Premonstratensian Order in England, found himself deprived of all control of elections in the houses of his order. It was Cromwell's agent, the formidable Dr. Leigh, who took charge of the election of the new abbot of the Norfolk house of West Dereham, and all that the Abbot of Welbeck could do was to grumble and acquiesce. 'I intend to do nothing but that shall stand with the King's grace's pleasure and yours, both humbly desiring to know your Mastership's pleasure in writing what I shall do herein', he wrote. The Archbishop of York, again, was obliged to waive his intended visitation of St. Mary's, York, in favour of the visitor-general and was thereby baulked of his intention to get the abbot's friend, Mrs. Robinson, out of the monastery.

So strong, indeed, was the visitors' position that they were able to extend their inquiries into the behaviour of the laity. 'Certain of the knights and gentlemen' (of Staffordshire and the adjoining counties), wrote Doctor Leigh,[1] 'and more commonly all, liveth so incontinently, having their concubines openly in their houses, with five or six of their children, putting from them their wives, that all the country therewith be not a little offended and taketh evil example of them.' He went on to say that he had threatened them that if they did not put from them their concubines and take back their wives he would have them sent up to Cromwell to show cause why they should not be compelled

[1] August 22nd, 1536, Wright, *Suppression*, p. 243.

to do so. A similar report was given by two of Cromwell's other agents about the state of affairs in Cheshire.[1] So far as the gentlemen were concerned they solved the problem by forcing those who were single to marry their mistresses. County society must henceforth have been of a very mixed kind. Were the newly married couples asked, one wonders, to garden or dinner parties? The visitors could not very well, 'the law being what it now is', as the Abbot of Reading said about clerical marriage, oblige the clergy to marry *their* mistresses, so they contented themselves with expelling the ladies from the parsonage houses. Old Parson Savage, who held for many years the family living of Davenham, seems to have escaped their clutches by an opportune demise. But his flock of children — Edmund Bonner, soon to be Bishop of London; John Wymmesley, Archdeacon of London (1543 — 54) and Middlesex (1554 — 56); George Wymmesley, Chancellor of Chester — made great careers for themselves in the church and so no doubt did his 'several other bastards'.[2] Large clerical families were already becoming the rule.

II

The general visitation of the monasteries began in July 1535, and lasted a little over six months. A vast amount of abuse has been levelled at Cromwell and his agents in connection with this visitation, a great deal of which is justified. This is especially the case in the matter of taking of bribes. It must, however, be remembered that that was no new thing in connection with episcopal visitations and with

[1] *L.P.*, VIII, 495 and 496.
[2] See the genealogy of the Savage family in Ormerod's *History of Cheshire*, II, 720.

elections of abbots or priors. Cromwell, in particular, had learned the practice only too thoroughly in the service of his master, the cardinal. It is impossible to measure the standard of public service which prevailed in those days with that which obtains to-day.

The agents who were employed by Cromwell for the work first of visitation and then of suppression, were lawyers; some clerical, some lay. Most of the clerical lawyers were also beneficed clergymen. Thus, the reverend Mr. Portinari, who took such delight in pulling down the great priory church of Lewes, held the rich living of Algarkirk in Lincoln-shire. Clergymen of this class had little liking for monks, who found in them their most formidable opponents. Their representatives invariably accompanied bishops in their visitations to act as their legal advisers. Sometimes, indeed, they took the bishop's place. When the Benedictine nunnery of Bungay, Suffolk, was visited on August 21st, 1532, the visitor was not the Bishop of Norwich, but Doctor Miles Spenser *vice et auctoritate dicti reverendi patris*. Nearly all Cromwell's agents were similarly experienced, both in visitations and in working deprivations and elections of abbots on behalf of the bishop or the founder. Doctor Layton, 'Your assured poor priest,' was only telling the truth when he informed Cromwell that 'there is neither monastery, cell, priory, nor any other religious house in the north, but either Doctor Lee or I have familiar acquaintance within ten or twelve miles of it, so that no knavery can be hid from us in that country.' After which he practically admitted that he meant to produce an unfavourable report. Now of what type were these agents? were they really the scoundrels that sentimentalist writers picture them? A sketch of the careers of the three foremost of them will perhaps give the answer to this question.

Doctor Richard Layton, already Archdeacon of Buckingham and later (1539-43) Dean of York, was a clergyman of that detestable type, the 'man's man'. Were he living nowadays he would be seen and heard in the smoking-rooms of clubs, slapping laymen on the back, listening to, if not repeating, the latest risky tale. In his own day he could have claimed to rival his fellow priest, the Reverend Prebendary Francis Rabelais, in impudicity and in much of his wit. It is to him that nearly all of the immodest tales about the religious are due. He loved gossip and like all gossips he wished to repeat, if not to amplify, what he had heard, whether from the religious about each other, or from neighbours who had a grudge against them. But nothing he said about them was as bad as, for instance, what the abbot of the Cistercian abbey of Warden was saying at this very time about his own monks;[1] and it is really difficult to believe that he invented the very circumstantial story of how he had to break in the door of the Abbot of Langdon's lodging, since he could make nobody hear, 'saving the abbot's little dog that within his door fast locked bayed and barked', with the subsequent misfortunes of the abbot and his gentlewoman.[2] But he could be fair enough when he liked. He could give a more favourable account of Durham — 'No women come in and no monks go out.' He was far less strict than his colleague Dr. Leigh in enforcing the injunctions to the religious houses, and nothing, surely, could be more admirable than his reformation of the University of Oxford;[3] a task which, as a Cambridge man, he must thoroughly have enjoyed. 'We have enjoined in visiting the religious students that no man for no manner of cause shall come within any tavern, inn, alehouse and . . . upon pain once so taken by day or by night to be sent immediately

[1] Wright, *Suppression*, pp. 53-5.   [2] Ibid., pp. 75-7.   [3] Ibid., pp. 70-2.

home to his cloister wherein he was professed' (in other words 'sent down'). In fact, what the university proctors had never been able to effect, he, as royal visitor, could put through.

If a 'man's man' is a detestable variety of clergyman, a clever and conceited young don is an equally hateful type of layman. Such was Dr. Thomas Leigh, the second in importance among the visitors. Persons of his type can be kept in check in the universities, whose admirable function it is to persuade their alumni that they know nothing and never can know anything. But nothing can exceed the terror which highbrow persons of Dr. Leigh's type excites among those who are known in the American language as 'hicks and hayseeds', in other words the 'barbarous rural persons' amongst whom Dr. Leigh's lot was now to be cast. This terror he exploited to the full. His narrow legal mind allowed for no give and take. Not only did he enforce the injunctions with no allowance whatever, but he tried to get Dr. Layton into trouble for being too lenient. His intolerable arrogance and what one of his colleagues, Dr. ap Rice, called his 'satrapic countenance', was a cause of offence to everybody, even to his cousin Bishop Lee of Lichfield. But though the Duke of Norfolk on one occasion described him as a 'vicious man' he seems to have had a reputation for personal disinterestedness; at any rate Sir Thomas Audeley, the Lord Chancellor, told Cromwell, 'I hear not but that he suith himself right indifferently in the execution of his charge'. He often put himself to considerable trouble — no doubt for a consideration — to secure ample pensions for the heads of the threatened houses. 'In him is all my trust,' wrote the Prior of Cokesford, Norfolk, to Cromwell; and the Abbess of Wherwell, in Hampshire, wrote hoping that 'Dr. Lee's learning and excellent qualities may profit us and our monastery'.

The third visitor of note was also a don, but of Oxford and not of Cambridge. Dr. John London, Warden of New College and Dean of Wallingford, has probably suffered more than any of the others at the hands of sobstuff writers. That unfortunate incident in the Warden's gallery in New College and the humiliating ride at Windsor, where he had procured the incarceration of three persons addicted to the 'new learning', and his death in the Fleet prison a few years later are brought up against him again and again. These stories were, in fact, put about by contemporary writers of the innovating party like Hall, or by John Foxe and his followers, in revenge for the zeal with which he enforced the provisions of the diehard conservative measure known as the Act of the Six Articles of 1539. What religion he had was conventionally conservative, and he would probably have said with Descartes that it was that of his King and of his nurse. Indeed, he often had to defend himself against the charge of going too slow: and when the Government was beginning to put down purgatory and pilgrimages and faith-healing images he was under the necessity of clearing himself of lukewarmness. His contemptuous attitude to certain of the more improbable objects of popular devotion has also served to blacken his character in sentimentalist quarters. That he should have disbelieved in the genuineness of the two heads of St. Ursula and of the jaw bone of the ass which slew Abel is surely to his credit. 'Doctor London,' wrote Thomas Bedyll to Cromwell, 'has done more for the reformation of ignorance and superstition than all the other visitors.' He was on the whole a kindly person and his letters to Cromwell both now and later show a great deal of sympathy for those whom he was commissioned to disendow. 'The Abbess of de la Pre by Northampton,' he wrote, 'is a good aged woman who has served the King well': and he beseeches Cromwell to ratify the generous provision he had made for her 'and to be good lord unto her and to her poor sisters for their pensions'. If he was rude to the Abbess of Godstow she was much ruder to him. As a Bulkeley of Beaumaris she looked down upon him socially, while in religion he was probably more conservative than she. At any rate she wished to be under no suspicion of keeping up old ways in the abbey, as her letter to Cromwell shows:[1] while her will, made in November 1559, shows no signs whatever of having returned to them. That Dr. London was a vigilant administrator of college property is shown by his letter to Cromwell of February 21st, 1538. 'In answer to your letter in favour of such bondmen as my college has in Colerne (Wilts) to be manumitted, it is against the statutes of the college to alienate either land or bondmen.'[2] It is obviously impossible to connect sentiments of this kind with innovating or liberalizing tendencies.

The other visitors, now or later, were of a colourless kind and may be dismissed in a few words. They were all of similar type to Doctors Layton and Leigh and London. Dr. John ap Rice was a milder edition of Dr. Leigh. If he was unable to believe that the coals on which St. Lawrence was roasted were really at Bury St. Edmunds, he could give great praise where it was due. When he visited the large house of Augustinian canonesses at Lacock in Wiltshire, he paid a very handsome compliment to the house and its occupants and he compliments the ladies on their attainments. He must not be confused with Doctor Ellis Price, whose visitations covered Wales only, and who laid himself open to misrepresentation by taking his mistress with him — scarcely a wise proceeding on the part of a reformer.

[1] *L.P.*, XIII (2), 911. For her genealogy and will, see Earwaker, *East Cheshire*, I, 204.
[2] *L.P.*, XIII (1), 324.

Dr. Bedyll, a fellow of New College, under Dr. London, and also a clergyman, had, as he confessed, little sense of humour. Doctor (afterwards Sir) John Tregonwell — another of the civil lawyers who worked the dissolution — was no innovator in religion, as the favour he was later to enjoy under Queen Mary shows.

Finally, of the provincials or wardens who undertook the visitation of the friars, and eventually (in 1538) received the surrender of their houses, one at least was a conservative in religion to the end. Dr. Edward Baskerville, last Warden of the Oxford Franciscans, was an intimate friend of Dr. London and travelled about with him on monastic business on more than one occasion. Dr. London described him as an 'honest man who had caused all his house to surrender and to change their papistical garments'. His dislike of successive religious changes brought him eventually to the Tower, where we find him at the beginning of Elizabeth's reign, for boggling at the oath of supremacy. His courage, however, soon failed him and the prospect of losing what he had amassed since the suppression of his house brought about a change in his views, and he died seven years later still enjoying all his preferments in Hereford Cathedral and elsewhere.[1] Indeed, of all the agents whom Cromwell employed, every one of them, except Dr. London, died in their beds in full possession of all their emoluments, ecclesiastical or legal.

IV

The likeness of the Vicar-General himself has been portrayed so often that there is no need to do more than touch on it here. Nobody in English history has been more

---

[1] For his career see *Essays in History presented to R. Lane Poole*, p. 463.

assailed than he, yet his chief fault was no more than whole-hearted devotion to a king who used and then slew him 'for heresy, treason, felony and extortion'. If he wished to read Italian books, why did he not study *Il Cortigiano* rather than *Il Principe*? It would have shown him a better way to deal with a man like Henry. If he took bribes, and spent money lavishly, it was not always on himself, and the memory of the numbers of poor who were daily fed at his gate long lingered in London, as Stow's *Survey* bears witness.[1] His religion was doubtless that of the *politiques*, and if he had his tongue in his cheek when he talked about the King's catholic garden, he had no sympathy with innovators of the Anabaptist type, with their dangerous anti-social doctrines. Still less did he appreciate indelicate speech or writings. Once an English undergraduate of the University of Padua, thinking to flatter him in the matter of his familiarity with the Italian language, sent him a copy of some improper verses which he had seen stuck on a church door. Cromwell was furious, and it was all that the young man could do to placate him and to stop his exhibition from being taken away.

A general visitation of the monasteries was a task which no bishop or archbishop, not even Cardinal Wolsey at the height of his power, had been strong enough to attempt. But it did not daunt Cromwell. However prurient Doctor Layton may have been and however insolent Doctor Leigh, it cannot be said that they did not follow precedents, both generally and in detail, or that their methods differed much from those of former visitors, except that they were more thorough-going. If the articles of inquiry,[2] eighty-six in number (the last twelve for nuns only), are examined carefully,

[1] See E. M. Leonard, *Early History of Poor Relief*, p. 17.
[2] Printed in Burnet's *History of the Reformation*, ed. Pocock, IV, 207 ff.

it will be seen that they are the same as those which bishops and other visitors had always used *in primis*: 'Whether divine service be solemnly said, observed and kept in this monastery accordingly to the number and the abilities thereof, by night and by day in due time and hours?' 'And how many be present commonly at Mattins and other services and who be absent and so unaccustomed to be without cause or sickness?' An advisable question which former visitors always asked without often getting a satisfactory answer, since the custom of taking part in the services by rotation forbade it. 'What was your suggestion and notice at the obtaining of your exemption from your diocesan?' This was an awkward question indeed, and one to which most of the bishops knew the answer only too well. 'Whether women useth and resorteth much to this monastery by back ways or otherwise?' 'Whether you do sleep all together in the dorter under one roof or not?' 'Whether ye do keep the fratry at meals?' 'Whether ye or any of you be, or hath been, in manifest apostasy, that is to say fugitives or vagabonds?' 'Whether the master of the house do use his discipline and corrections and punishments upon his brethren with mercy, pity and charity without cruelty, rigorousness and enormous hurt, no more favouring one than another?' 'Whether the master of the house makes his brethren privy to the state and condition of the house and makes his accounts annually? What about due reparations, a detailed inventory, debts and leases? Whether the master of the house be wont to give under his seal of office or convent seal, farms, corrodies, annuities and offices to his kinsfolk, alliances, friends or acquaintances . . . to the hurt, hindrance, damage and impoverishment of this house? Whether rewards are taken at the reception of novices? Whether the novices have a preceptor to teach them grammar and good letters? Does any of the seniors teach them the rules of the order?'

Every one of these questions had been asked by the bishops for years, nay centuries: but how often had they been satisfied with the answers they got to them? It has been said that the visitations of the royal commissioners were too hasty to be of any value. But they were no more hasty than those of a bishop, who, as it has been pointed out, could often manage to visit two monasteries in a single day. Just as the bishop knew a great deal about the internal affairs of a house before ever he set foot inside it, so did Cromwell's agents, as the letter of Doctor Layton, already quoted, shows. The royal visitors followed the precedents of episcopal visitors down to the last detail. If Doctor Leigh insisted on being received with a procession, so did all former visitors, and so for that matter did the lay patron of a monastery. It was no new thing for a layman to be accorded such a compliment. If the religious were examined by the visitors apart and individually, so as to worm their secrets out of them, how otherwise had the bishop acted?

Just as the bishops made secret inquiries, so did they give injunctions based upon them to the religious. The royal visitors followed their example. Their injunctions[1] are to a great extent based on those which bishops had been wont to issue, but which were now tightened up. 'No monk or brother of the monastery by any means to go forth of the precincts of the same', was, for example, harsher than of yore, because permission to go forth could formerly be granted by the head of the house.

But the clauses relating to the exclusion of women, the closing-up of back doors and the obligation to use only the great foregate of the monastery, were rules which the bishops had long sought to enforce. So were those enforcing

[1] Printed in Burnet, IV, 217 ff.

the distribution of alms according to the foundation, the sumptuary regulations, which forbade the abbot and his guests having an 'over sumptuous table, full of delicate and strange dishes', the insistence that the broken meats should go to the poor, instead of to the monks' kinsfolk, or to the 'valiant, naughty and idle beggars and vagabonds as commonly use to resort about such places, which rather as drove beasts and mychers should be driven away and compelled to labour, than in their idleness and lewdness against the form of the King's grace's statutes in that behalf made, cherished and maintained to the great hindrance and damage of the common weal'. 'That no man suffer or profess to wear the habit of religion or he be twenty years of age.' Were not the bishops always trying to enforce this rule? 'That if either the master or any brother of this house do infringe any of the said injunctions, any of them may denounce the same to King, visitor general or his deputy.' This was a reprehensible clause, but delation had always been a recognized part of visitations. Delation arising out of internal quarrels eased the visitors' task enormously. The complaints which disgruntled monks had sent to superior authorities, whether ecclesiastical, like the bishop, or lay, as the founder or high steward, were now to go to the visitor general, either directly or through his visiting agents. These complaints might be formulated by the head of the house against his own subordinates. 'Immediately after the King's grace's visitation was executed,' wrote Abbot Emery of Warden,[1] 'by his commissioners Master Doctor Leigh and Master John ap Rice, and certain injunctions by them to me and my brethren delivered to be observed, my said brethren took occasion against me thereat and said amongst them that I was the causer why they were

---

[1] Wright, *Suppression*, p. 53.

enclosed within their monastery, to this intent (as they did imagine) that I might do outwardly what I would and they should not know it.' The abbot went on to say that nothing would induce his monks to come to the divinity lecture ordered by the injunctions, and that they would not learn the grammars he had bought for them. 'What did Dom Thomas Warden do when I sent him out on the business of the house, but sit in the alehouse at Shefford all night? When I tried to correct him he said I had no authority to do so. He and Dom Christopher (a common drunkard) threatened me to such an extent that I got my servants to watch my chamber four nights after till their fury was somewhat assuaged.' The abbot's further details about the behaviour of the monks when they were outside the walls of the monastery show how much they must have disliked the 'gating' injunction.

The priors of the 'cells' or houses subordinate to great monasteries had now a fine opportunity for airing their grievances against their abbots. The monks could get up a set of 'articles' against their head, such as those of Cerne got up against Abbot Corton, the extent and nature of which might have surprised Doctor Layton himself.[1] Sometimes the revelations were made in the course of the visitation, as were those made by a monk of the neighbouring abbey of Abbotsbury about Abbot Rodden.[2] Internal quarrels caused all kinds of strange stories to be related to the visitors. The monastery of Worcester had long been rent by dissensions, which an absentee prior had done nothing to heal. The former cellarer, William Fordham, anxious to be restored to his post, took it upon him to defend all the King's acts. 'In this reign no man has suffered, but he has said', "I deserve to suffer", 'and divers might have lived if they

---

[1] L.P., VIII, 148.   [2] L.P., IX, 1087.

would. His most merciful pardon was always ready and it was their own folly which caused their undoing.' Cromwell, evidently impressed by this argument, ordered the convent to restore him. They were in despair and wrote to the Vicar-General: 'He is a most troublesome person. He ran the house into debt and borrowed money to such an extent that the Prior was arrested in London in convocation time. He has a fell disease so badly that no man may abide him. What with physics for his disease, prowling to his friends and other misuse, we think he will be the ruin of the house.'[1] Another monk of this monastery was 'comperted by many of our convent for incontinency' to the visitors.

Quite apart from such ecclesiastical sources of information Cromwell and his agents could always rely on lay help, especially from members of county families who were familiar, as practically all of them were, with the internal affairs of the monasteries. And here the doings of the convent of Worcester may well furnish us with another example. Prior More and the chamberlain of the priory, Dom Roger Neckham, were at daggers drawn. The latter was doing all he could to procure the prior's forced resignation. Great ladies could never resist interfering in matters of this kind, so Lady Margery Sandys, taking the part of the prior, wrote to Cromwell: 'Don't pay any heed to what that wretch Doctor Neckham says. The Prior was elected by the whole house and gift of Doctor Foxe, Bishop of Winchester, without giving a penny for his promotion.'[2] The fact that the lady lays such stress on this shows how unwonted such procedure was. Bishop Foxe had been Lord Privy Seal at the time of Prior More's election, and was therefore in a position to receive bribes of this kind in accordance with precedent. Wolsey and Cromwell were

[1] *L.P.*, IX, 653.   [2] *L.P.*, IX, 656.

not so scrupulous. It is to be noted that these letters were written while Doctor Leigh and Doctor ap Rice were actually visiting the monastery in October 1535. Indeed they seem to have got very much bored with all the quarrels. 'They say,' wrote one of the complainants, 'that I am unreasonable.'

Since Cromwell and his deputies had the power of dismissing anybody who applied to them for release, the visitation was naturally welcome to religious who were discontented with their lot. That there were numbers of such persons cannot possibly be doubted. How could it be otherwise when one considers the methods by which the monks were recruited? The problem of 'what to do with our boys' was as acute in the sixteenth century as it is to-day. Entering on the religious life was too often looked upon as the first step on the ladder of ecclesiastical promotion and to a successful career. 'People are tempted,' said a preacher at the time of the visitation of some religious house, 'by the splendour of the monasteries to compel their children to take the vows. They say, "My child or kinsman, if thou shalt be a monk or canon then thou shalt have plenty of delicious meats. Then ... when you become prior or abbot thou shalt be able to help me and my kindred. If thou wilt not be a religious man I am not able to find thee in thy learning and therefore thou shalt go to plough: then thou shalt fare hardly".'[1]

It must have been hard indeed to resist arguments so powerful as these. But they are hardly consistent with a sense of vocation. Indeed, there is plenty of evidence of the tragedies into which lives so manipulated were plunged. When Doctor Leigh visited the large house of Augustinian canons at St. Osyth, near Harwich, one of the young canons

[1] *L.P.*, VII, p. 523.

confessed at his examination that his vows meant nothing to him. Dr. Leigh told him to write to the Visitor-General, and his letter to Cromwell puts his point of view very clearly. 'I received the habit at 13 and was professed before I had completed my 14th year. For twelve years I have never willingly borne the yoke of religion. I would rather die than live any longer such a miserable life.'[1] He asserts that he was only induced to take the vows by threats of his school-master. This looks as if he had been one of the boys in the almonry of the priory, and there can be no doubt but that pressure of a very pronounced kind was often put on them to enter religion. 'I was bound apprentice at the age of 13 and sold by my master to the abbot in the first year, who shaved my head and put on me a white coat,' said Edward Paynter, monk of Jervaulx.[2] This unwilling votary was naturally led into apostasy, flight to Essex and marriage. Not unnaturally the abbot wrote to Cromwell that the convent did not want him back. 'Now my most gracious lord and most worthiest vicar that ever came amongst us,' wrote a young monk of Pershore to Cromwell, 'help me out of this vain religion and make me your servant, handmaid and bedeman and save my soul.'[3] 'I was enticed here by fair promises when I was fourteen years old,' wrote a monk of Winchcombe.[4] 'I mean,' said a young monk of St. Albans, 'to leave the monastery for the uncharitableness I find there and I claim to have the King's authority by which all men under 22 should be put forth.'[5]

Instances of this kind could be multiplied. And when Dr. Leigh says that he had given leave to half the Cistercian house of Sawtry in Hunts to depart, or when Dr. Rice gives the numbers of unwilling religious at Bury, they were

[1] *L.P.*, ix, 1157.   [2] *L.P.*, v, Appendix 34.   [3] Wright, *Suppression*, p. 132.   [4] *L.P.*, vii, 1367.   [5] *L.P.*, xi, 354.

probably telling no more than the truth. The married abbot of Walden half emptied his house by persuading his monks to leave.[1]

V

The visitors again were greatly helped by a movement of which episcopal visitors had had but little experience. For the last ten years the doctrines of the 'new learning', whether in the form advocated by Martin Luther, or, in its more radical aspect, by William Tyndale and his associates, spread more and more widely, first among the religious who were studying at the universities and then through them in the monasteries themselves. In the later years of Wolsey's tenure of power there had been a great deal of trouble on this score both at Oxford and Cambridge. Dr. London reported to the cardinal in 1528 that among the scholars who were infected by it were two monks of Bury St. Edmunds and one of Glastonbury.[2] Bishop Longland had two monks in his house whom he proposed after penance to commit to their monasteries.[3] One of the Bury monks was Dr. Rougham,[4] who certainly did not hide his opinions and whom he got back to Bury. At any rate, a few years later he and Dr. Brinkley the warden of the local house of Franciscans got into trouble for resorting to the preaching of the later martyr, Dr. Rowland Taylor, rector of Hadleigh, while a monk of Bury called Bayfield was burned at Smithfield in 1531. A great part of the abbey of Reading was corrupted. The prior had brought from Oxford no fewer than sixty of the new books and conveyed them to the

---

[1] *L.P.*, ix, 661. According to Wriothesley, *Chronicle*, 1, 63, Abbot Barrington was married to 'Mistress Bures, nun of the minories' (i.e. the Minoresses of Aldgate). The abbot quaintly calls her his 'remedy' in his letters to Cromwell.
[2] *L.P.*, iv, 3962.   [3] *L.P.*, iv, 4418.   [4] *L.P.*, iv, 4125.

abbey,[1] and not long afterwards the cardinal had him conveyed to the Tower in the hope that he might be 'converted'. The abbot vainly tried to get rid of him by asking him to take a living in the abbey's gift. Moreover a married canon of Westacre was appointed to teach the monks divinity, much to the abbot's grief. It is significant that in later years most of the monks of Reading of whose later careers we have any information took to themselves wives, a course hardly in harmony with their original profession. A few years later one of the Oxford scholars, Thomas Coventry, monk of Evesham, wrote to Cromwell to beg that if the monastery should be dissolved his exhibition might be continued. 'I study Greek, Latin and Hebrew and refute papistical sophistry.'[2]

At Cambridge things were not much better. The Bishop of Norwich reported in 1530 that Gonville Hall (the resort of many Cluniac monks) was full of heretics: 'No monk who has lately come out of it but smelleth of the frying pan.' When these young gentlemen went back to their monasteries they naturally held forth freely on their new spiritual experiences, and thus a new kind of unrest was spread in most of the great houses. Some of them revolted against the godly discipline of the Church and especially in the matter of fasting. The Archbishop of York complained to Cromwell that one of the monks of the great Benedictine abbey of Selby had been heard railing at this laudable practice.[3] Another great Benedictine abbey, that of Winchcombe in Gloucestershire, had more than its share of monks of this kind. 'Two of my monks,' wrote the abbot to Cromwell, 'Walter Aldhelm and Hugh Egwin, have been eating flesh in Advent and say they will eat it on Friday if they may have it.'[4] 'Please excuse me,' wrote another of

[1] L.P., IV, 4004. [2] L.P., XIV (2), 437. [3] L.P., IX, 742. [4] L.P., IX, 934.

his monks to Cromwell, 'rising for Mattins. I cannot endure the straitness of this religion.' The fact is that it was all very well to prohibit the heretical books; above all, Simon Fish's *Supplication of Beggars* and John Frith's *Disputation of Purgatory*, but everybody was reading them — even, as we shall see — the nuns. On the plea of going about the country preaching the Gospel, some monks got leave from Cromwell to leave their monasteries. Such was the case with another great Gloucestershire abbey, that of Kingswood, a Cistercian house. Here the prior had written a treatise in favour of the royal supremacy. One monk got leave of absence to preach, while the abbot can scarcely have been loyal to the old ideas since he ended his days as a married man, leaving a fortune to his wife and children.[1] At another of the Gloucestershire Cistercian abbeys, that of Hayles, there must have been a similar movement brought in from its students in Oxford. We may indeed credit Archbishop Whitgift's statement that he had learned his faith from his uncle, the last abbot of Wellow (Grimsby).[2] It is probable that Cromwell and his agents more than winked at, even if they did not actively forward, their movement. And it is of some significance that former friars preaching the new doctrines were sent to serve parishes contiguous to monasteries.

What was the proportion of religious disgruntled or caught up by the 'new learning', it is, of course, impossible to say. It may, however, be taken for granted that few of those who let their tongues run away with them had any idea of what was in store for them. That it was generally understood that a certain measure of suppression was im-

[1] *Transactions of the Bristol and Gloucestershire Archaeological Society*, vol. XLIX (1927), p. 88.

[2] Strype, *Life of Archbishop Whitgift*, I, p. 4. Abbot Robert Whitgift became Vicar of Ketton, Rutland, in 1538, and was buried at St. John's, Peterborough, January 11th, 1565.

pending may be inferred by the voluntary surrender of half a dozen small houses (one of them Langdon, upon whose state Dr. Layton had made merry) between November 1535 and February 1536. The inmates were treated in the same way as those of monasteries destined to be suppressed by the Act of 1536 and in accordance with medieval pro- cedure. That is to say, the master was pensioned off and the rest of the convent given the choice of transference to other houses or of taking up work as secular clergymen. Until arrangements could be made for them they remained in their abbeys until the King's pleasure was known.

'On Saturday in Ember week,' wrote a London clergy- man to his friends in Plymouth, 'the King's grace came in among the burgesses of parliament and delivered them a bill and bade them look upon it and weigh it in conscience, for he would not, he said, have them pass on it nor on any other thing because his grace giveth in the bill, but try to see if it be for a common weal to his subjects and have an eye thitherward.'[1] It is generally agreed that this bill was that providing for the suppression of the smaller monas- teries, that is, of all those whose revenues did not amount to £200 a year. Now though the preamble of the Act[2] states without more ado that 'manifest sin, vicious, carnal and abominable living is daily used and committed among the little and small abbeys,' it may very well be doubted whether the reports of the visitors had much weight with the House of Commons, even if, as is more than doubtful, they were ever seen by its members. Those visitation reports had dealt just as severely with the large as with the small monasteries.

Yet according to the Act the great and solemn monasteries

[1] Wright, *Suppression*, p. 38.
[2] Printed in Gee and Hardy, *Documents Illustrative of the History of the English Church* p. 257 ff.

(thanks be to God) were well kept and observed religion. Nobody in the House could have taken this distinction between the small and the great houses seriously. Neither need Bishop Latimer's famous statement that 'when their enormities were first read in the parliament house, they were so great and abominable that there was nothing but down with them' be trusted. The bishop had a perfervid imagination. Not only was he not present in the house, but he was preaching more than twelve years later. It has been calculated that after the lapse of such a space of time not more than fifteen per cent of truth can be reckoned upon in the statements of anybody about a past event, so distorted has recollection become owing to a variety of causes. Edward Hall was, on the contrary, a member of the house. He disliked monks at least as much as the bishop did, and all he says on the subject is this: 'And in this time was given unto the King by the consent of the great and fat abbots, all religious houses that were of the value of 300 marks and under, in hope that their great monasteries should have continued still.' The truth would seem to be that at this stage people believed the statement put forth by the Government that there was no intention to interfere with the greater houses. But even at that time one said in the parliament house 'that these were as thorns, but the great abbots were putrified old oaks and these people must follow', and 'so will others do in Christendom,' quoth Doctor Stokesley, Bishop of London, 'or many years past'.[1]

On the whole, then, it seems unlikely that even if the visitors' statements were known to the House of Commons that they had much effect. Similar reports could doubtless have been made on all institutions, on the secular clergy or

[1] Hall, *Chronicle*, II, 268.

on the laity. A visitation of the House of Commons itself conducted on the lines of the visitation of Cheshire[1] would certainly have produced devastating results. The simple explanation of the case with which the bill went through is that members of the House of Commons saw that they would be more popular with their constituents if they could manage to shift increased taxation on to the Church.

[1] See above, p. 122.

CHAPTER VI

SUPPRESSION OF SMALLER MONASTERIES AND THE PILGRIMAGE OF GRACE 1536-37

I

THE parliament which passed the Act of Suppression, one of the most far-going experiments in nationalization that has ever been known in this country, and legalized the creation of the Court of Augmentations to deal with the spoil, was dissolved on April 14th, 1536. Ten days later, local commissioners were appointed by the King to make a new survey of each of the doomed houses, some 220 in number (160 of monks and canons and 60 of nuns), to estimate the value of their property, movable and immovable; to provide against waste and to inquire into recent leases, sales, etc. So far as the inmates of the houses were concerned, the important clauses were the fourth: 'What number of persons of religion be in the same and the conversation of their lives: and how many of them be priests, and how many of them will go to other houses of that religion, or how many will take capacities;'[1] and the nineteenth, twentieth and twenty-first: 'The said commissioners in every such house, to send such of the religious persons that will remain in the same religion, to some other great house of that religion, by their discretion . . . and the residue of them that will go to the world, to send them to my Lord of Canterbury, and the Lord Chancellor for their capacities, with the letter of the same commissioners. To those that will have capacities,

[1] Dispensations to serve as secular clergymen. See below, p. 151.

some reasonable reward. The governor (i.e. the head of house whether prior or abbot) to resort to the Chancellor of the Augmentations, for his yearly stipend or pension.'[1]

Although the commissions included the legal element, the leading spirits in them were not lawyers but country gentlemen, with a wide and tolerant outlook on life, and an extensive knowledge of the internal affairs of the monasteries upon whose state they had to report. As magistrates they were perfectly familiar with 'inquisitions' of all kinds and had often sat on commissions of a somewhat similar kind before. Most of them, too, or their near relations, held offices of some kind in the monasteries: their daughters were being brought up in the nunneries or had become nuns themselves. They were not gossips like Dr. Layton, or insolent like Dr. Leigh, and consequently their reports were on the whole more favourable than those of the inquiry of the previous year. But they were not proceeding on the same lines. They conducted no visitation of the houses with which they were concerned and gave as a rule a sort of general certificate of good character.

In Sussex seven houses were reported on;[2] of the forty-two monks and canons in them, no fewer than thirty-eight wished to have 'capacities', and only four to remain in religion. It can hardly be pretended that zeal for the religious life was rife in the county. On the other hand, less than half a dozen of the inmates were 'noted' for incontinence. A great deal of misconception has arisen about the fate which awaited the inmates of the doomed houses. Yet the procedure was quite simple and is clearly laid down in the 1536 Act. 'His Majesty is pleased and contented . . . to provide to every chief head and governor of every such

---

[1] Printed in Burnet's *History of the Reformation*, Ed. Pocock, vol. IV, pp. 304-7.
[2] *L.P.*, XI, Appendix 2.

religious house, during their lives, such yearly pensions and benefices as for their degree and qualities shall be reasonable and convenient,' with special favour to those who preserve the goods and ornaments without spoil, waste or embezzling, to the King's use. As to the rest of the community, 'the convents of every such religious house shall have their capacities, if they will, to live honestly and virtuously abroad and some convenient charity disposed to them towards their living, or else shall be committed to such honourable great monasteries of this realm ... the chief governors and convents of (which) shall take and accept into their houses from time to time such numbers of the persons of the said convents as shall be assigned and appointed by the King's highness and keep them religiously during their lives ...'

There are, therefore, three classes of persons to be considered: (1) the pensioned abbots or priors; (2) the religious who wanted to leave their habit and return to the world to serve as secular clergymen; (3) those whose religious vocation was strong and who desired, therefore, to be transferred to houses which were left standing. The reports of the commissioners who took the surrender of the smaller monasteries in the later part of 1536 are only extant in part, so it is impossible to say how many of the religious were transferred to other houses and how many went to the world. The procedure was, in fact, the same as that followed by the Kent commissioners in the previous autumn after the surrender of the three Kent monasteries of Langdon, Dover and Folkestone. 'We have left the canons and monks still in their houses, without any clear discharge of them, but have put them at their liberty and choice whether they will abide there until the King's grace's pleasure be further known therein, or else to go from thence to their friends, *whereof the most part desire to have capacities*[1] *and some to be assigned over to other places of religion.*'[2] A few weeks later the prior of Christ Church, Canterbury, wrote to Cromwell: 'We will receive into our house two religious men of the priory of Dover, according to the King's command,'[3] while another of the Dover monks went to the neighbouring abbey of St. Augustine's.

The pensions to the heads of houses were on a generous scale. Not only were they equal to, if not greater, than those paid to retired abbots in the past, but they were probably more certain. It has been already pointed out that it was often very difficult for retired abbots to get their pensions paid by their successors. Those who lost their posts as a result of the Act of 1536 had far less difficulty in getting them paid by the Court of Augmentations. Some of them took the opportunity of continuing their studies and retired to one or other of the universities to complete their education, as the phrase is, though whether anybody has ever succeeded in doing so may well be doubted. Thus Abbot Alynge of Waverley, which, though the earliest Cistercian abbey in England, had come under the Act, went to Oxford and took up his abode at the college of St. Bernard, which belonged to his order.[4] His pension and income arising out of the rectory of Yoxall in Staffordshire, to which he was presented in 1539, were amply sufficient to pay his expenses at the university. Abbot Austen of Rewley, in the suburbs of Oxford, took the odd fancy of going to Cambridge. A cheerful letter written a short while after the suppression of his house, shows that he was then at Trinity Hall, 'studying

---

[1] To serve as secular clergymen: only a minority wishing to remain in religion.
[2] *L.P.*, IX, 829.   [3] *L.P.*, X, 13.
[4] His will (proved January 5th, 1539/40) in the Prerogative Court of Canterbury, shows that he was then head (Provisor) of that college. He left books to three former monks of Hayles, then scholars of the college, and desired to be buried in the church of St. Mary Magdalene, Oxford.

the word of God sincerely'.[1] This phrase probably means that he had thrown in his lot with the 'new learning'; at any rate no political or ecclesiastical changes were going to make him sacrifice any of his emoluments, for he held the rich living of Whatcote, Warwickshire, from 1542 to his death in 1571. Since his pension was £22 and the living was worth £12 in the King's books, he can hardly be said to have been ill-treated. His income from these two sources would have amounted nowadays to some £800 a year, surely adequate sustenance for a single man.

There could be no question of giving pensions to the rank and file of the religious. They had, as has been said, their choice of remaining in religion by being transferred to one or other of the larger houses or of becoming secular clergymen. The reports of the commissioners on this head vary enormously. In some houses not one member was willing to persevere in religion; in others all wished to do so. It may be reckoned, however, that Cistercian monks were the most fervent and the Augustinian canons the most indifferent. Thus of the Cistercian abbey of Stanley in Wiltshire all the monks desired to remain in religion and we find them, in fact, at other Cistercian houses, Beaulieu in particular, at the suppression of the great houses. On the other hand not a single one of the canons of the large Augustinian priory of Westacre in Norfolk wished to go on.[2]

II

That the opportunity of returning to the world was taken by such a large proportion of the religious is not altogether to be wondered at. To the discontented and to those who had no real vocation the chance naturally appealed. Many,

[1] *L.P.*, XII (2), 1320.   [2] *L.P.*, XIII (1), 101.

too, doubtless saw the red light and shrewdly suspected that the still existing houses would fall in their turn. But even for those whose natural inclination it was to remain in religion, the idea of being shifted to a strange house, often in a distant part of the country, must have been hateful. The monks' birthplaces were nearly always in the immediate neighbourhood of the abbey to which they were professed: local ties in the Middle Ages were very strong and it is striking to notice how many of the religious returned after the suppression to the place of their birth. To be shifted, as was the case of two monks of Quarr, from the Isle of Wight to the wilds of Dartmoor at Buckland, must have been very distasteful and to have been to them an exile as great and distant as one in Central Africa would be nowadays.

Nobody can suppose, either, that they were other than unwelcome in the monasteries to which they were assigned. Supposing that in our day some of the smaller and more obscure colleges at Oxford and Cambridge were suppressed, and the fellows given the choice of being shifted to a larger college or of going out into the world. It is terrible to think of the reception which these poor creatures would get at the high tables of their new abode. They would certainly prefer to give up the learned profession and to go elsewhere to earn their living. In point of fact, this is exactly what did happen to some at least of the monks who chose the alternative of remaining in religion. When the Cistercian abbey of Salley (or Sawley), on the borders of Lancashire and Yorkshire was suppressed, four of the monks were shifted to the neighbouring abbey of Furness. Were they made welcome there? Not at all. The Abbot of Furness refused to keep them and drove them out on the ground that the rooms were wanted for 'Lords', and also that he was not bound to receive them because they had taken 'capacities' and were therefore no longer in religion.[1] But this must surely have been a subterfuge on his part. It must have been easy enough to find places for them. Very few of the monasteries had their full complement of numbers at this period, and after the visitors of 1535 had given leave to any monk who wished to go to do so, and had dismissed all those below the age of twenty, there were a great many vacant places in all the great monasteries. A study of the pension list[2] of the large Cistercian abbey of Beaulieu in the New Forest will illustrate this. Of the twenty-two monks who were present at the surrender in 1538, nearly half had come in from Cistercian abbeys in Hampshire and the neighbouring counties, e.g. Quarr, Waverley, Netley and Stanley. These discontented outsiders were apt to stir up a good deal of trouble in their new abodes and were either quarrelsome, like the ex-abbot of Quarr at Beaulieu, or seditious, like Robert Morreby, 'monk of a suppressed abbey in Wales', whom the Council of the North reported in 1538 to have spoken seditious words at the table of the Abbot of Fountains.[3] It must be noted, however, that they enjoyed to the full the privileges of their new house; and when the time came for it to fall in its turn, they received pensions on the same scale as those of the monks who had been there all along.[4] And, as we shall see, these privileges were accorded to the monks of all the abbeys which fell by attainder (like Whalley) or otherwise, right up to the final disappearance of the religious houses three years later.[5]

A large proportion — probably more than half — of the monks and canons of the houses which fell as a result of the

---

[1] *L.P.*, XII (1), 841. [2] *L.P.*, XIV (1), 1355. [3] *L.P.*, XIII (1), 941. [4] See below, p. 255.
[5] The only exceptions were Reading, Colchester, and Glastonbury, whose monks got pensions, because it was not possible at that date to transfer them to other houses. See below, Chapter VII., p. 179, note.

Act of 1536 did not choose to remain in religion. They preferred to become secular clergymen, or as the expression of the day went to 'take capacities' to serve as such. Dispensations to do this had long been in vogue and many religious were already holding livings. That was the case rather with the regular canons than with the monks, though there are a few instances among them, and in some houses of the Augustinian, Premonstratensian and Gilbertine orders a fair proportion of the canons were no longer resident, but were installed in the rectories or vicarages of benefices which were in the gift of their house. St. Frideswide's, Oxford, one of the houses which were suppressed by Cardinal Wolsey, had half its canons scattered in Oxfordshire or Buckinghamshire parishes. Many of the Premonstratensian houses were half empty from this cause. Indeed, their Visitor-General, Bishop Maxey, the Abbot of Welbeck, confessed to Cromwell that they could scarcely carry on but for this additional financial help. Archbishop Warham accused the religious of choosing to serve the rich livings in their gift and not the poor. 'If,' he wrote to Wolsey in July 1528, 'there be any good vicarages, the religious obtain faculties from the Pope to have them served by religious.'[1] When Cromwell's visitors came into Chester they found two of the canons of the Augustinian abbey of Norton serving as vicars of Great Budworth and Runcorn respectively 'under a general capacity from the Bishop of Rome'.[2] Dispensations of this kind were so frequent that they seem to have been the cause of much merriment among the religious. Thomas Clare, one of the monks of the great Benedictine abbey of St. John, Colchester, was lamenting on one occasion that he had not obtained one. 'Pooh,' answered his colleague, John Flyngate, 'things like that are hung up

---

[1] *L.P.*, IV, 4631.   [2] *L.P.*, VIII, 496.

in apothecaries' shops in Rome, with a blank for the buyer's name.'[1] They contributed not a little to indiscipline in the religious houses, because monks and canons were apt to obtain them with the aid of lay patrons and without consent of their superiors. 'One of our monks,' wrote the abbot of the Cistercian house of Holme Cultram in Cumberland to Cromwell, 'has got a dispensation from Rome that he may be *capax beneficii* without our consent or that of our order. By this dispensation he has become the Earl of Northumberland's chaplain, contrary to the rule of our religion.'[2] These dispensations were, however, anything but cheap. Their cost at Rome was very high, and amounted roughly to the equivalent of £100 to £120 at present-day values. As the result of the breach with Rome and of the Act for the exoneration from exactions paid to the see of Rome (1533) these dispensations had no longer to be imported, but were produced at home.[3] Henceforth it was the Archbishop of Canterbury who issued them. Whether the religious gained anything by this change may well be doubted. Probably the only difference was that English lawyers pocketed the fees instead of Italian ones. Fee-snatching is not a wholly foreign practice. But Canterbury was nearer than Rome and travelling expenses were naturally far less onerous to applicants. In some ways, however, the expenses must have gone up, especially when, in November 1536, dispensations from Rome, together with all papal bulls and faculties, were called in to be examined by three Masters in Chancery and reissued at further expense to the holders.[4]

The monks and canons who had not chosen to remain in

---

[1] *L.P.*, VII, 454.   [2] *L.P.*, VI, 781.
[3] For the question of dispensations generally, see *Essays in History presented to R. Lane Poole*, p. 439, especially Note 4.
[4] *L.P.*, XI, 1217, Grant 22.

religion naturally desired to obtain employment as soon as possible. To do this it was obligatory to them to obtain a dispensation[1] from the archbishop and these were sent to them (or they went to fetch them) within a very few days after the suppression of their houses.

The necessity of obtaining this confirmation was often misunderstood by the religious who were seeking dispensations. An unfortunate Carthusian who had got his 'release' from Witham priory told Cromwell that he had written to the Archbishop, thinking that he had sufficient authority and not knowing that he had to get the King's consent as well.[2]

The religious, then, who had deliberately chosen to return to the world and become secular clergymen when they could have continued in religion could not expect pensions. No monk or canon who had taken a dispensation in former years had ever had a pension and why should they have one now? They did not, however, leave their houses without being given any provision, as writers of lachrymose disposition would have us to believe. Their wages, long in arrear, were paid and a 'reward' or species of bonus was given as well. This sum was to go towards the purchase of clothes suitable for their new careers as secular clergymen and to tide them over generally until they got a new job. Rewards for the religious were on a generous scale. The nine Augustinian canons of Grimsby (Wellow) had between them £8 in rewards and nearly £7 arrears in wages.[3] They thus each received what would nowadays amount to about £50. Nevertheless the religious were not generally satisfied with this provision: to their discontent may be attributed one of the causes of the risings in Lincolnshire which began in the autumn of 1536 and of the far more

---

[1] For an example of these dispensations, see Oliver, *Monasticon dioecesis Exoniensis*, p. 216.
[2] *L.P.*, VII, 577.　　　[3] *V.C.H. Lincs*, II, p. 161.

serious rising in Yorkshire which followed closely upon it. That those whom the Duke of Norfolk called 'the naughty religious persons', dissatisfied with their financial condition, had a considerable share in fomenting smouldering discontent of all kinds, there can be no doubt. Bishop Mackarel, Abbot of Barlings, who was destined to be executed for his share in the Lincolnshire rising, said at his trial that he had sold the abbey plate because his canons did not think that their 'rewards' were large enough.

Nobody likes being turned out of house and home, and the upshot of the dispersion was that those religious who had been shifted into the larger monasteries stirred up trouble in them, while those who had chosen to return to the world were apt to hang about the neighbourhood and form centres of disturbance. It was a monk of the suppressed Cistercian abbey of Louth Park who had taken a 'capacity' himself and distributed others, who wrote the Lincolnshire 'articles' which embodied the demands of the rebels. 'When the abbey was dissolved in September 1536,' said he in his evidence at the trial, 'I got my capacity at Bourne on Holy Rood Day [September 14] and brought back with me seventy-six other capacities given me by one of the canons of Bourne. After this I went in the habit of a secular [clergyman]. I went on to Markby and Hagnaby [respectively an Austin and Premonstratensian house] and then to Grimsby to deliver capacities to certain canons of Wellow resident thereabouts.'[1]

The canons of the suppressed Augustinian house of Lanercost in Cumberland were reported as lurking in the neighbourhood in their white coats 'very unseemly'. 'The monks who were suppressed,' wrote Sir William Fairfax from Yorkshire to Cromwell, 'inhabit the villages round

[1] *L.P.*, XII (1), 380.

their houses and daily "wag" the people to put them in again.'[1] The activities of these disgruntled religious seriously perturbed the Government, and when the Cistercian abbey of Whalley was suppressed and its abbot attainted early in the next year the King wrote to the Earl of Sussex, his lieutenant in the district, 'Turn out the religious who have been restored and send them to other houses of their rule, or treat them as vagabonds and tell people that if they won't go into houses they vary from their profession of wilful poverty, chastity and obedience. Husbandmen,' went on the King, 'have to labour in all weathers, while monks and canons are sure at all times of good food.'[2]

The after-careers of the religious who were dispersed in 1536 are more difficult to trace than those of their companions whose sense of vocation led them to accept transference to the larger monasteries, and who were eventually able to claim a pension. What most of them did was to accept small posts, as stipendiaries, chantry priests and so on, all the while looking out for any living which might fall vacant. After the suppression of the small Augustinian priory of Michelham (none of whose canons wished to remain in religion) its inmates all took posts in Sussex, some as chantry priests, some as country parsons.

III

It is not my intention to go into the details of the risings of the autumn of 1536, the most dangerous months to Henry of his whole reign. The interests of so many classes had been affected by recent legislation that if only the

[1] *L.P.*, XII (1), 192.   [2] *L.P.*, XII (1), 302.

conservative leaders had been united, the red rose might again have given place to the white. But the natural leaders of the white rose party, the Poles, did not stir and the King was soon to employ with overwhelming success the familiar tactics of sowing discord between the different sections and classes of the rebels and so bring about their speedy overthrow. 'The indiscreet multitude,' wrote Archbishop Warham to Wolsey in the midst of the taxation crisis of 1525, 'is easily moved to ill by every light tale', and so it proved now. Fears that the parish churches would follow the monastic to ruin, fears that their treasures were to be seized (a foreboding which was to come true a dozen years later) were in all minds. Besides that, evidence of what the suppression really meant was visible to all eyes as the royal commissioners began to pull down the churches of the condemned religious houses.

The fire of local patriotism was everywhere kindled. 'The temples of God ruffed and put down', as Robert Aske said at his trial in April 1537. Riots, such as those which followed on the suppression of Bayham Abbey by Cardinal Wolsey, now broke out in many places. 'This year, 1535 [*sic* 1536] by a parliament held at London, all religious houses of the sum of 300 marks [=£200 and] under, were given to the King: and Sir John Tregonwell, Sir Thomas Arundell and others were appointed to be commissioners for the same in the west parts: who came to this city [Exeter] in the summer time to execute their commission, and beginning first with the priory of St. Nicholas: after that they viewed the same they went to dinner, and commanded one in the time of their absence to pull down the rood loft up the church. In the meanwhile, and before they did return, certain women and wives, in the city . . . minding to stop the suppressing of the house, came in at last to the said church: the door being fast, they broke it open, and finding there the man pulling down the rood loft, they all sought the means they could to take him, and hurled stones unto him, insomuch that for his safety he was driven to take the tower for his refuge, and yet they pursued him so eagerly that he was enforced to leap out at a window and so save himself, and yet very hardly he escaped the breaking of his neck: but yet broke one of his ribs.' An alderman who went to try to pacify the women was received by a fore-runner of (the mythical) Jennie Geddes, who gave him a blow and sent him packing. Finally the Mayor of Exeter was forced to break into the priory, to lay hands on the obstreperous women and send them to ward: whence they were soon released at the intercession of the royal visitors themselves.[1]

Local patriotism of this kind was shown all over the country. 'Rather than *our* house at St. Agatha should be put down we shall all die,' said some of the commons of north-west Yorkshire, while others put back the monks who had been ejected from the Cistercian Salley, and to the effect on popular opinion may be added that of the disgust which those demolitions inspired in great personages whose ancestors' tombs and monuments adorned the monastic churches. 'I have,' wrote Lord La Warr to Cromwell, 'a poor house called Boxgrove [Sussex], very near to my poor house, whereof I am founder, and there lieth many of my ancestors and also my wife's mother: and because it is of my foundation, and that my parish church is under the roof of the church of the said monastery, and have made a poor chapel to be buried in, whereof if it might stand with the King's grace's pleasure for the poor service I have done his highness, to forbear the suppressing of the same . . . I

[1] Oliver, *Monasticon dioecesis Exoniensis*, p. 116.

beg your favour.'[1] This request of Lord La Warr was not granted; but his alternative petition was, and he was able to buy not only the lands, but to preserve the monastic church, in which his ancestors' tombs can be seen to this day. Not all the great families, however, were so lucky, and the pulling down of the priory church of Bisham and the destruction of the monuments of the Poles' ancestors was certainly one of the reasons which embittered that family with the royal policy and led them to go forward with the intrigues which were shortly to prove their ruin.

The disturbances which followed the suppression of the lesser monasteries began in the autumn of 1536 and ended before the spring of 1537. Apart from sporadic outbreaks such as those in Cumberland, the three main movements were the Lincolnshire rising, which began on October 1st and was put down by the middle of that month; the first Yorkshire rebellion, or Pilgrimage of Grace proper, extending from October 9th to early in December; and the renewed outbreak, crushed almost immediately, in the East Riding in the following month. If it had not been for its repercussions all over the country, the Lincolnshire rising would not have differed much from movements to which medieval kings had been familiar. Indeed, the risings of the Cornishmen under the blacksmith, Michael Joseph, in the reign of the King's father bore many resemblances to that of the shoemaker, Nicholas Multon, 'Captain Cobbler', at Louth. 'That we may be no more taxed' was the ingenuous demand of the rebels; and the burning of books of taxation which had been a leading feature of Wat Tyler's rebellion was repeated here. The killing of Archbishop Sudbury in the Tower was paralleled by the pulling of an unfortunate ecclesiastical dignitary, old and sick, off his horse to be

[1] Wright, *Suppression*, p. 119.

beaten to death; while a tax collector, with a bull skin on his back was baited to death by dogs.

Dislike of existing taxation, fear of future — as the rumour that the King would have all unmarked cattle showed — operated promptly on the minds of the laity. The clergy were equally alarmed by more stringent rules for the collection of first fruits and tenths, and by the increasing circulation of New Testaments in English and of innovating books such as Frith's *Disputation of Purgatory*, while for no apparent reason they classed their own bishop with prelates addicted to the 'new learning' like Cranmer and Latimer; and it was natural that the monks and canons of the suppressed houses should be in sympathy, active or passive, with the rebels. That there was much agreement with them in the rest of the country is shown by a letter of Sir William Fitzwilliam to Cromwell written on October 7th from Guildford: 'All, old and young, pray God speed to the rebels.' But it was not long after that Sir William himself was at Lincoln helping the King's brother-in-law, the Duke of Suffolk, to put things straight after the collapse of a rebellion which had lasted no more than ten days. 'God being your grace's friend,' wrote the Duke to Henry, 'the traitors of the rebellion shall be punished to the fearful example of all others.' But in the following month the King wrote to the Earl of Rutland that he had pardoned all the Lincolnshire men, except the wretches in ward at Lincoln, the Vicar of Louth and Nicholas Leech of Horncastle. The said 'wretches' included the Abbot of Kirkstead (a Cistercian abbey rich enough to have escaped suppression), three of its monks, six monks of the Benedictine abbey of Bardney and four çanons of the Premonstratensian abbey of Barlings, and seven secular priests. Abbot Harrison of Kirkstead was executed at Lincoln on March 7th and the others, announced Sir William Parr, were to be removed next day to suffer at Louth and Horncastle, the two chief centres of the rebellion. Whether they were *all* executed may perhaps be doubted, for one of the secular clergy was still vicar of his parish two years later,[1] and even in the sixteenth century last-minute reprieves were common enough. At the end of the month the Abbot of Barlings, William Morland, monk of Louth Park, three secular clergy, including the vicar of Louth, and seven laymen were tried in London, found guilty of levying war on the King and sentenced: 'execution to be at Tyburn: to be hanged, cut down alive, disembowelled, their entrails burned while they were still alive, and beheaded.' 'As the gates of London are full of quarters not consumed,' wrote the Lord Chancellor to Cromwell, 'I have ordered the heads of these prisoners to be set up over London Bridge and at every gate.' 'God pardon their souls,' wrote the chronicler Wriothesley piously, but without further comments.

The rebellion in Yorkshire which broke out just as that in Lincolnshire was being quelled, was far more dangerous. The gentry of that shire were not such 'a sight of asses, so unlike gentlemen for the most part' as those of Lincolnshire were represented to be: and whereas practically none except Lord Hussey were involved in Lincolnshire, a great many flung themselves into the movement in Yorkshire. The commons, too, were more numerous and determined, and had been stuffed, not only with the tales which had done the conservative cause good service farther south, but in addition with such fantasies as that the King would allow nobody to eat white bread, goose or capon without paying toll to the Crown and that a noble (nearly £10 nowadays) would be charged for every christening, wedding, and

---

[1] William Smythe, Rector of Donington on Bain.

funeral. It was no wonder that less than a week after the first outbreak, Sir Brian Hastings had to report to Lord Shrewsbury that there were 40,000 rebels and that most of the northern lords (including the Earl of Cumberland, of all people, for he was the most hated landlord in the north) had been sworn to them, and with the banner of the Five Wounds of Christ this 'rebellious garrison of Satan' occupied York. Before the end of October it was facing the King's ill-equipped army at Doncaster. Yet before the end of the month Lord Shrewsbury was able to report that 'we have stayed the commons of Yorkshire, and every man has returned home'. It is not necessary to account for this by the 'great miracle of God'[1] which caused the waters of the Don to rise to a height, deepness and breadth such as nobody had ever known before. Divisions among the rebels had already begun and the King and the Duke of Norfolk were able, the one to grant, the other to proclaim, a general pardon, or rather promise of pardon, early in December. The most dangerous movement in Henry's reign had fizzled out in two months. Whether the promise of pardon would have been kept may be left in doubt. But the foolish revival of the rebellion at Hull and its neighbourhood in January 1537, and disturbances in Cumberland, Westmorland and Richmondshire in the following month, all of which were suppressed by the Duke of Norfolk with the greatest ease, gave him and the King an excuse for infringing it.

Henry owed his victory chiefly to two men, the Duke of Norfolk and the Earl of Shrewsbury. It is important to note that neither of these great personages had any sympathy whatever with ecclesiastical changes of any kind, and that they disliked all that Cranmer and Latimer stood

---

[1] Hall, *Chronicle*, II, 276.

for as much as the pilgrims of grace did. Three unfortunate adherents of the 'new learning' were once brought before the Earl 'defamed of heresy'. He spoke to them in terms which he would hardly have used to poachers. 'Come near, thou heretic and kneel near. Ha! thou heretic, thou hast books here!'

'Yea, my Lord, the New Testament I have.'

'The New Testament nought thou hast,' and repeated very often that it was nought, adding, 'Thou art an heretic and but for shame I should thrust my dagger into thee. Thy sentence is seven days' dungeon.'[1]

The Duke was as much opposed to innovations in other people's religion as he was to reforms in his own morals. Miss Elizabeth Holland had taken up her abode with him and his half-crazy wife was put to it to subsist, while her maids sat on her chest till the blood came. Nobody was more responsible than he for the savage Act of the Six Articles which preceded Cromwell's fall less than three years after the collapse of the Pilgrimage of Grace; yet he had no sympathy with those who were mixed up in it, spoke of the abominable living of religious men, and when he condemned a poor London Carthusian in Hull for denying the royal supremacy, his only objection was that the execution was not to take place in the South because people in these parts are 'clean turned against the Bishop of Rome'.[2] Nobody, again, was more conservative in religion than Bishop Tunstal of Durham, yet nobody was more fierce in his denunciation of the adherents of the pilgrimage as traitors. Archbishop Lee of York was also a conservative and was suspected of being secretly in sympathy with the rebels; but he had no mind to be a martyr like his predecessor, Archbishop Scrope, and he did all he

[1] *L.P.*, XII (2), 436.   [2] *L.P.*, XII (1), 777.

could to stifle among the monks of Mountgrace, and elsewhere, objections to accepting the King as supreme head of the Church of England. Lord Latimer and Lord Scrope had, perhaps willynilly, been with the rebel army, but they felt no scruple in buying or leasing abbey lands from the Crown. The two men of noble birth who did suffer, Lord Darcy and Sir Robert Constable, were not followed in their politics by their families: they seem to have been personally unpopular, and the Duke of Norfolk was probably right in saying that their death was little regretted. Both had sought armed aid from foreign powers, and so had irredeemably damaged themselves in the eyes of patriots like the Duke. The real leader of the rebels, Robert Aske, was single-minded and disinterested, but his head was turned by his brief term of authority and his countenance became as 'satrapic' as that of his fellow-lawyer Thomas Leigh, the King's visitor; and his bullying and insolent behaviour was that so often seen in a certain type of provincial lawyer. Sir Francis Bigod, the leader of the renewed rebellion of January 1537, was an incredibly fanatical and feather-pated person, who dashed from one extreme to another, both in religion and politics, and who thoroughly deserved his end, if only on account of the number of people he brought down with him.

The number of religious persons who perished as the result of Bigod's rebellion, and its repercussions in Cumberland and the vicinity, was not so large as might have been expected in an age so merciless towards treason. Very little sympathy can be felt for some of them. Ex-Abbot Thirsk of Fountains, and ex-Prior Cockerell of Gisburn wanted to be restored to the posts of which they had been deprived early in 1536. The accusations of the King's visitors, assisted by the Earl of Northumberland, against the former of stealing jewels and conveying them to a receiver in London may or may not be true.[1] But the charge that he was 'a very fool ànd a miserable idiot' was corroborated by his successor, Abbot Bradley, 'the wisest man in England of that coat', who wrote to Cromwell to protest against the large pension which Doctor Leigh and Doctor Layton had assigned to him and to suggest that it should be drastically reduced: 'the Statute of our rèligion is that if an abbot has ruled ten years well, he is to have a competent pension, but this one has ruled naughtily.'[2]

There was another northern abbot who was in the same position as ex-Abbot Thirsk and ex-Prior Cockerell, namely, ex-Abbot Kirkby of Rievaulx. The Earl of Rutland, patron of that abbey, had been so dissatisfied with this abbot's behaviour that three years before he had, as we have seen, applied to Cromwell for a commission to examine and do justice on him. The commission, consisting of the Abbots of Fountains and Byland, forced him to resign and assigned him a pension of £44.[3] He found it as difficult to acquiesce in what was to all intents and purposes a dismissal as in obtaining his pension out of his successors. That he sought redress from the rebels is shown by a letter of the Duke of Norfolk written to Cromwell in October 1537, in which the Duke says that it is at *his* orders that the present abbot has not paid the pension to his predecessor, who had 'showed himself false and traitorous during the late business'.[4] Indeed, he was for a time in the Tower of London with the *quondams* of Fountains and Gisburn; either because he had only been implicated in the first rebellion and not in the second, and was therefore protected by the pardon, or because he bought a pardon, he escaped further punishment,

<hr>

[1] Wright, *Suppression*, p. 100.   [2] *L.P.*, x, 424.
[3] See above, p. 92.   [4] *L.P.*, xii (2), 822.

and two years later accepted from the abbot and convent of Westminster the vicarage of Newport in Essex.[1]

His was no isolated instance, and the failure to recognize that many of those who were condemned managed in one way or another to escape the penalties of the law has caused the period to be looked upon as more cruel than it actually was. A typical example of this is the case of Lawrence Cooke, prior of the Carmelites of Doncaster, who was attainted in parliament for adhering to the rebel, Aske, specially exempted from pardon in July 1537, reported by the French ambassador to have been executed in July 1540, yet who in October that year received a pardon for all offences committed before August 8th last.[2] A somewhat similar case is that of John Dakyns, archdeacon of the East Riding and rector of Kirkby Ravensworth, who had got into trouble for writing a letter to the prior of the lately suppressed monastery of Cartmel, urging him and his brethren to return to their house; yet in the event he suffered nothing either in life or goods and died in possession of all his offices, a few days before the accession of Queen Elizabeth. Nobody had been more implicated in the rebellion than Abbot Bolton of Salley, the great Cistercian abbey on the borders of Lancashire and Yorkshire. He and his monks had been restored by the rebels in October 1536. He was certainly condemned to die, as Sir Stephen Hamerton in a statement made on April 25th, 1537, shows.[3] But what evidence is there that he actually suffered? It is certainly curious that his name does not appear on the list of attainders for treason which was drawn up in 1540 and which includes the names not only of all the other abbots and

---

[1] Edward Cowper *alias* Kirkby, Vicar of Newport, 1539-46. Vicar of Kirkby Misperton (close to Rievaulx), 1543-57.
[2] *L.P.*, XVI, 220, grant 7.
[3] *L.P.*, XII (1), 1034. The term 'late abbot' need not necessarily mean that he was dead.

priors, nine in number, who perished in the years 1537 — 39, but that of Thomas Cromwell himself.[1]

The abbots of Jervaulx and Whalley seem to have been the victims of the intrigues of others. Abbot Sedbergh of Jervaulx had taken no part in the first rebellion, and, only the year before, had been reported to have behaved like a true man when one of his monks had interrupted a sermon against the pope which was being preached in the abbey church. Unluckily for him, ex-Abbot Thirsk of Fountains, leaving his free quarters there which were part of his pension, came to live at Jervaulx as a 'sojourner'[2] (or paying guest); there he seems to have worked hard to incite the neighbourhood to rise afresh, offering money to be restored to Fountains, of which, he asserted, he had been unjustly deprived by the visitors. The upshot was that both he and his host, Abbot Sedbergh, had a most unpleasant journey in London. They were drawn on hurdles from the Tower to Tyburn and executed there on May 25th, 1537.

Abbot Paslew of Whalley similarly kept free from the first rebellion, but unluckily one of his monks had a brother who was professed at the neighbouring abbey of Salley and chaplain to the abbot of that house. When it was suppressed, he was either sent to, or went of his own accord to, Whalley, and so must have involved the abbot in a charge of harbouring the King's enemies.[3] Abbot Paslew pleaded guilty of treason at his trial in the following March and was executed at Lancaster. There were tried with him Richard Eastgate of Salley and his brother John Eastgate of Whalley, Henry Banaster, another monk of Salley, and William Haydock, monk of Whalley; but of these only the first and

---

[1] *L.P.*, xv, 937.   [2] *L.P.*, xII (1), 1011 and 1012.
[3] For the executions at Whalley and Cartmel see *The Narrative of the Indictment of the traitors of Whalley and Cartmel*, in *Chetham Miscellanies*, New Series, vol. v (1931), by the Reverend Canon J. E. W. Wallis.

last were executed: the second was acquitted and desired to go to be received at Neath abbey in Wales, while the third seems to have evaded arrest. The neighbouring priory of Cartmel also provided four victims among the canons and two husbandmen of the place. They had been put back by the commons and nothing would probably have happened to them if they and some of the yeomen had not stirred up a fresh commotion two months after the pardon. Three others escaped and two were acquitted at their trial at Lancaster in March 1537. That the two canons who had been acquitted soon reconciled themselves to the course of events is shown by the fact that one of them died curate of Cartmel so late as 1585, having buried his wife three years before, while the wife of the other was buried at Cartmel in 1593. The later careers of the monks of Whalley were of a like kind, and one of them was still serving the curacy of Haslingden so late as 1574; another was vicar of Whalley from 1537 to his death in 1558, and a third, vicar of Blackburn from 1536 to 1555.

The foolish renewal of the rebellion in the East Riding involved a few more religious, including Prior Wood of Bridlington, three canons of the Gilbertine priory of Watton, two of the Augustinian priory of Warter, and a Dominican friar named Pickering, who seems to have been the chief means of getting the prior into trouble, and he was hanged at Tyburn in May, 1537. On the other hand, Prior Roundell of Healaugh Park, who with one of his canons was committed to ward in York Castle after successfully pleading that he had been enforced and compelled against his will by the commons to enter again into his monastery in 'the late commotion time' was not only released, but became rector of St. Saviour's, York, and held the living till his death in 1550.

'Ye shall be drawn from the Tower of London unto Tyburn and there ye shall be hanged a whole day and after to be taken down and your heads smitten off and set on London Bridge,' and so it was done. The Prior of Launde and eight friars minor, whereof one was a master of divinity, were drawn and hanged for treason at Tyburn, and the master of the friars, an old man, made a devout sermon on the theme *In manus tuas, Domine.* Four Franciscans having been captured by the Earl of Westmorland his men stripped and debagged them (*femoralia detrahebant,* as the chronicler has it).[1] The ill-treatment of these friars was not by Henry the Eighth, but by Henry the Fourth, the most orthodox of all English kings. Such were the treason laws of the middle ages.

[1] *Eulogium Historiarum* (Rolls Series), III, 407.

CHAPTER VII

FROM THE PILGRIMAGE OF GRACE
TO THE FINAL SUPPRESSION 1537-1540

I

'DIVERS and great solemn monasteries of this realm, wherein (thanks be to God) religion is right well kept and observed' were in existence, and in great numbers, when the
northern rising was crushed. That the act of dissolution of
1536 should speak of them in these terms seems to show,
first, that there was not at that time any fixed intention on
the part of the King and Cromwell to destroy all the surviving houses; and secondly, that not much reliance was
placed on denigration, for the royal visitors had made
reports on some of the larger monasteries (Battle in
particular) which were far worse than anything they had
said about the smaller. Even when their fate as religious
houses was determined, there was still a chance of the
survival of a great many of them in a changed form, as
cathedral bodies or as educational establishments. In
May, 1539, the French Ambassador told King Francis that
'the reduction of certain abbeys is imminent, which they
wish to make bishoprics and foundation schools for children
and hospitals for the poor'. It is apt to be forgotten not
only that the King could vie in learning with many scholars
— indeed, that he was almost the first theologian in Europe
— but that he had inherited much of his grandmother's zeal
for education. When he reorganized the chapter of
Winchester Cathedral on a secular instead of a religious
basis in 1541, no fewer than four of the former monks were

provided with scholarships at Oxford at a salary of £10 (say £300) a year, a number which the prior and convent had never been able to afford. The scheme for new bishoprics drawn up in 1539[1] shows that he was equally anxious to extend the system to them. Had it eventuated there would have been a bishop for nearly every shire. The churches of Bury St. Edmunds, St. Albans, Colchester, Shrewsbury and Leicester abbeys; and of Waltham, Dunstable and Bodmin priories would have become cathedrals, while a Bishop of Fountains would have ruled Lancashire and north-west Yorkshire, with his seat in Fountains Abbey, assisted by a dean, six prebendaries, six minor canons and masters of grammar and song schools. Other great houses like Thornton, Burton-on-Trent and Thetford were to become — and in fact the two first did for a short time become — colleges.

That these schemes fell far short of their original aims and that in the end only six bishoprics were founded and most of the educational provisions given up was due to repercussions oversea. Social reforms had to give way to rearmament. Once the northern rising was put down there was not much danger to be feared at home. The King walked along his ecclesiastical *via media*, hanging some rash persons who had eaten flesh on Friday against his command, arresting others for traitorously naming that venemous serpent, the Bishop of Rome, to be supreme head of the Church of England, going to mass twice on holy days, arguing with persons of innovating religious opinions before sending them to be burned, causing the King of France to smile at a proclamation allowing Englishmen to eat eggs in Lent and to say that he thinks Henry will want to say mass next, and making all Europe to laugh over his matrimonial adventures. Poor Anne Boleyn's head had

[1] *L.P.*, XIV (2), 428-30.

been parted from her body less than six months before the northern rising began. She had not fulfilled her function of producing a male heir: the birth of a daughter (for who could foresee the future of that daughter?) was surely bad enough, but when she followed that blunder by a worse one and brought forth a stillborn child, her other indiscretions could no longer be overlooked and she perished. Her successor, Jane Seymour, the only wife to whom Henry seems to have been really attached, lived only long enough to provide the longed-for boy, and died in October 1537. The Duke of Norfolk caused a thousand masses to be said for her soul. Requiem masses were said at Hampton Court chapel on successive days by seven abbots and two bishops. In the choir of St. George's Chapel, Windsor, to which the body had been taken, was the Archbishop of Canterbury *in pontificalibus*, assisted by six bishops and by the abbots of St. Albans, Westminster, Reading, Waltham, Tower Hill and Stratford. It is strange to think that in the course of the next few years, no fewer than three of the officiants were to die as martyrs: Archbishop Cranmer and Bishop Latimer at the stake, and Abbot Cook of Reading on the scaffold.

For the present, however, the policy of making the Church of England a convenient mixture held good. The birth of a weakly prince did not make the succession to the Crown any too sure, and Henry was soon on the look-out for a new wife who should provide him with sons, on whom by way of anticipation he bestowed the dukedoms of York and Gloucester. His ambassadors sent reports about marriageable royal ladies from all the courts of Europe. Great artists were commissioned to paint their portraits and Holbein was given a retaining fee of £30[1] a year. Had Cranach, the Duke of Cleve's court painter, only painted

---

[1] About £900 nowadays.

the portrait of Anne instead of Holbein a great deal of trouble would have been saved (for did he ever make those who sat to him anything but frights?); she need never have had to exchange the titles of wife and Queen for those of servant and sister to Henry, and Cromwell need not have lost his head. But the King was horrified, not only by her face, but by the hideous German clothes in which she and her ladies were habited (he sent hastily to Paris to get the latest fashions for them) and by the fact that her knowledge of cards was limited to the complicated game of skat, still so popular in the Fatherland. *Her* divorce, at any rate, gave very little trouble.

'The Government,' wrote Castillon to Francis I, in January 1538, 'don't wish for such enemies as you. They only seek to put the country in order, which they have begun to do with the abbeys and other benefices as peaceably as they can: whatever countenance they may put on they do not wish for trouble. Moreover in my judgment it would be dangerous to them.' About the same time Cromwell was writing to one of the great abbots (perhaps Glastonbury) to deny that there was any fear of suppression and saying that no surrender would be taken unless overtures were first made.[1] That none of the monasteries survived, whether in their original form or 'altered', and that the scheme for new bishoprics which would have saved so many of the abbey churches came to nought was due to the Government's financial embarrassments produced in great measure by the fear of foreign invasion in the years 1538 and 1539, and the costly defence measures which this involved. In August 1539, Sir Brian Tuke, the Treasurer of the Chamber, had to admit that the treasury was practically empty.

[1] *L.P.*, XIII (1), 573.

If there was one individual more than another who contributed most to the war scare, it was the King's cousin, Reginald Pole, whose efforts, literary and diplomatic, to discredit and ruin Henry fill these years. Pole was a very good example of the saying that no man is the wiser for his learning. He combined in almost unique measure single-heartedness with simple-mindedness, and he paid no attention to Bishop Tunstal's warning that his simplicity would be taken advantage of in Rome. His life was really one great tragedy: he spent his life in the ultramontane service and ended it by being branded by zealots as little better than a heretic. He exhibited all 'the irritability and self sufficiency of the successful scholar', was touchy to a degree, and so naively conceited as to offer to surrender the cardinalate which Pope Paul III had, very imprudently, conferred on him in December 1536, on condition that Henry should give up his title of supreme head.[1] He was never a match for an opponent of Henry's ability, and anything which he undertook was always months, if not years, behindhand. He awoke to the possibilities of the Pilgrimage of Grace months too late, and when, in March 1537, he was appointed papal legate to organize a crusade against England the whole movement had collapsed. And what a failure was his mission! Refused audience by the King of France, finding no more success with the Emperor in the Low Countries, he had to return to Italy. Henry, he wrote plaintively in January 1538, had spurned the salvation he wanted so much to secure for him, had got one prince to expel him from his realm and another to refuse to admit him. Unluckily for his family he continued to correspond with them and with other 'wounded minds' in England. The arrest of his brother, Sir Geoffrey Pole, in August 1538,

[1] *L.P.*, XII (1), 429.

and the execution of another brother, Lord Montague, in the following December, was the result. His mother, the old Countess of Salisbury, was still in the Tower: yet he proceeded to incite Henry's fury still further.

Encouraged by a temporary drawing together of the King of France and the Emperor, he set forth on yet another mission to raise up a coalition against England, which proved as vain as the former one. He got no help in Madrid; King Francis refused to receive him and he had to return to Italy, crying despairingly that God will punish Henry if men won't. But God did not punish Henry: the threatened coalition against him fell to pieces. There was no 'great filibuster' like William III at hand to undertake an expedition against England, and the only results of Pole's activities were, first, to rally conservative opinion in this country to the King and to excite feelings of nationalism and anti-popery, and secondly, so to deplete the royal treasury, by reason of the necessity of rearming the Kingdom, as to bring about further depredations at the expense of the church.

'The cankered and cruel serpent, the Bishop of Rome, working through that arch traitor Reginald Pole, enemy to God's word and his natural country.' Such was the opinion of the radical chronicler Edward Hall; but Englishmen of all shades of opinion were equally vehement. Sir Thomas Wyatt, ambassador at Madrid, refused to shake hands with him as a traitor. The spirit of nationalism which was to reach its highest point under Elizabeth is reflected in many letters written in these years. Lawyers like Sir Thomas Dennis, the recorder of Exeter, were convinced of the royal claims by Bracton's book written nearly 300 years before and which called the King *Vicarius Christi*. Peers, like Lord Morley, discovered the works of Machiavelli; the History of

Florence, he wrote to Cromwell, is somewhat like the King's cause; 'Note how little the Florentines reputed the Bishop of Rome's cursings,' and 'do show his *Prince* to the King, surely a good thing for your lordship.'[1] Somewhat superfluous advice, since Cromwell knew the Italian author's work and acted on his maxims, almost as thoroughly as Mussolini does to-day. Among the bishops, Stephen Gardiner could refer to that 'traitor Pole', while the hierarchy generally strove to purge their dioceses of foreign clergy.

This was not of course new. Bishops of Winchester had often refused to admit French clergy to their dioceses. But it now took a sharper form, and Bishop Shaxton of Salisbury issued the very sensible injunction that no French or Irish priest who could not speak English properly was to hold a cure in his diocese.[2] This dislike of Irish clergymen seems to have been general. When Sir Edward Guilford, the Kentish magnate, heard that the trustees of the chantry of Biddenden had appointed an Irishman to the living he hastily wrote to Cromwell to have the presentation annulled on racial grounds.[3] Not only did the cardinal's intrigues bring about the ruin of his own family and that of his cousin, the Marquis of Exeter, but there is little doubt that they were to involve also two of the most prominent abbots in England. The fate of the abbots of Glastonbury and Reading is best understood in the light of a report made by the French Ambassador, Marillac, to King Francis in November 1539, in which he says of the two abbots that he cannot learn any particulars of what they were charged with 'except that it was the "reliques" of the late Marquis'.[4] That they should have been involved at all seems to have come upon the Government with surprise. They were both

[1] *L.P.*, xiv (1), 285.
[2] Burnet, *History of the Reformation*, Ed. Pocock, vi, 210
[3] *L.P.*, v, 1678.   [4] *L.P.*, xiv (2), 607.

royal nominees: and had both acknowledged the royal supremacy.[1] Naturally they wished to retain their positions but there was no reason to suppose that they would prove less pliable than the rest of their cloth. At Glastonbury the corrody vacated by the death of Sir Thomas More was bestowed on Cromwell, who was the abbot's proxy in the parliament of April 1539, while the Abbot of Reading, though loth to surrender himself, was only too ready to consent to the suppression of the important 'cell' at Leominster, with whose prior he was on the worst possible terms. He had, however, the bad luck to take in a paying guest who was to be his *âme damnée*, just as the former abbot of Fountains had been that of the abbot of Jervaulx.

There was a prebendary of Chichester Cathedral of the name of John Rugge, who had been residing for some years in Reading Abbey. Now Chichester was a centre of opposition to government. Bishop Sampson was of the old way of thinking: so was Lord de la Warr at Halnaker, near by. Old Lady Salisbury's house at Cowdray was only a dozen miles away, while that of her son, Sir Geoffrey Pole, was even nearer. Furthermore, the abbot had been a great friend of Sir Geoffrey's elder brother, Lord Montague, whose Buckinghamshire and Berkshire seats of Bockmere and Bisham were only about a dozen miles distant from Reading. When Prebendary Rugge was examined in September 1539, there were found in his rooms at Chichester and the abbey, not only a relic called St. Anastasius' head (though the King had sent his visitors to suppress idolatry in the abbey), but also one book against the royal supremacy and another against the royal divorce. Since there are

---

[1] The acknowledgment of the abbot and convent of Glastonbury on September 19th, 1534, is extant. That of the abbot and monks of Reading is not. But it is obvious that they must have taken it, or they would have shared the fate of the Carthusians.

no records of Abbot Cook's trial, it is impossible to say what were the exact charges against him. The note in Cromwell's memoranda: 'The Abbot of Reading to be sent down to be tried and executed at Reading with his complices, similarly the Abbot of Glaston at Glaston' has rightly been characterized in the way it deserves. But a recent writer has well observed that these notes have been over-emphasized. 'A man might write down, in a private note intended only for himself "to be tried and executed", meaning "if found guilty (as I suppose they will be)". Cromwell had indeed reason enough for practical certainty.'[1] The Abbot of Glastonbury was examined 'upon certain articles', and so, without doubt, was the Abbot of Reading.

That Abbot Cook and perhaps Abbot Whiting, through the medium of the 'blind harper', had been induced to correspond with each other and with the Pole family was probably the real cause of their fall, coupled in Whiting's case with an attempt to secrete the treasures of his church. Henry's avarice was one of his chief failings, while his hatred of the Poles amounted to a monomania; and it had just been excited to frenzy by the discovery of Lady Salisbury's coat of armour blazoned with the arms of England and by the scheme for marrying Cardinal Pole to the Princess Mary. Taking all these circumstances into consideration it would seem that these two abbots were being treated as political and not as ecclesiastical victims and that their case differs widely from those of the Carthusian and Marian martyrs.

A few words may be added on the fate of the three other heads of houses who suffered in the period between the collapse of the Pilgrimage of Grace and the suppression of

---

[1] Pickthorn, *Early Tudor Government: Henry VIII*, p. 374, note 1.

the last of the religious houses. The case of Abbot Hobbes of Woburn has recently been investigated afresh: and Miss Scott-Thomson[1] has been able to fix the date (June 20th, 1538) and place (Woburn, not Bedford) of his execution. It stands quite apart both from the Pilgrimage of Grace — with which it had nothing to do — and from the Pole plot of that year. The commission which tried him consisted of nine neighbouring peers, knights and esquires, some of them (like John Gostwike) diehard conservatives in doctrinal matters. He was found guilty, first, of offending against the Supremacy Act of 1534 (though he must have taken the oath, or he would have been in trouble before) by upholding the lawfulness of the authority of the Bishop of Rome in England, and secondly, against the Succession Act of 1536, by referring to Katharine of Aragon as the King's true and undoubted wife. He made no defence and was executed, in all probability outside his own abbey gate. The cases of the Prior of Lenton, Nicholas Heath (executed April 16th, 1538) and of the Abbot of Colchester, Thomas Marshall (executed December 1st, 1539) are very similar. The first had quarrelled with 'certain men of Nottingham' and the second not only with his own servants, but with his medical man, all of whom were seemingly only too willing to repeat their master's rash utterances about the King's avarice, and the unlawfulness of putting down the greater religious houses. The conflict of evidence was, however, great. Whereas, for instance, the accusers maintained that the abbot had said that the Bishop of Rome was supreme head, the abbot himself asserted that he thought the King had good right to be supreme head and that the Bishop of Rome's supremacy originated in human law. On the whole, it may be said that of the five abbots or

[1] *Translations of Royal Historical Society*, Fourth Series, vol. XVI (1933), pp. 129 ff.

priors who suffered in 1538 and 1539, the abbot of Woburn was most entitled to be called a martyr for ecclesiastical opinions.

They were not, however, followed to the scaffold by their monks, except at Glastonbury, where two monks suffered (one the treasurer); Woburn, which also provided two victims; Lenton one; Reading and Colchester none at all. As to the rest of the monks of these houses very little is known about the fate of those of Woburn or of Lenton. Presumably they were given the choice of going to surviving Cistercian or Cluniac houses respectively, or of obtaining dispensations to serve as secular clergymen. In any case they were later absorbed into the ranks of the parochial clergy. Indeed, one of the Woburn monks was still holding a living in Northamptonshire nearly fifty years after the suppression of his abbey. The monks of Reading, Colchester and Glastonbury had no choice but to go into the world, and over forty of them were still in receipt of pensions and serving parishes seventeen years later.[1]

At Walsingham there was some trouble in 1537 and the treasurer of the priory, Nicholas Mileham, came to his end. He had not boggled at taking the oath of supremacy three years before, but the stripping of Our Lady's image of her jewels was too much for his equanimity and he dabbled in treasonable correspondence. It has been already pointed out that one difficulty in estimating the number of victims is that many of those who were imprisoned and even condemned to death received a pardon. This was the case with the Carmelite friar, William Gibson, who was involved in this affair. Two of the houses suppressed in 1536,

[1] The names of twenty-five monks of Glastonbury, thirteen of Reading, and four of Colchester are on the pension list of February, 1555-6, known as Cardinal Poles. (*P.R.O. Exchequer, K.R.*, Misc. books, vol. XXXI.) It was the Court of Exchequer and not the Court of Augmentations which paid the pensions of attainted abbeys, see Giuseppi, *Guide to the Public Records*, I, p. 139.

Hexham in Northumberland and Norton in Cheshire, offered armed resistance. But as there are no records of the trial, much less of the execution of any of the inmates, it is to be supposed that their offences were overlooked as occurring before the pardon of December 2nd, 1536. The Duke of Norfolk went to Hexham in February 1537, 'dissolved the house to the very good contentation of the inhabitants, avoiding the canons' and put the King's farmer, Sir Richard Carnaby, in possession. The abbot and three canons of Norton were imprisoned, first in Halton Castle and then in the King's jail at Chester, by the High Sheriff of Cheshire, Sir Piers Dutton, who was anxious to execute them. Several of the local gentry interested themselves in their behalf and in the late summer of 1537 one of them, Sir William Brereton, wrote to Cromwell: 'I lately received your order for the discharge of the abbot and canons of Norton and have done so on their giving sufficient securities.'[1] There is no record whatever of further proceedings against them. It is very difficult to understand on what principles the Crown went in dealing out executions or pardons, or of ignoring accusations altogether. Delation on the part of personal enemies of heads of houses (whether their own monks or outsiders) was as frequent in these years as it had been in the past.

Yet while one, such as the Abbot of Woburn, whose offences amounted to no more than verbal treason, was taken, others, against whom similar or worse charges were levelled, were left. Of this, old Abbot Stonywell of Pershore is a good instance. This abbot was a harsh and unpopular man, in constant trouble with his neighbours and friends. In April 1538 one of the local gentry heard the

---

[1] *L.P.*, XII (2), 597. The last abbot, Thomas Birkenhead, had been in office since at least 1525. Beamont, *History of Norton*, p. 182.

abbot say at his own table: 'I trust and I pray to God that I may die one of the children of Rome.' His guest answered that for his part he thought that 'the usurped power of the Bishop of Rome was not given by God, but rather of the devil'. The talk went on about northern affairs. 'I think,' said another of the abbot's guests, 'the King has been too merciful; why, he could have put 40,000 to death.'[1] No notice seems, however, to have been taken of this accusation, and the abbot peacefully surrendered the abbey less than two years afterwards. Abbot Love of the Cistercian house of Coggeshall, Essex, had quarrelled with his monks, who sent up 'articles' against him to Cromwell in 1536.[2] They accused him of maintaining the power of the pope 'contrary to our oath and the statute', removing jewels and evidences against the visitation, using a key by a book to know things to come, of obtaining his office by simony, of saying that he would go to the devil for money and that Cromwell was the head of all heretics. 'God keep the King, Queen Anne, Princess Elizabeth and Master Cromwell, general visitor of all religious' ends the convent's petition. Two neighbouring magnates, the Earls of Oxford and Essex, were ordered to inquire into these charges. They were pretty well acquainted with the internal affairs of this abbey and were perfectly well aware that the real author of the accusation was Abbot Love's predecessor, John Sampford, who had not acquiesced in being deprived of his post nine years before, and the Earls reported that there was no truth in the charges. Abbot Love was indeed deprived, but he came to no harm, accepted the neighbouring vicarage of Witham, which he held till his death in 1559, and was buried in the choir of his parish church. Abbot Peryn of Tavistock was reported,

---

[1] *L.P.*, XIII (1), 822.   [2] *L.P.*, X, 164.

in 1536, to have said at table in the presence of Sir Thomas Arundell, 'Lo, the King sends to suppress many houses of religion, which is a piteous case: so did the Cardinal in his time, but what became of him? What end he made for so doing, all men know.'[1] It is difficult to imagine a more dangerous outburst, yet the abbot had a pension at the surrender of £100, and died peacefully at Tavistock in 1550.

II

Not all the monasteries suppressed under the Act of 1536 perished as the result of that Act. A considerable number of them bought from the Crown, at a very high price, leave to continue. Besides this, all the houses of the Gilbertine canons, whether they were above the value of £200 annually or not, had been spared through the influence of their late master, Doctor Holgate, now Bishop of Llandaff, and, from 1538 on, President of the Council of the North. There yet remained in existence, therefore, some two hundred monasteries and fifty nunneries, all of which were to disappear during the next four years. The surrender of the great Augustinian abbey of Waltham, Essex, on March 23rd, 1540, marked the end of the process.

A certain number of these monasteries survived, but in an altered form. Just as in the eleventh century secular canons were turned out of many cathedrals to make way for monks, so now monks were turned out to make way for secular canons, or to become secular canons themselves. The earliest change of this kind came about at Norwich, where by the charter of May 2nd, 1538,[2] the prior became dean, five of the monks prebendaries, and sixteen minor

[1] *L.P.*, x, 1221.   [2] *L.P.*, xiii (1), 1115, grant 4.

canons. In addition to their stipends the dean had leave to hold two benefices, and each prebendary one, and to be non-resident upon them. It was hardly to be expected that the monks would be other than willing to fall in with an arrangement so favourable to themselves. They threw off their monastic habits and appeared in the dress of secular clergymen. The late prior and new dean grew a long beard, and wore a full surplice, which caused him to look like an old-fashioned early Victorian clergyman; the prebendaries duly provided themselves with livings in their own gift, leaving them to be served by ill-paid curates. The other cathedrals which had hitherto been served by monks were treated in a slightly different manner. The priors and convents were induced to surrender and, after an interval of a few months, a dean and chapter were established; included in the new staff were a number of the former monks, who became prebendaries or minor canons. The bishops of the new sees, which the King founded in 1541, all had their thrones in former monastic churches.

At the end of 1539 royal commissioners went down to Gloucester to receive the surrender of St. Peter's abbey. This abbey was surrendered by the prior[1] and convent on January 2nd, 1540. The commissioners had drawn up a scheme[2] for its governance, which shows what 'alterations' meant. 'Of 32 religious persons, 14 be despatched, 4 students of Oxford, 14 remaineth there of the King's majesty's reward.' That is to say the abbey had become a collegiate church. The college consisted of a warden, sub-warden and two assistants, a reader in divinity, eight seniors, ten juniors, and four scholars of Oxford, all except the reader of divinity former monks of the abbey. The remain-

---

[1] Abbot Parker had died a few months before.
[2] Printed in *Transactions of the Bristol and Gloucestershire Archaeological Society*, vol. XLIX (1927), p. 81.

ing fourteen monks were 'despatched', but not without ample provision being made for them. The prior had a pension of £20 (say £600) a year, and the others pensions of amounts varying with their length of service, chiefly ranging from £8 (over £200) to £10, while most of them had livings as well, many of which were in the gift of the Dean and Chapter of Gloucester, that is to say of their former colleagues. One of them, for example, the reverend Walter Stanley, was given the rectory of Taynton in 1545, married Miss Joan Cutler, sister of the vicar of Newent, and died as parson in 1550. The collegiate foundation was not destined to last very long, for in the following year the see of Gloucester was founded. The abbot of Tewkesbury became the first bishop. The deanery would probably have been given to Prior Bisley of St. Guthlac's, Hereford, the first warden of the now defunct college. But he died the same year and was buried in the collegiate church. The first dean had therefore to be sought elsewhere and the post was bestowed on Prior Jenyns of the Augustinian house of St. Oswald in the suburbs of Gloucester. Three former monks became prebendaries of Gloucester and several more minor canons. The rest of the collegiate body were given pensions of £6 a year and went off to serve curacies: the four Oxford scholars got no less than £10 by way of pension, a sum which was equivalent to the full amount of their exhibition and £4 more than the abbot and convent had given to one of their monk scholars before the dissolution. They too were soon absorbed into the ranks of the parochial clergy and many of them took to themselves wives.

There is no need to go into similar details in respect of the other new foundations. The arrangements were roughly the same at all the cathedrals formerly served by monks or regular canons, whether of the old or of the newly formed sees. As these numbered eight of the former and six of the latter it is obvious that a considerable number of monks were provided for by these establishments. Had the original scheme of bishoprics been carried out a great many more would have become cathedral dignitaries.

Nevertheless, these represented a very small proportion of the religious who were still in occupation of their houses at the beginning of 1537. There were still some 3000 monks and regular canons, and 800 nuns, while the friars had so far been left untouched. The belief which had been expressed in the Act of 1536 that good religion was kept in the greater monasteries was now beginning to wane in government circles, and three years later it was thought that 'the slothful and ungodly life which hath been used among all those sorts which have borne the name of religious folk' was such that their possessions would be better employed in setting forth God's word, bringing up children in learning, nourishing clerks in the universities, building almshouses for poor folk, road repair, poor relief and the like. All of these objects had, of course, been the concern of pious persons for centuries past. There was, however, a significant omission from the list. There is no mention of prayers.

Early in 1537, the great abbey of Furness in Lancashire gave the signal for surrender. The abbot and monks had narrowly escaped being involved in the fate of their neighbours at Whalley, and they thought it best to give themselves up at discretion. 'I expected,' wrote Richard Southwell, the commissioner for taking the surrender,[1] 'to find the monks ready to disperse on receiving their

---

[1] *L.P.*, XII (2), 205.

capacities. They don't think they are getting enough money. However, I gave them forty shillings (say £60) on the King's reward, which seemed the least I could give,' considering that the traitors of Whalley got no more. The only thing to do with them would be to deny them their capacity, alleging that the King wanted to send them to some religious house unless they were unfit to persevere in religion. This threat seems to have frightened them out of their wits and they gave no more trouble. Towards the end of the year the example of Furness began to be followed by other monasteries. In November the great Cluniac priory of Lewes gave itself up and in the following month the large Cistercian abbey of Warden, Bedford-shire; all through 1538 this process continued and the parliament of 1539 legalized these and all future surrenders and assured their property to the Crown. After this it was merely a question of time before the remaining houses gave themselves up, and as has been mentioned already, by the spring of 1540 not one remained.

III

It is hardly to be supposed that the surrender was as voluntary as the forms in which it was expressed would make it appear. But if the fall of the religious houses was inevitable, was it not wiser to go with the times and get what terms one could? After all, those terms were not to be despised. For the abbots or priors, huge pensions, with all manner of perquisites in the way of country houses, plate, jewels, and the like often thrown in; for the monks, first, large bonuses or 'rewards', arrears of wages paid up and then pensions for life. When the Abbot of Pershore wrote to Cromwell, 'I am willing to resign and leave the

monastery in good case in return for a pension for myself
and my monks', he was not deceived in his expectation.
He did not think it wise to risk losing such a chance as a
pension of £160 (between £4000 and £5000) a year with
garden, orchards and pool, all of which he was destined to
enjoy for another fifteen years. Would his fourteen
colleagues have been wise to refuse to acquiesce, when
they were assured of pensions which brought them in
nearly £200 a year each and which they could supplement by holding other ecclesiastical preferment? and so in
fact *they* were destined to do. (Indeed the bishops looked
upon the pension as so sure a source of income that they
were prepared to ordain former monks on the title of
their pensions.) The rest of Abbot Stonywell's monks
occupied ·Worcestershire or Warwickshire benefices as
long as they lived.

The abbot and convent of the Cistercian abbey of
Bittlesden in Buckinghamshire had come under the Act
of 1536, but had bought an exemption from suppression
from the Crown. Their respite lasted two years, at the end
of which period they discovered that it was time to give
up the 'pretensed' religion they had practised. They
expressed regret that they had accepted the constitutions
of foreign potentates, such as the Bishop of Rome and the
Abbot of Citeaux, instead of that of their diocesan bishop
(the Bishop of Lincoln) and saw that it was expedient for
them to be governed and ordered by their supreme head
under God, the King's most noble grace. Anticipating
the supreme head's wishes they surrendered their lands to
him, asked that in return for their obedient behaviour they
might be granted under letters patent, some annuity or
other manner of living whereby they may be assured to
have their sustenance in time coming: and further to grant

them freely, licence to change their habits into secular
fashion and receive such manner of living as other secular
priests be wont to have. Finally, they all prayed unto
Almighty God long to preserve his grace with increase of
much felicity. This curious document (varied according
as it was to be applied to the different orders of religions)
was produced in all the monasteries and in almost every
case it effected its purpose; the King got the lands and the
abbots and monks got their pensions. Like the monks of
Pershore, most of those of Bittlesden soon fitted themselves
into neighbouring benefices in Buckinghamshire and
Northamptonshire: while of the others one had a living in
Gloucestershire, which had been once in the gift of his
old abbey, and another proved a very expensive pensioner
indeed, by remaining rector of Dauntsey in Wiltshire
from 1547 till his death in 1601.

The more subservient the abbots and monks were, the
more secure would be their future livelihood. Abbot Pope
of Hartland was doubtless aware of this when he wrote to
Cromwell in May, 1538, 'Rumours are common that more
houses are to be put down, there are so many papistical
persons trusting in the abominable monster of Rome that
they daily infest these parts'. The meaning of this was that
his rival, the old Abbot Prust, was trying to get restored to
the abbey with the help of the founders, the Arundell
family.[1] Abbot Pope felt himself by no means secure: he
had lavishly rewarded Sir William Courtenay and his
family for the share they had taken in making him abbot.
'Please,' wrote Sir William's son, Peter, to Cromwell,
'send to the Abbot and convent for the grant of £6 they
promised me under their convent seal in consideration of
the favour shown to them by my father to the present

[1] See above, p. 62.

abbot, by which he came to his promotion.' And so, early in 1539, Abbot Pope surrendered the abbey, assured by the royal commissioners, Doctors Tregonwell and Petre, of a pension of £60 (over £1500) a year. Two months after the surrender he received a dispensation[1] from Archbishop Cranmer to leave the religion in which he had been professed, to assume the habit of a secular clergyman and to take a living. He soon availed himself of this permission and in 1541 accepted the rectories of South Pool and Portlemouth in South Devon. Since these two benefices, valued in the King's books at £23 and £30 respectively, were in the gift of a private patron, their acceptance involved neither loss nor diminution of the abbot's pension. He must, therefore, have been in the enjoyment of an income which would nowadays amount to some £3000 a year. Nothing so far had gone wrong with his career. Unluckily he did not foresee the early death of King Edward VI and he had the imprudence to take a wife. The accession of Mary meant that he had to give up his livings, and presumably his wife; but he was still enjoying his pension in 1556.

How much more satisfying was it to follow Abbot Pope's example, and, so long as they did not toy with treason and run the risk of being disembowelled, there was no reason why all the heads of the religious houses should not enjoy equal advantages. And so practically all of them did. A vast deal of nonsense would have been spared us if only these elementary facts were considered. Abbot Reeve of Bury St. Edmunds, a merry old man, fond of the ladies, fond of his glass, fond of the gardens in his numerous country houses, was granted a pension of 500 marks (some £9000) a year. 'He died six months later without having

[1] Printed in Oliver, *Monasticon dioecesis Exoniensis*, p. 216.

touched a penny of his pension,' moans a super-senti-mentalist writer. So is history made. The abbot's pension, which was paid half-yearly, was not even due: and it was not grief or starvation that killed him, but gout and old age. Abbot Bradley of Fountains was not going to follow his predecessor's example. Abbot Thirsk did not wish to go to London: for his visit meant to him the Tower and Tyburn. Neither did Abbot Bradley want to go thither: but that was only because he was lame. He wrote: 'I will accomplish the King's will as cheerfully and well as if I were present.'

In other words, instead of going to London to make a 'privy surrender' of his house as so many other abbots were doing, he was prepared to carry out the royal wishes at home. His pension of £150, a nice house at Ripon, a prebend in the collegiate church at Ripon, the mastership of St. Mary Magdalene's Hospital, Ripon — his head on his shoulders instead of on London Bridge — was it not worth while to 'accomplish the King's will'?

The last thing that Abbot Segar of Hayles wanted to do was to give up his great abbey in the Cotswolds. But he saw the uselessness of resistance and the advantages of compliance. He was, therefore, converted to the 'new learning'. 'I am glad,' he wrote to Cromwell, 'to live in the light. I should never have come to the truth if I had not the liberty to read the Scriptures in English,' a truly surprising statement considering that he had been a scholar of Oxford and could presumably read them quite easily in Latin. A few months later he coupled a request that his house would stand with a petition that 'the feigned relic called the Blood may be put down'.[1] The first part of his appeal was in vain. Next year he went to London to make a 'privy surrender'. See what an advantage this was to

[1] *L.P.*, XIII (1), 347.

him. A pension of £100, a fine country-house and garden and other perquisites, to which next year was added the rich rectory of Avening in Gloucestershire, a chaplaincy to the King with all the pay and prospects which such a post offered, a prebend of York Minster and leave to reside at Oxford or Cambridge to continue his studies. So well off indeed was he that the King was able to borrow a large sum of money from him. Among the sums repaid for the King's use just before Henry's death was £66 13s. 4d. to Mr. Segar, late Abbot of Hayles.[1] He had no wish to follow the example of his old master, Abbot Paslew of Whalley (of which abbey he had once been a monk), and have portions of his anatomy displayed to the public gaze in Lancashire towns. Nor had most of his monks, as is shown by the career of Doctor Philip Brode, whom he took with him to the North and who succeeded him in his York prebend. Indeed, of the twenty-two monks of Hayles who signed the surrender only one seems to have remained steadfast. In 1557 Queen Mary restored the monks to Westminster: among their number was Richard Eddon, formerly monk of Hayles, who resigned his living in Somerset and his prebend in Winchester Cathedral to don a black (since he could not don a white) habit.

Abbots and priors could almost everywhere rely on powerful friends among the laity to secure for them their pensions or to get these increased. Sir Thomas Wriothesley, soon to become Earl of Southampton, and high in favour at court, was very useful indeed to many of the abbots with whom he was in touch. When the abbey of Titch-field was dissolved at the end of 1537, one of the conditions on which Sir Thomas was granted it was that he should pay the pensions of the abbot, ex-abbot and eleven canons.

[1] *L.P.*, xxi (2), 775.

Since the abbot was to have annually £66, and the canons £45 between them it was obviously to Sir Thomas's interest to use his influence to get them 'promotions' elsewhere. Just the very thing turned up for him a few months later. He received a letter from Abbot Salisbury to say that he was then at Norwich 'to abide the alteration concerning the monks. Yarmouth is better than I deserved. Thanks for it'. In other words Sir Thomas had got for his pensioner the one prebend of Norwich which had not been reserved for former monks of that church. Abbot Stephens of Beaulieu was under very similar obligations to Sir Thomas Wriothesley, who had protected him against his own monks, headed by the ex-abbot of Quarr, and who, after the surrender, lent the abbot one of his country houses and got him a good Hampshire living to supplement his pension.

There was in Northamptonshire a large Cistercian abbey called Pipewell. One of its neighbours, and also its seneschal, was Sir William Parr, brother to the lady who was so venturesome as to become the King's sixth wife and himself destined to become Marquis of Northampton. Now Sir William was not normally a friend of monks. He had early imbibed the 'new learning', which was to get him into sad trouble in Mary's reign. He must, however, have been under financial obligations to the abbey, or the abbey to him, and in July 1538 he wrote to Cromwell to say that the abbot would give £200 to let the house stand. 'He and the convent,' said Sir William, 'are of virtuous disposition and live according to their profession. People hereabouts are relieved by their hospitality and good deeds.' At the same time he was looking to the future. So he went on: 'I think I can get them to forsake their habits and take the habits of secular priests.' If we may judge by another letter to Cromwell which was written a little over a week later, the Lord Privy Seal must have suspected Sir William's motives. 'I am moved,' he protested 'by no pity or desire for gain. It is true that they did give me the lease of a farm, but really I shall get nothing out of it.' By the end of September he had given up hope of saving the house, so he thought he had better look after his own interests. 'May I,' he wrote, 'have the preferment of the house and domain. Please be good lord to the abbot and brethren for their pensions. I never knew nor heard but that they used themselves like honest men.' Cromwell was good lord to them, so was Sir William. The year after the surrender he presented Abbot Gwillam to the neighbouring rectory of Ashley. Curiously enough this living had been in the gift of Pipewell Abbey, and that abbey had given or sold the next presentation to him. That he and the abbot had an understanding in that matter cannot very well be doubted.

IV

'It is true that they did give me the lease.' If any historical student should want to undertake a piece of work which should combine research with amusement, an investigation of leases of this kind may be recommended. The religious of all ranks got a great deal more out of the dissolution of their houses than is generally recognized. It was not only the courtiers who were greedy. The country gentry and lawyers who had the management of the monastic estates were not going to waste their expert knowledge if they could help it; neither were their clients. Just as great nobles, like the Duke of Norfolk, got into touch with the Lord Chancellor and other officers of the Crown with the object of getting what advantage they could out of the suppression, so with a similar object in view did the country gentry get into touch with the monastic bodies whose officers they were.

Towards the end of 1537 a Norfolk gentleman, called Charles Wingfield, came to the great Augustinian priory of Westacre and told the prior and canons that it was the King's pleasure that they should sell to him and his heirs the monastery and its possessions to hold good as the King pleases.[1] But the King did not please. Gentlemen like Mr. Wingfield seem to have forgotten that they were living under a left wing government which was bent on the nationalization of monastic lands. It was to the last degree improbable that the Crown lawyers would overlook a case of this kind, particularly as Mr. Wingfield happened to be the prior's brother. Cromwell got wind of the affair and at his orders a commission, consisting of Sir Roger Townshend and two other Norfolk gentlemen, went to the priory and sequestered its goods. They found a strange state of things there, as their report of January 1538 shows. The prior and convent had been getting rid of the lands at a great rate to the neighbouring country gentlemen. Such was their cunning that the commissioners had to confess themselves baffled: and although they effected a surrender of the priory they could see no way to upset the bargains, the lands having been transferred to the wives of the purchasers in dower, just as persons approaching bankruptcy nowadays transfer property to their spouses. The prior had received for his share in the business £489 (say £12,000 of our money) while the canons had divided £84 (say £1400) between them. The commissioners' report was endorsed 'For the destroying of Wingfield's bargain': but they confessed that they could recover very little of the

---

[1] *L.P.*, XIII (1), 85.

money and the parties concerned were able to stick to most of it. Prior Wingfield had a good friend in Sir Philip Calthorp, a neighbouring gentleman who had had much experience of financial dealings with the priory. Two years after the surrender he presented the former prior with the valuable living of Burnham Thorpe, and so enabled him to add to his pension of £40 a benefice worth nearly £20 in the King's books. He, like Abbot Pope of Hartland, got ensnared by the fair sex. Sixteen years after the surrender a report was sent to the Exchequer concerning the whereabouts and behaviour of all the pensioned religious of the diocese of Norwich. It contained the following item:[1] 'Mr. William Wingfield, of Burnham Thorpe within the county of Norfolk, lately prior of Westacre in the said county, lately married, and now divorced from his woman, and suspended from celebration of divines, has a yearly pension of forty pounds paid unto him at the feasts of the Annunciation of Our Lady and Saint Michael the Archangel by equal portions and possesseth nothing more than his said pension to live upon. He is a quiet man.'

Nothing more to live upon than £1200 a year, and no wife to feed and clothe! What had happened to Mrs. Wingfield in the meantime? And did the Prior go to hear mass in Burnham Church said by his supplanter, the Reverend Peter Stancliff, who had himself just been deprived of *his* living and *his* wife? Did Mrs. Wingfield go off and marry somebody else, as Mrs. Stancliff did?[2] and did the prior take her away from her second husband when Queen Elizabeth came to the throne, as Mr. Stancliff did his? We are not given to know.

The royal commissioners of 1538 had reported of this priory that all (twenty) the canons want 'capacities and

---

[1] *English Historical Review*, vol. XLVIII (1933), p. 212.   [2] Ibid., p. 46.

that none of them are willing to enter again into religion'. None of them indeed seem to have chosen to be transferred to any of the larger monasteries, which, like the neighbouring Walsingham, still survived. They preferred to settle down as country clergymen in the neighbourhood, many of them following their prior's example and marrying.

The Act of 1539, which granted all religious houses which either had surrendered or would in future surrender to the King, contained a proviso that leases and grants must 'within one year next before the dissolution be annulled'. But one year was a very short term. The granting of favourable leases to relatives and friends had, as has been pointed out already, been a regular practice on the part of' heads of houses for centuries. Now it was extended as a form of prudential assurance against the suppression, which was obviously close at hand. How extensive this system was may be illustrated by the example of the large abbey of Augustinian canonesses at Lacock in Wiltshire. It had an excellent report from the lay commissioners of 1536. The inmates were stated to be seventeen in number: 'by report and in appearance of virtuous living: all desire to continue.' Nor had Doctor ap Rice found anything amiss. But when the house gave itself up in January 1539 Doctor Petre, the commissioner who took the surrender, reported that the demesnes had been all leased out and that he was inquiring into the circumstances which accompanied the grants. And well he might. Abbess Temmes was not a member of a great Wiltshire family for nothing: and what careers for her younger brothers could she not hold out? So she made her brother Robert steward of the courts of her manors at a handsome fee. Her brother Christopher was steward of the demesne with a fee of £6 13s. 4d. (say £150). Her brother Thomas had a long lease of the abbey property in the Isle of

Wight. Her brother-in-law, Robert Bath, had a ninety-nine-years lease of one of the manors. Her first cousin, Sir Edward Baynton, a very influential person, was chief steward of this abbey, as well as of that of Malmesbury. It is obvious that the above-mentioned clause in the 1539 Act affected none of these leases: and the Temmes family continued after the suppression in occupation or possession of a large proportion of the abbey lands. The abbess herself lived for many years on a handsome pension of £40 (say £1200) a year. Brother Christopher was steward for the Crown of all the former possessions of the monastery. Brother Thomas still had his lease in the Isle of Wight in 1561, while the former abbess's brother-in-law had bought Bishopstrow Manor from the Crown and made it his residence.[1] This is a very good example of how a family could be permanently enriched by the association of its members with the management of monastic estates. Investigation of the administrative staff of any monastery would tell the same tale.

When Doctors Tregonwell and Petre were suppressing monasteries in the West in February 1539, they found themselves obliged to call in a great many leases which had lately been granted by the abbots and convents. But commissioners were here to-day and gone to-morrow, just as bishops had been in respect of their visitations.

The large Augustinian priory of Bodmin in Cornwall will give us a very good instance of how the religious and their rich friends could get the better of the Crown.[2] This house had long been ruled by a prior of a great local family, Doctor Thomas Vivian, Bishop of Megara *in partibus*, a very

[1] For further details see W. L. Bowles and J. G. Nichols *Annals of Lacock* (1835).
[2] The early part of this account is from an Exchequer Deposition of 1577 (No. 134, 18 Eliz.) a transcript of which has been kindly lent me by Mr. A. L. Rowse. The rest is from earlier depositions printed in Sir John Maclean's *Deanery of Trigg Minor*, I, 133 ff.

haughty and arbitrary person, who, by his enclosures and neglect of the parishioners' interests, had made himself very unpopular both in the town and priory. His relations with his canons were so bad that when he was on his deathbed he sent for his servant, Nicholas Prideaux, and said to him, 'There is not a single one of the canons who is fit to succeed me. I know of a very good man at Merton Priory, near London. His name is Thomas Munday. Please see to it that he is elected'. He was not. A neighbouring potentate, Sir John Arundel, had another candidate in view, and him he got the canons to elect. Prideaux hurried off to London and 'so laboured and dealt in the same cause with the Lord [*sic*] Cromwell and others' that he got the new prior 'removed, put out and displaced' (on a pension of £40) and so made the way clear for Thomas Munday. A few days later Prideaux rode to London a second time and announced the news of his election to the new prior. Thomas Munday belonged to a family whose members were most of them 'something in the City'. He inherited all their business instincts and was determined to make what he could for himself and his relations out of the suppression of his priory which was obviously approaching. In the summer of 1537 he assembled the canons in the chapter house and said: 'I hear that the King's Majesty will take his pleasure upon our house and so I think it good to give unto such as be good to the house' (in other words, Nicholas Prideaux and his friends) 'some leases or other preferments to the intent they should be better to us hereafter.'

See how easy it all was. The prior and convent granted one manor on a ninety-nine-years lease to one John Munday. Now John Munday happened to be the prior's brother, a merchant prince from London. Another lease went to one Lawrence Kendall: now he happened to be betrothed to

Miss Katharine Munday, the prior's niece, and the lease came in very well for a marriage portion. Young Mr. William Prideaux had married Miss Joan Munday, another of the prior's nieces; he and his father Nicholas got the Manor of Padstow. All these leases had, of course, to be sealed with the consent of the convent, and how were the canons to be induced to agree to the enrichment of the prior's family? However, the prior found a very simple way out of the difficulty. 'I will promise each of you £20[1] if the leases hold good,' said he, 'five pounds in hand without conditions, and the advowsons of benefices in the gift of the priory to go to each of you severally, to the intent that you may be the rather agreeable unto the sealing and granting of the said leases.' Of course they were agreeable. The advowson of Padstow was eventually transferred to the sub-prior, Richard Oliver, who became vicar of that parish in 1547 and held it till his death in 1564. The vicarage of Bodmin went in 1550 to another canon, John Dagle, who was buried as vicar in 1564. He had been presented to it by the son of Sir John Chamond, a neighbouring knight to whom the priory had given one of their best manors, to be 'better' to one of the canons 'hereafter'.

Finally, Nicholas Prideaux, the gentleman who had engineered the prior's election, got leases covering a period of one hundred and eight years between them of the tithes in four parishes of which the priory was patron. It is to be noted that all these arrangements infringed the Act of 1539, since the leases were granted less than a year before the surrender of the priory. It was not, however, for another seven years that any inquiry was made by the Crown, and although one of the under stewards of the manors told the commissioners that he had been dismissed from his post by

---

[1] About £600 to-day.

the prior and convent because he would not be a party to writings craftily made with ante-dates, the leases seem to have been allowed by the Chancellor and Council of the Court of Augmentations. The Munday family and the canons had, to use a modern phrase, 'got away with it'.

The practice of making ante-dated leases seems to have been followed in most of the religious houses just before the suppression.[1] Early in the reign of Queen Elizabeth a gentleman called John Whitney was called to give evidence about some disputed property formerly belonging to the Cistercian abbey of Dieulacres in Staffordshire. He presumably knew what he was talking about, since he was the brother of the last abbot and had been chamberlain of the abbey: in fact, all his family had held some office of profit there. He told the commissioners that four or five days after the surrender of the abbey he saw several blanks having the convent seal. 'My brother said to his secretary, "write out leases with ante-dates on these forms".' Here again the abbot and monks seem to have succeeded in their efforts.[2]

In the year 1582 a very old clergyman, named John Roper, was summoned by a royal commission to give evidence at his rectory of West Stafford in Dorset about the validity of some disputed leases at Axminster in Devonshire. The property was by then in the possession of Lord William Howard, son of the Duke of Norfolk, who had lost his head ten years before, but it had once belonged to the Cistercian Abbey of Newenham. The reverend Mr. Roper told a strange tale. 'After the dissolution of that abbey, of which I was once a monk,' said he, 'my former superior, Abbot Gill, used often to come and bother me to

---

[1] At Tywardreth they were smoked before a fire to give them a venerable aspect – see above p. 55 for reference.
[2] Sleigh, *History of Leek*, p. 64 ff.

agree to the making and sealing of some other leases and grants under the convent seal of lands which were parcel of the said monastery. I answered that I would do nothing of the kind.' Two years later there was another meeting of the commission. Mr. Roper appeared again and said that he knew that all the leases and grants that were lawfully made by the abbot and convent were written in a register book which was now, he thought, at the Exchequer, sealed with the new silver seal of the abbey. There was, however, an old and disused latten seal still in existence. The abbot and one of his servants named Morris thought they could make some use of it to their advantage and to that of the monks generally. So they patched it up and glued it together, after which they proceeded to get to work. The abbot was quite able to look after himself. To his large pension of £44 (£1200) he added the rich Devonshire livings of Farway and Offwell, which he held (with his pension) till his death in 1573. The patron of Offwell was a gentleman called John Drake of Musbury, who had been under great financial obligations to Abbot Gill and who had provided William Parsons, one of his monks, with the family living. Another monk, by name John Riche, also benefited by the old seal. It was not exactly wise to ante-date a lease to him, since as a monk he could not legally hold it, so it was made out to his sister, the widow Ferris. And so matters went on for years, but at last there was a quarrel between Mr. Morris and another old man, and the other old man went about saying, 'I know too much about Mr. Morris's doings. *Why, he had a false convent seal*'. So it all came out.[1]

This was perhaps a unique case. But behaviour such as that of Prior Munday of Bodmin and his convent was

[1] James Davidson, *History of Newenham Abbey* (1843), p. 105.

probably followed by every monastery in the country. It was easy enough to procure rich and powerful friends by similar methods. But it is doubtful if all monasteries were so far-sighted as the abbot and convent of Thorney in Cambridgeshire, who on May 20th, 1539 (a little over six months before their surrender) granted[1] their cell of Deeping to Elizabeth Holland, daughter of Thomas Holland of Swineshead, Lincolnshire, Esquire, on a forty-years lease. Now Miss Elizabeth Holland was the first and principal mistress of the Duke of Norfolk. Since the Duke had a grant of the lands in question, the very next year, it is to be presumed that his lady friend's interests were not affected in any way by the suppression of Thorney Abbey. It is to be noted that most bargains of this kind seem to have been allowed by the Court of Augmentations to stand: for example, that which the dowager marchioness of Dorset made with the monks of Tilty in Essex, where she was in residence. She bought the place and kept it. From all parts of the country reports came in that the monasteries were making leases and alienating goods in anticipation of suppression. The prior and convent of the Augustinian house of Launde in Leicestershire had, for example, sold off all their sheep, cattle and household stuff. The prior and convent of Bath in the course of a couple of years sold the right of presentation to all the advowsons in their gift. That some of these sales were made to ensure provision for the monks is shown by the fact that Sir Walter Dennis — one of the grantees — gave the living of St. Mary Stalls, Bath, to one monk of that abbey, while Sir Henry Champneys gave that of St. Mary, Northgate, to another. It is obvious that such appointments were not fortuitous, but were the result of a bargain.[2]

[1] Dugdale, *Monasticon*, IV, 171. [2] Full details are given in MS. Harleian, no. 3970.

This chapter may fitly be ended with a sketch of the career of a certain Welsh abbot: it should dispose effectually of the legend of persecuted and starving monks. The Cistercian abbey of Basingwerk had as its last abbot one Nicholas Pennant. He was the son of his predecessor and had himself begotten a son whom he wished to set up in life. The abbey had in its gift the rich living of Holywell, all the richer because the offerings from the renowned faith-healing well of St. Winifred went with it. What more could young Master Pennant want. Unluckily for him the Bishop of St. Asaph did not see things in quite the same light. He nominated (though by what right does not seem clear) a clergyman called Pigott and duly instituted him. One day Mr. Pigott was returning home after collecting his tithes when he saw an armed rabble coming towards him. Perhaps it occurred to him that it contained farmers who boggled at paying tithe. But when he saw among the crowd the prior of Basingwerk and another monk armed with great quarter staves, two members of the Pennant family and their retainers to the number of twenty-one, and more, having bills, bows, stubbs, swords and bucklers, he quite understood that the abbot had decided to get rid of him by force. He took refuge in a neighbouring house, where he had to withstand a siege until he was rescued by his flock. He then appealed to the Star Chamber, that sure refuge for the poor and oppressed. Incidents of this kind were of course frequent enough. The historical value of this one is that it shows how an abbot, supported by his relations, rooted firmly in monastic lands, could make his power felt and defy the bishop and even the Crown. The two abbots Pennant, father and son, had plundered the property of the monastery for the benefit of their family to such an extent that it became and still is one of the most important and wealthy in North Wales. The suppression of the monasteries made no difference whatever to the Pennant family in this case,[1] or to similarly situated families in the case of other monasteries. The records, not only of the Exchequer but of all the sixteenth-century courts, Star Chamber, Court of Requests, Court of Augmentations and the like teem with cases of this kind. They well deserve extensive research.

[1] See the article by Arthur Jones in *Historical Essays in honour of James Tait*, p. 169 ff.

CHAPTER VIII

NUNS

I

WHEN the former Cistercian monk, John Hooper, soon to become Bishop of Gloucester, wrote that there were after the suppression ten thousand former nuns, not one of whom was allowed to marry, he was indulging in the customary exaggeration of religious enthusiasts. He had multiplied by more than five. There were in fact, well under two thousand. These numbers were far below those of the earlier centuries; in many houses they had gone down by more than half. To take examples from Oxfordshire alone, the Benedictine priory of Studley numbered fifty in the thirteenth century and only ten just before the suppression, while the Augustinian canonesses of Goring were seven in 1530, several of whom were unprofessed, in place of the thirty-six of 1300. In Yorkshire the Benedictine nuns of Wilberfosse had diminished from twenty in 1310 to eleven at the suppression, while at Watton there were half the number of Gilbertine nuns to what there had been two centuries earlier. Even the great and rich abbey of Shaftesbury had just over fifty nuns in 1538 instead of the hundred who were there in 1300.

The duties of the nuns in respect of prayers, hospitality and alms were the same as those of the monks. That the nunneries were just as, if not more, useful as inns for ladies on their travels goes without saying. Like the monks, too, they sometimes set up alehouses in the precincts to cater for

NUNS

travellers.[1] The alms were given in the same haphazard way as in the monasteries, and gave a considerable amount of relief, especially on anniversaries and the like. Such was the case with the Augustinian canonesses of Burnham, Buckinghamshire, where every day one poor person received half a bottle of beer and a loaf for the sake of the founder's soul. There do not seem to be the same complaints about the diversion of alms as was the case with the monks. The nuns were sometimes accused of owning pet dogs and even of taking them into church,[2] where their yappings and snarlings disturbed divine worship, but they did not keep, like so many of the monks, packs of hounds to devour the broken meats which were the perquisite of the poor.

Probably the sphere in which the nunneries were most useful was that of education. It was not only great houses like Shaftesbury and Barking which had a great reputation in this respect. Nothing could be more handsome than the tribute paid by Bishop Lee of Lichfield — no friend of monks — in his capacity of President of the Council of Wales to the merits of the small house of Aconbury in Herefordshire: 'where gentlemen of Abergavenny . . . Brecknock and adjoining parts of Wales have had commonly their women and children brought up in virtue and learning';[3] or than the report of the Warwickshire commissioners of 1536 about the abbey of Polesworth under its 'sad, discreet and religious' Abbess Fitzherbert, where the gentlemen's children and sojournes (paying guests) 'do live to the number sometime of 30 and sometime 40 and more, that they be right virtuously brought up.'[4] But we must be careful to avoid over-statement about the services which the

[1] As at Esholt, Yorkshire. *V.C.H. Yorkshire*, III, p. 162.
[2] As at Rosedale, Yorkshire, in 1315. *V.C.H. Yorks*, III, p. 175.
[3] *L.P.*, XI, 1370.   [4] Wright, *Suppression*, p. 139.

nunneries performed in this matter. They had no idea of educating poor girls. Just as the monasteries took in hand sons of the nobility and gentry, so did the nunneries in respect of the daughters. In an age when there were so few opportunities for female education, they performed undoubtedly a most useful task. The young ladies were certainly in a far more respectable atmosphere than that which they would have found in the royal or noble households to which they would otherwise have been consigned. The abbesses seem to have taken great personal interest in them. 'I allowed your daughter, Bridget,' wrote Abbess Shelley of Nunnaminster in Winchester to Lady Lisle, 'to go on a visit to Sir Andrew Windsor to sport her for a week. She hasn't come back. Please tell me the reason.'[1] Now Miss Bridget Plantagenet was a young lady of the first consequence. She was the granddaughter of a king; her mother was a great landed proprietress in Devonshire. Among her twenty-six companions was Miss Mary Pole, daughter of Sir Geoffrey Pole and granddaughter of the formidable Margaret, Countess of Salisbury, while the rest of the young ladies were of equally high birth.

No doubt, but for the suppression, some at least of them would have developed a vocation. The list of nuns of Shaftesbury in 1539 contains the names of nearly all the great county families of Dorset and Wiltshire. Had not Cardinal Wolsey himself chosen this abbey to place his daughter in as a nun?[2] Barking — then a fashionable suburb of London — took in great ladies from the eastern counties, while St. Helen's, Bishopsgate, and Dartford seem to have catered more for the *nouveaux riches*, the daughters of

[1] *L.P.*, XI, 478.
[2] She passed under the name of Dorothy Clansey (*L.P.*, IX, 228) and had a pension of £4 at the suppression of the abbey. She was living in 1556, since her name is on Cardinal Pole's pension list, but what happened to her seems unknown.

the merchant princes of London. It is obvious that these young women were not being educated for nothing. 'Four children, two boys and two girls, are in the convent,' complained the Abbess of Burnham to the Bishop of Lincoln, at his visitation of 1530, 'and they pay nothing for their commons.' 'John Jervis, gentleman, has a daughter being brought up in the priory and pays nothing for her,' said the nuns of Thetford to the Bishop of Norwich.[1] Altogether the nunneries must have made quite a respectable income out of their young ladies, not to say also out of the small girls and boys up to the age of eight who were occasionally allowed by the bishop to be taken in.

What kind of education these young ladies got must be a matter of doubt. The nuns would certainly know no Latin, as the care with which bishops furnished them with English translations of injunctions and like documents shows. Bishop Stapleton of Exeter, in 1320, was so painfully aware of the deficiencies of the nuns of Polslo in this respect that he recommended them, should they have to use that language, to do so without regard to grammar.[2] They were hardly in a position to teach it! Their French was probably of the Stratford-at-Bow kind, over which Chaucer had made merry. At Lacock, a large Augustinian house in Wiltshire, Doctor ap Rice reported that the nuns knew French well and could even read their rule, though it was written in old French like that of common law. It may be doubted, however, if the nuns themselves attempted any form of instruction. They were living before and not after St. Vincent de Paul. It is far more likely that the young ladies were taught by governesses, just as the young gentlemen in abbeys were instructed by schoolmasters. Indeed.

[1] *Norwich Visitations*, p. 304.
[2] Oliver, *Monasticon dioecesis Exoniensis*, p. 163.

the Dominican nuns of Dartford were authorized by the Minister General in 1481[1] to engage a preceptor for this purpose.

With the bishop's leave the nunneries were also able to add to their income by taking in paying guests.[2] But the bishops were usually chary in giving permission, for visitors of this kind might quite well become a great nuisance, and sometimes the bishop ordered them to go after a month's stay. And how could the service in Langley Priory Church be performed reverently when Lady Audeley insisted on coming to church accompanied by no fewer than twelve dogs, as a visitation of Bishop Alnwick of Lincoln shows? That the nunneries were havens of refuge to widows in poor circumstances is shown by a moving letter of the dowager Lady Dudley to Cromwell in which she dilates on the kindness of the good prioress of Nuneaton who 'gave me. and my daughter meat and drink free of cost and afterwards harboured the other children. I should indeed be in poor case but for the help we got there,' she added.[3]

What has been said about lay interference in the monasteries applies equally to the nunneries. The founders were partly an advantage, partly a nuisance. Not many of them went so far as Lady Clinton, at Maxstoke, who in the fourteenth century had got herself elected prioress. But they were constantly planting their relations or dependents on them. It was one way of getting rid of illegitimate daughters. The Ward family seem to have provided a prioress to Esholt, a Yorkshire house of their foundation, in this way.[4] Queens sent them discarded ladies-in-waiting. It cost Elizabeth of York, Queen of King Henry VII,

---

[1] *V.C.H. Kent*, II, p. 187.
[2] *Perhendinatrices* was the formidable word which described them.
[3] *L.P.*, XIII (2), Appendix 6.
[4] *V.C.H. Yorkshire*, III, p. 161.

£6 13s. od. to make her attendant, little Anne Loveday, a nun at Elstow.[1]

The estates of the nunneries were managed by the same class of persons as were those of the monasteries and here again one notices the opportunities for advancement which relations of the abbess or nuns enjoyed. How Abbess Temmes of Lacock provided for practically her whole family has been related already.

The country gentry or other neighbours interfered in the elections and espoused the cause of different candidates. Queens thrust their dependents on nunneries as Kings did on monasteries and these corrodians or pensioners must have been a great nuisance. So must the buyers of annuities have been. How this system worked in nunneries may be illustrated by the case of a widow who bought an annuity from the Yorkshire nunnery of Arden in 1524. In return for a payment of £12 she had for life her own chamber, the same meat and drink as the convent (and much better too than she could have got at home or at an inn), either at the nuns' common table or at her own; and also meat and drink for her chaplain at the table of the prioress and a chamber next the frater.[2] The system was, as has been pointed out, open to many abuses, especially when the annuities went to the relations of the head of the house, and the bishops had often to interfere to stop this practice. 'You are to stop giving corrodies, especially to your brother George Thomson and his children,' wrote the Bishop of Lincoln to the Prioress of Nun Cotham in 1530. 'Don't you grant any leases above five years,' went on the bishop. This lady's relations were evidently in clover.[3]

The bishop had powers of visitation of the same kind as

---

[1] *V.C.H. Bedfordshire*, I, p. 354.   [2] *V.C.H. Yorkshire*, III, p. 115.
[3] The bishop's injunctions to this and other houses are printed in *Archaeologia*, XLVII, p. 55 ff.

he had in the monasteries. Indeed more, since he was able
to visit Cluniac and Cistercian nunneries, so that only the
Premonstratensian and Gilbertine canonesses, the Minoresses
and the Dominican nuns of Dartford were exempt from his
attentions. The visitation was carried out in exactly the
same way as was the case with the monasteries. Perhaps the
bishops were more drastic in their treatment of nunneries,
judging by the number of cases where they took the administration out of the hands of the nuns and appointed lay
administrators. The fact is that the nuns gave the bishops a
great deal of trouble. 'Had I,' wrote the Bishop of Winchester to Cardinal Wolsey, '*your* authority I would inure
[immure] and enclose them according to the ordinance of
the law, otherwise there will be no surety for the observance
of good religion.'[1] 'I despair,' wrote Doctor Bennet to
Wolsey, 'of ever getting the nuns (of Wilton) enclosed', and
the new abbess, who had been put in to effect reforms,
was no more sanguine. 'I will try to make the sisters be
enclosed, but they show many considerations against it,'[2]
wrote she to the cardinal.

How hard it was to effect reforms may be seen by the
difficulties in which the Bishop of Lincoln was involved in
the abbey of Elstow, near Bedford, the residence of a very
fashionable band of nuns, who had got wholly out of hand.
His chancellor, Doctor Rayne, had visited the abbey on
August 25th, 1530, and found himself bound to suspend the
abbess, to deprive the prioress of office, and to appoint a
new and stricter one. In the following summer the vicar-
general appeared again. There had been a dreadful
disturbance in the interval. The sub-prioress and eight
nuns had refused to obey either the prioress or the abbess
herself, and had left the chapter house. 'And I would do it

[1] *L.P.*, IV, 3806.   [2] *L.P.*, IV, 4950.

again, for all my Lord says,' observed Dame Barbara Grey, 'and though my Lord did command my Lady Snow to be prioress I cannot find it in my heart to obey her as prioress and I would rather go out of the house than obey her. She makes every fault a deadly sin,' and so testified several other nuns. The Chancellor, finding that nothing he could do would move them, was obliged to appeal to Bishop Longland himself, who made one of his rare visitations in person, rated the nuns soundly and ordered them to accept his nominee as prioress on pain of excommunication. Seven years later the 'households' in which they entertained their friends in the abbey had to be given up and they had to give their little parties in Bedford.[1] Internal quarrels of this kind occupied much of the bishop's time; and one may well sympathize with the remark of the Bishop of Lincoln's secretary in 1301 at a visitation of Goring about the proneness of nuns to quarrel.[2]

The abbess or prioress was a personage of the highest possible consequence, addressed as 'My Lady', riding about with as numerous a retinue as that of a great noble, often connected with the greatest families of the land. Even the head of a very small house put on the most arrogant airs. When the Abbot of Burton sent his bailiff to collect some rents of which the Prioress of Derby was twenty years in arrear she assailed him furiously and said that any churl who should come against her should be nailed with arrows; 'For I am a gentlewoman come of the greatest of Lancashire and Cheshire (she was a Stanley) and that the Abbot shall know right well.'[3] The Prioress of Easebourne in Sussex, when she rode about the country, had a train of attendants and wore furs whose value would nowadays come to £100

[1] *Lincoln Visitation*, Longland MSS., folio 47. The Bishop's injunctions to the nuns are printed in Wigram, *Chronicles of Elstow*, p. 130 ff.
[2] *V.C.H. Oxfordshire*, II, 103 and 104.   [3] *V.C.H., Derby* II, p. 44.

or more. Some of the smaller nunneries were almost a
family perquisite, so eager were their heads to benefit their
own relations, and so the frequent occurrence of nuns with
the same surname as that of the abbess shows. The abbess's
relations were often a great cause of trouble. Often they
lived with her, as at Studley, Oxfordshire, where her
brother and sister-in-law were in permanent residence. The
great offices of a nunnery were usually distributed among
her relations, as at Lacock, or at Dartford, where Prioress
Vane had a habit of granting leases on most advantageous
terms to members of her family. Sometimes the abbess was
ruled by some man, under whose influence she had fallen.
At the Cistercian nunnery of Stixwould in Lincolnshire
there was in 1525 considerable trouble on these grounds.
The prioress was entirely ruled by the seneschal of the
house, who was feathering his own nest and sleeping on the
precincts. At the bishop's visitation several of the nuns
complained about this and the prioress's most severe critic
was Dame Alice Cranmer, who had evidently already
imbibed her more famous brother's reforming propensities.[1]

The head of a house had many eyes on her and the
sharpest were usually those of former abbesses or prioresses
who had board and lodging on the precincts, on part payment of their pension. These old ladies were often a great
nuisance and spent much of their time intriguing against
their successors. For who would go so far as to admit that
one's successor is a success? On the other hand these aged
women often had the greatest difficulty in getting their
pension or its equivalent honoured. 'Please remove our
supposed prioress;' wrote the nuns of Stratford-at-Bow to
Cromwell in 1533, 'since our petition to the King we have
been treated worse than ever for meat and drink. The old

---

[1] *English Historical Review*, LI (1936), p. 287.

lady who was prioress is like to die for want of sustenance. She can get no meat or drink or money.'[1]

The rank and file of the nuns had the same grievances against the head of their house as had the monks: non-payment of stipends or allowances for clothing, reading the letters they addressed to their friends, reception of colleagues uncongenial to them. Why should we have a dumb and deformed nun in our house? cried those of Thetford. 'The Prioress,' complained the nuns of Greenfield, Lincolnshire, in 1525, 'wants to make one Agnes Kittel a nun, though she is a malicious gossip, foments quarrels everywhere and is utterly unfit to be a religious.'

Since many of the nuns were of equally high birth with the abbess or prioress they could, through their relations, exercise a considerable influence on the fortunes of the house. Some remained unprofessed for years notwithstanding all that the bishops could do; others on the other hand were professed at ages which seem amazingly young, even allowing for the greater speed with which people grew up in those days. The records of visitations undertaken by the bishops immediately before the general suppression seem to indicate that what Bishop Foxe had complained of was justified, and that a spirit of independence, not to say insubordination, was widely spread. There was, for example, an almost universal tendency to set up separate 'house-holds', in other words for the nuns to have their own apartments — one might almost say flats — and at the large Benedictine nunnery of Redlingfield in Suffolk the refectory was reported in 1514 as disused for years.[2] At Godstow the nuns were reported in 1432 to have feasts in their rooms, and a visitation of a few years later[3] seems to show that invita-

---

[1] *L.P.*, VI, 1692.   [2] *Norwich Visitations*, p. 139.
[3] *V.C.H. Oxfordshire*, II. 73.

tions to these functions were extended to undergraduates of the neighbouring university of Oxford. The dormitory, too, seems to have been equally deserted for separate rooms, judging by the inventory of the Benedictine house of Minster in Sheppey (of which Archbishop Cranmer's sister was the last prioress). Here the rooms are described as those of the several nuns, and the feather beds and the 'great bath' would scarcely have received the approbation of St. Scholastica.[1] Bishop Foxe's remarks about the difficulty of enclosing the nuns is shown by many visitation reports. *Wanderlust* often seized them, which they tried to satisfy on plea of going on pilgrimage, while it was very difficult to stop them wandering about the country or into the neighbouring towns.

II

It is impossible to pass any judgment on the general state of the nunneries in the period immediately before the dissolution. Sentimentalists would have us believe that all the houses were like the Northamptonshire priory of Catesby, the report on which by the commissioners of 1536 has been so often quoted: 'in very perfect order, the prioress, a sure, wise, discreet and very religious woman, with nine nuns under her obedience as religious and devout and with as good obedience as we have in time past seen or be like shall see.'[2] Scavengers would have us suppose that they were all like Littlemore, near Oxford, where at the 1519 visitation the prioress was having her illegitimate child brought up in the convent, at the convent's expense, while the nuns had broken out of the house and gone to

[1] *L.P.*, x, 562. [2] Wright, *Suppression*, p. 129.

their friends;[1] or like Easebourne, which has been described as 'a kind of reformatory for young women of good family who had strayed from virtue'.[2] The truth was between the two. Probably the larger houses were more satisfactory than the smaller, and even the royal visitors had little to say — indeed much to commend in them. Moreover they only occasionally reported cases of nuns who wished for release. There must, however, have been many who had no vocation.

When the old Countess of Salisbury, Cardinal Pole's mother, lost her son Arthur, she did not wish his widow to remarry, and so deprive the family of her great fortune. Lady Salisbury and her son, Lord Montague, bethought themselves of a good way out of the difficulty. They forced the widow to 'take the mantle and ring', in other words to become a novice. The lady had no wish to proceed farther in the religious life, so she betook herself to the new Bishop of St. Asaph, who was residing in his priory of Bisham, where the Poles had one of their country houses. She said to Bishop Barlow, 'Can I leave the veil at pleasure?' 'Yes,' said he, 'for all religious persons have a time of probation. You are only a novice and could leave your nun's weeds at your pleasure. I bind you no further.'

The lady took the bishop's advice, and married Sir William Barentyne. A few years later (1543), in fear of being prosecuted under the Act of the Six Articles, she and her husband were obliged to procure an Act of Parliament to declare their children legitimate.[3] This cannot have been an isolated instance and Doctor Leigh may well have

---

[1] *V.C.H. Oxfordshire*, II, 75.   [2] *V.C.H. Sussex*, II, 85.
[3] *L.P.*, XVIII, 67. The date at which the Poles were carrying on these intrigues is not mentioned, but it must be the beginning of 1536. The 'Bishop of St. Asaph' mentioned in the document can only be Bishop Barlow, who was elected Bishop of that see in January 1536, and transferred to St. David's the following April. He had been Prior of Bisham for about a year.

spoken the truth when he asserted that many of the nuns of Denny in Cambridgeshire, besought him on their knees for release.[1] They had been reading heretical books and had doubtless become unsettled.[2] Nevertheless, the dismissal by the visitors of all the religious women under the age of twenty-four must have involved great hardship. Five of the nuns of the Aldgate house of Minoresses wrote to Cromwell to say that as they were under twenty-four they had been dismissed and were now in secular clothing. 'May we be re-vested and come again into our religion, or have licence to be in the cloister till we are twenty-four and then to be professed again if God shall call us?'[3] The reports of the royal commissioners who were carrying out the suppression of the smaller houses in 1536 show that, as in the case of the monasteries, there was a great difference of opinion on the question of remaining in religion, or of taking dispensations. In some houses there was unanimity in favour of persevering; in others, especially in Norfolk, of giving up. The great majority were, however, in favour of continuance, and most of the nuns would have subscribed to the petition which the Prioress of Legbourne in Lincolnshire and her nuns sent to Cromwell, in his capacity of patron of the priory, early in 1537, in which they urge that their house might be spared.[4] They did not succeed in moving him, and they were dispersed and dispensed. Eighteen years later Prioress Missenden was living in the neighbouring village of Corby. She had by this time made the best of a bad business and had become Mrs. Otley. Her pension of £7 (£200 nowadays) must have made a useful addition to the family income.[5]

---

[1] *L.P.*, IX, 694 and 708.   [2] *L.P.*, IV, 4282.
[3] *L.P.*, IX, 1075. The name of the house is not given: but it can be identified by its surrender list.
[4] Wright, *Suppression*, p. 116.   [5] *P.R.O. Exchequer*, 101, 76/26.

III

The nuns of the convents which were suppressed under the 1536 Act were given the same choice as the monks. They could either take dispensations or be transferred to one of the larger houses. Those who took the former course got a sum of money down ('rewards') to enable them to buy secular clothing and to tide them over until they had settled down. When the small Benedictine priory of Cannington in Somerset was suppressed the prioress got a pension, and of the five professed nuns, three were sent to Shaftesbury in Dorset and one to Polslo in Devonshire, and their names duly appear in the pension lists of those houses, which had themselves to surrender three years later. Shaftesbury was indeed the last of all the nunneries to be dissolved.

What happened to the nuns after the suppression? It is obvious that their lot was far harsher than that of the monks. 'You have not,' wrote one of Cromwell's servants to his aunt, a former nun of Sion, 'been cumbered with the world, and know not the travail, pain and study you ought and must have in the governance of a house.'[1] Had she become a lady housekeeper? And Fuller, in his *Church History*, wisely remarks that fathers and elder brothers were the chief sufferers by the suppression of the nunneries. He means, of course, that the former nuns had to be dowered at the expense of the family, instead of at that of the church. Many did, in fact, return to their homes. Sir William Paston, the head of a great Norfolk house, had a daughter named Margerie, whom he had placed in the fashionable nunnery of Barking, near London. Fifteen years after its suppression we find her 'dwelling with her father'.[2] But she was able to

---

[1] *L.P.*, xv, 757.   [2] *English Historical Review*, vol. XLVIII (1933), p. 214.

contribute to the household expenses since she had a pension of eight marks (say £150). Another nun of Barking, Gabrielle Shelton, was living in Carrow Priory near Norwich,[1] which her father, Sir John Shelton, had bought from the Crown. She had a slightly larger pension than that enjoyed by Miss Paston. Some nuns were not so lucky as to have homes to which they could return. In this same year, 1554, there were two of the former Dominican nuns of Dartford living together at Walsingham,[2] to which no pilgrims came any longer. The image of Our Lady of Walsingham, which had brought so many visitors in the past, had gone, so why should they have settled there? However, next year Queen Mary refounded their house at King's Langley, and the names of both these ladies are found on the list of the new house.[3]

All the nuns who were in the houses which surrendered between 1537 and 1539 got pensions. These pensions were awarded in any case, whatever the former reputation of the pensioner may have been. Prioress Wells of Littlemore, notwithstanding the illegitimate daughter to whose existence she had confessed to the bishop in 1519, was awarded by Cardinal Wolsey a pension of £6 13s. 4d. (nearly £200) a year.[4] When Doctors Leigh and Layton visited the Cistercian nunnery of Basedale they reported that one of the nuns named Joan Fletcher had had a child. And so she had. She had been giving trouble to the Archbishop of York for years. She had once run away, so he sent her to the neighbouring priory of Rosedale to do penance. So bad was her example that she had to be sent back again to Basedale. The archbishop begged the prioress to receive her affectionately, but not to allow her to go outside the precincts without his

[1] *English Historical Review*, vol. XLVIII (1933), p. 228.   [2] Ibid., p. 211.
[3] *Downside Review*, 1908, p. 138.   [4] *L.P.*, IV, 1138.

219

leave. She was still there at the suppression and received a handsome pension, which she was still enjoying twenty years later.[1]

The pensions of abbesses and prioresses were large, in the case of rich houses very large indeed. Abbess Bodenham of Wilton's £100 pension would amount nowadays to nearly £3000; in addition she had a country house at Fovant. Abbess Barley of Barking had an even larger pension, while Abbess Zouche of Shaftesbury with her £133 pension enjoyed the equivalent of some £4000 a year. These great ladies lived on in their country houses in great state, with chaplains and large staffs of servants. Abbess Bulkeley of Godstow was sister to the great North Wales magnate, Sir Richard Bulkeley of Beaumaris. She leased the parsonage of Cheadle church, Cheshire, from her brother John (the absentee rector), lived, apparently, in the rectory, spent large sums on the repair of the church, and was buried in it early in the reign of Elizabeth. Her will suggests that she, along with the rest of her family, had accepted the 'new learning', or at any rate acquiesced in it.[2] Prioress Lawson of St. Bartholomew's, Newcastle, was buried in the parish church of that town in 1566. Her will shows, not only that she could afford to keep a chaplain, but that she had a large house at Gateshead, besides flocks of sheep and herds of cattle.[3] She must, indeed, have been an early example of a lady farmer. Abbess Russell of Tarrant, Dorset, who was buried in Bere Regis Church in 1568, left a great deal of money, plate and jewels, some to her cousin, the second Earl of Bedford; while to various ladies of her acquaintance she bequeathed her costumes, 'my best gown of silk chamlet, my kirtle of satin, my scarlet petticoat, my best bonnet of

[1] *Yorkshire Archaeological Journal*, XVI, 434.
[2] Earwaker, *East Cheshire*, I, p. 204.
[3] *Surtees Society: Wills and Inventories*, V (1), p. 232.

velvet'.[1] What would the visitors of the Cistercian order have thought of these garments?

The provision which was made for the rank and file of the nuns does not seem adequate, even after generous allowance has been made for the difference in cost of living between then and now. But when the rich Benedictine abbey of Malling was about to be dissolved the abbess did not suggest a pension of more than £4 for her nuns. When Edburga Stratford, formerly nun of Nunnaminster in Winchester, made her will[2] in 1552 she stated that her board from September 30th to March 21st was, at the rate of one shilling and twopence a week, twenty-five shillings and fourpence.[3] As she had a pension of fifty-three shillings and fourpence, she had therefore very little to spare. Her former colleague, Agnes Bachcroft, the former sub-prioress, who made her will four years later, was living in the same parish in Winchester, while Abbess Shelley was buried in Winchester College Chapel; and this looks as if some of the former nuns of this abbey lived together in a sort of community, but there is no direct evidence of this.

When the nuns left their houses they received dispensations from their vows. The reports of the commissioners who carried out the suppression leave no doubt as to this. In January 1537 the priory of Blackborough in Norfolk was dissolved. The prioress had a pension. All the ten nuns had expressed a wish to have dispensations and not to be transferred to other houses, and the commissioners duly noted that 'they have dispensations'.[4] The great Benedictine abbey of Romsey had among its nuns two sisters, the ladies

[1] *Somerset and Dorset Notes and Queries*, v, p. 268.
[2] The Baigent MSS. in Winchester Cathedral library include transcripts of the wills of several former religious.
[3] The lady was seemingly a poor hand at arithmetic: perhaps she was trying to get the better of her landlady!
[4] *P.R.O.*, S.P. Dom., IV, 130.

Katharine and Jane Wadham. They were daughters of an influential gentleman, Sir Nicholas Wadham, and nieces of a very rising man at court, Sir Edward Seymour, and of his sister, Queen Jane. These ladies and the steward of the abbey, John Foster, engineered the surrender in collusion with the Seymour family. Their uncle, Sir Thomas (later Lord) Seymour, got the lands and paid the pensions. Very shortly after the surrender of the abbey one of the sisters, Jane, married the steward. She justified herself on the ground that she had only done so after she had been released from her vows. This raises a difficulty. What was the form of the dispensations which were given by the Archbishop of Canterbury to the nuns? It could not have been that which was given to the monks, since nuns could not, naturally, hold a cure of souls. It is most likely that it simply gave them leave to wear secular clothing, and so, automatically, to revoke the vows of poverty and obedience. That of chastity was, however, a different question, and so the newly made Mrs. Foster found to her cost.

The Act of the Six Articles, which was actually in force when Romsey surrendered at the end of 1539, contained a clause which was fatal to the lady's position. Parliament had finally resolved, accorded and agreed, 'that vows of chastity or widowhood, by man or woman made to God advisedly, ought to be observed by the law of God', and 'that if any man or woman which has actually vowed chastity, do actually marry or contract matrimony with any person he or she shall be deemed a felon' and suffer pains of death and forfeiture of goods. Nuns who had married were now liable to be prosecuted in the church courts for incest, while husbands who had married them were apt to take advantage of the act in question, and to seek a divorce on the ground that the marriage was null.[1] Mrs. Foster's case was so prominent that a special commission of two bishops was appointed in 1541 to investigate it.[2] It is doubtful if the savage provisions of the Act were, or in existing circumstances could be, carried out; and it would not appear that anything serious happened to Mrs. Foster as the result of her breach of the law. At any rate, in the will which the vicar of Romsey made in May 1558 there is a mention of Jane Foster, gentlewoman, who is no doubt to be identified with the former Miss Wadham.

Very early in the reign of Edward the Sixth the Act of the Six Articles was repealed, and its repeal was quickly followed by the acceptance by convocation and the legalizing by parliament of clerical marriage. It was now possible for the former nuns to marry lawfully and a considerable number of them seem to have taken advantage of the change of affairs. Archdeacon Harpsfield says that, notwithstanding the frailty of their sex, and in contrast with the male religious, there were few backsliders. It is not possible to give even a guess as to what proportion of them did take husbands. Few of them were by this time in their first youth and most of them must have been distinctly antiquated. Nevertheless, a report on the pensioned religious which was sent to the Exchequer early in 1555[3] shows that in the diocese of Lincoln quite a number of former nuns had married, including the prioresses of Gokewell, Legbourne and Ankerwyke, and nearly half the nuns of the Gilbertine priory of Sixhill. The pensions of Mrs. Keale, Mrs. Barnby, Mrs. Pratt, Mrs. Buston and Mrs. Grisby, formerly nuns of Sixhill, must have been found very useful.

---

[1] *English Historical Review*, vol. LI (1936), p. 504.
[2] For further details about this curious case see H. Liveing, *Records of Romsey* (1906).
[3] *P.R.O. Exchequer*, 101, 76/26.

Queen Mary's vision of the restoration of the religious houses generally was frustrated by the vigilance of her parliament. But she was able to refound two small establishments, and to put back Brigittine nuns at Sion and Dominican at King's Langley (in this case in place of friars). Catharine Palmer, one of the former nuns of Sion, became abbess there, and no doubt others became her colleagues. Similarly, a former nun of Dartford, Elizabeth Cressner, became prioress of the new foundation of Langley, and was followed there by four or five of her former colleagues. Their new houses were not destined to keep them long and early in Elizabeth's reign they withdrew, those of Sion to Antwerp, those of Langley to Bruges, there to carry on the religious life. A representative of another religious order of women can also be traced oversea in the person of Elizabeth Woodford, canoness of the Augustinian house of Burnham, Buckinghamshire. She appears to have gone oversea as early as 1548, to join the house of her order at Louvain.[1] These exiles form a very small proportion of the whole number of nuns or canonesses who were still alive at Mary's death. It is comparatively easy, as we shall see, to trace the after-careers of the male religious. Those of the female provide a far harder problem. And a great deal more research will have to be done before it can be solved.

This chapter may well end with a list of nuns of the great Bedfordshire abbey of Elstow (the birthplace of John Bunyan) where the nave of the nuns' church is still in use. Abbess Boyville retired to live at Bedford, close by, on her pension of £50, and so did three other nuns, the dates of whose burials were recorded in the registers of St. Mary's Church. In 1555,[2] one was living at Elstow itself, and most of

[1] Dom Adam Hamilton, *Chronicle of Canonesses Regular of Louvain*, p. 24.
[2] *P.R.O. Exchequer*, 100, 76/26.

the others in villages around. Only one of the original nuns of Elstow had gone far afield, namely to Lincolnshire, and she produced letters from Abbess Boyville to show that she had been professed a nun at the age of sixteen on August 24th, 1529. Another, who was living in Northamptonshire, had been a nun of one of the smaller houses, probably Catesby, and had been transferred to Elstow in 1536. Finally, the statement of Archdeacon Harpsfield about marriage is justified in the case of Elstow, for of the twenty-five nuns who received pensions, only one had committed matrimony.

Apart from reports of pension commissioners, wills, parish registers and a few brasses are almost our only sources of knowledge about the lives of the nuns after the suppression. Sometimes the burial registers state definitely that the deceased had been a nun. At the suppression of Godstow Abbey in 1539 a nun called Margery Higgins received a pension of £3. Nine years later she was reported to the receiver of the Court of Augmentations — i.e. the pensions commissioner — for Oxfordshire to be living in Pontesbury, Warwickshire (a mistake for Shropshire).[1] Twenty years after that, namely on April 22nd, 1568, the burial registers of Pontesbury record the burial in the parish church of that village of Margeria Higgins *olim monialis*. Brasses show that the former nuns had reverted to secular costume. In Dingley Church, Northamptonshire, there is a brass to Anne Borough. 'Sometime professed at Clerkenwell near London,' died 1577, aged 75. She is not represented in the habit of a religious, but in the ordinary female costume of the early part of Elizabeth's reign, i.e. a gown with a scarf and band fixed round the waist, and a veiled head-dress, but no wimple. On the other hand there is a

---

[1] *P.R.O. Augmentation Office*, Miscellanea, Bundle 26.

brass in another Northamptonshire church (that of Rothwell) to Clementia Tresham, daughter of Sir Thomas Tresham (died September 6th, 1567), which represents her in a nun's habit and which has a prayer for her soul in the old form. Many wills, whether of former religious or of their relatives, give particulars of interest. Abbesses and prioresses were apt to leave small sums to their former colleagues. When Abbess Kingsmill of Wherwell in Hampshire made her will in 1569 she bequeathed her soul to 'God, my only maker and redeemer' (she does not go on to Our Lady and the holy host of heaven); to her sister-in-law, Lady Kingsmill, a feather bed; a feather bed, bedding, cushions, sheets, etc., to six of her former colleagues; finally, to Elizabeth Hacker (another of the former nuns) 'now wife of Edmund Bath, a worsted cassock and carpet cushion'.[1] The abbess does not, then, seem to have objected to Mrs. Bath's marriage.

Printed in *Hants Notes and Queries*, VI, 91.

CHAPTER IX

THE FRIARS

I

THE four orders of friars (Dominican, Franciscan, Carmelite, and Austin) were in a very different position to that of the 'possessioner' religious. Their landed possessions extended to little more than the site of their house, with a garden, a meadow or two and, perhaps, a little house property. It is obvious, therefore, that they could not perform two of the three duties prescribed for the others, namely, alms and hospitality. On the other hand, their prayers were of the highest possible importance. It is a natural, and indeed a healthy, conviction of laymen that the ministrations of poor clergymen are more efficacious than those of rich ones. It is true that the numbers of the friars had seriously diminished since the thirteenth century.[1] The London Franciscans had twenty-five friars at the surrender instead of the hundred of early years,[2] and those of Chichester seven instead of twenty-five. But they remained to a high degree popular, and right down to the suppression few wills of persons of standing failed to provide in some way or other for the prayers of one or more house of friars or for burial in one of their churches. Indeed, as an additional precaution, it was sometimes stipulated that the body of the deceased should be shared by more than one order of friars. A Duchess of Buckingham, for example,

---

[1] A rough calculation from the surrender lists may put their numbers at a little over 1500. Dominicans about 450, Franciscans 550, Carmelites 250, Austin 250. To which must be added about 50 Trinitarian friars and a dozen Crutched friars.

[2] Kingsford, *Grey Friars of London*, p. 26.

left her heart to the Grey Friars of London and her body to the Carmelites of Bristol.[1] The friars, naturally, reaped much benefit from these activities. In return for a daily mass for his soul and those of his relations, a London alderman paid for the repairs of the Franciscan church.[2] When a Knight of the Garter died, his colleagues were bound to have so many masses said for him by friars, and a certificate to that effect had to be sent to the Registrar of the Garter by the wardens of the convents concerned.[3] Their popularity with the laity is shown, too, by the difficulties which the royal visitor, Bishop Ingworth of Dover (himself a Dominican), found in getting true reports of the condition of their houses just before the suppression.

Like the monks, the friars' houses were used as banks, repositories for title deeds, jewels, plate. Thus 'a chest of evidences belonging to divers gentlemen' figures in an inventory of the Bodmin Franciscans. Many houses were places of pilgrimage, and contained wonder-working images of great value in more ways than one, like that of Our Lady in the Carmelite church at Doncaster, to which many bequests were made. They preserved many relics of an out-of-the-way kind, such as that which the Bishop of Dover says he found in Wales, namely, 'Malchus's ear that Peter stroke off'.[5] An image at Bangor was, he says, worth to the Black Friars yearly twenty marks (say £300 to £400 nowadays) in corn, cheese, cattle and money. At Telsford in Warwickshire, the Trinitarian friars had an image which cured headaches and kept the hair on ageing widows' heads. 'They put,' said Doctor London, 'a peck of oats into the trough under the image, and when they are slid under

---

[1] Kingsford, *Grey Friars of London*, pp. 208-11.
[2] *Collectanea Franciscana* (2), p. 139. (British Society of Franciscan Studies, vol. x.)
[3] *L.P.*, XII (1), 947. [4] *L.P.*, XIII (2), 170. [5] Wright, *Suppression*, p. 212.

the altar, the friars steal them out from behind and the sick must pay a penny a peck for those oats.'[1]

The services which the friars had once rendered to education had to a great extent petered out. Their houses in the universities no longer produced scholars of the stature of Roger Bacon, though, as Archbishop Cranmer testified, they still had a large number of learned men at Cambridge. That they undertook a certain amount of private teaching is shown by the fact that Thomas Hammond, who was elected Prior of the London Austin Friars in 1533, had been 'a teacher of young children'. One of the most eminent medical men of the sixteenth century, Dr. Simon Ludford, had been a Franciscan friar and there are other instances of the kind.

Finally, their reputation in the pulpit still held good, but it is doubtful if the quality of their sermons was kept up. That good conservative, Bishop Gardiner, is very contemptuous of their methods, 'ever barking against the parish priest': their 'scoffing friarlike wit', 'some petty conceit to entertain the audience', are some of the terms he uses, ending up with an expression of satisfaction (he is writing just after the suppression), 'Now they be gone with all their trumpery'.[2]

Interference from outside was probably less galling to the friars than to the monks. Since they had no lands they required no steward, or the assistance of country gentry and the like. But the representatives of the founder's family had the same rights as in the monasteries: and they were accorded the same honours. Their arms were seen everywhere, on buildings, seals, vestments, etc. They had

---

[1] *L.P.*, XIII (2), 719.

[2] The Bishop's account of his dealings with the late Doctor Barnes, a former friar (printed in Muller, *Letters of Stephen Gardiner*, pp. 164-78), is a very good example of the dislike which the secular clergy had for the friars.

lodgings in houses of their foundation, as at Ipswich, where the Franciscan friary had a 'chamber where my Lord Wentworth's [the founder] servants lay'. In the towns, the founders were often the burgesses themselves, and at the dissolution of the friaries many of the town councils petitioned for the materials on this ground. 'The Grey Friars of Bristol,' wrote the Mayor in 1538, 'is of the foundation ... of the town, built by ancient burgesses at their cost; we should like it to repair the walls and quay and to make a wharf.'[1] Many of the houses were of royal foundation and had to furnish the king and his officers with lodging. This opened the door to a good deal of perilous interference on the part of the king's officials. 'Please,' write the Grey Friars of London to Henry IV, 'tell the Sheriff of Essex to have search made for one of our friars and restore him to our order', and not long before the suppression we find Queen Katharine of Aragon complaining of the doings of the Dominican prior of King's Langley. 'The Queen,' wrote the Bishop of Lincoln to Cardinal Wolsey, 'insists, as foundress, on the reformation of the house. Little religion is kept there and the house is in utter decay. The prior has married his woman to a servant of his.'[2]

Another cause of outside interference arose from the fact that the friars were wont to lease parts of their precincts to outsiders. 'In this house' (of the Reading Franciscans), wrote Doctor London to Cromwell, 'there are three pretty lodgings. The Warden keeps one, Mr. Ogle the King's servant another, and an old lady, called Lady St. John, the third.'[3] Sometimes these lodgers were the cause of considerable difficulty to the friars. The London Dominicans, for instance, had an unpleasant experience with one of their tenants, a drunken woman, who all but set her house in the

---

[1] *L.P.*, XIII (2), 322.   [2] *L.P.*, IV, 4315.   [3] *L.P.*, XIII (2), 346.

precincts on fire and whose language was too awful for words. They had to appeal to the Lord Mayor to get her expelled.[1] Nearly all the friars' houses added to their incomes by taking in (to use a modern phrase) paying guests. In the precincts of the Coventry Carmelites there were no fewer than thirty-one houses and eleven gardens leased out to tenants, and in 1532 the Provincial of the Austin Friars had given Thomas Cromwell himself (a tenant far more dangerous than any drunken woman) 'two messuages late new builded within the precinct or close of the said [London] house of friars', while the Grey Friars of London in 1531 let their gardens and a tenement to a London citizen and his wife. Nearly all the friars' houses had tenants, whether male or female, of this kind, or were used as private hotels. A Yorkshire gentleman and his wife used to stay in the house of the Franciscans of Beverley when they wanted a change of air. And we meet with a number of cases of people coming in to drink with the friars, presumably after the public houses had closed.[2] Further, their precincts were often used for public purposes of various kinds. The Mayor and Corporation of Norwich used, as they use now, the great Dominican church for municipal purposes: while the University of Cambridge used the Franciscan house for its convocation.

The friars were almost wholly free from episcopal interference. Indeed, the only occasions on which they had any dealings with the bishop were at their ordination, or when they got from him licences to preach. It required a papal legate, and in the end a royal visitor, to deal with them. I do not think that any reports of visitations by the Ministers-General of this period survive, so that it is very difficult to

[1] *L.P.*, XI, 231.
[2] 'Sitting in the buttery drinking' is a frequent expression in accounts of the friars' houses. See *L.P.*, XIII (1), 658.

judge what the real state of the friars was. Nor do we get any information from the general visitation of the friars undertaken by George Brown and John Hilsey, Provincials of the Austin friars and Dominican friars respectively, in 1534, the records of which seem to be lost. Their numbers had, as has been already mentioned, seriously diminished since the thirteenth century. Moreover, they were getting less and less confined to their convents. A glance at episcopal visitation lists of this period shows that a number of them were serving as assistant clergy. Indeed, a report on the Winchester friars at the time of the suppression shows that they were nearly all 'serving abroad',[1] that is, in parishes or elsewhere. The discipline in many of the houses seems to have been sadly relaxed. A great many of the inmates were mere boys. The Earl of Rutland, for example, reported that at Grantham there was one friar of eighteen years of age and a novice of thirteen. About the same time it was reported of the Austin Friars of London that many of them were children, more like wild beasts in Sherwood than friars; that whereas there were formerly thirty masses by twelve men, now there are only one priest and five or six children; that the friars sit in the beerhouse from six in the morning till ten at night 'like drunken Flemings'; that there is no common refectory, and that the friars dine in parties in their rooms.[2] This order in particular seems to have got quite out of hand, though it is to be hoped that not all its priors were like him of the Austin convent at Northampton, 'a great dicer and reveller, who has made away with £100 worth of plate'.[3] The friars, like other people, seem to have dealt extensively in necromancy and the spiritualism which was usually connected with it. A Dominican of Oxford, one Christopher Threder, was convicted in 1536 of conjuration

---

[1] *L.P.*, XIII (1), 1456.   [2] *L.P.*, VI, 1670.   [3] *L.P.*, XIII (2), 719.

of spirits,[1] and we find a Franciscan of Chichester taken by the sheriff of Sussex for disposing of stolen goods.[2]

II

The houses of the friars were not suppressed piecemeal like those of the monks. They were all dissolved in the course of a single year — 1538 — the chief instrument employed by the Crown being a Dominican, Richard Ingworth, Bishop Suffragan of Dover, and formerly Prior of King's Langley. The suppression was carried out with comparative ease. The bishop pretended that he didn't suppress any houses, but only received the surrender of those who couldn't go on, because of poverty and debt. It was probably true that people, seeing which way things were going, had to a great extent ceased to subscribe towards their upkeep. 'People see through their manner of living,' wrote Doctor London to Cromwell, 'and few give them alms. Your Lordship would do well to reduce them to live like honest priests.' 'I want,' wrote the Bishop of Rochester,[3] 'to get the London Dominicans to change their habits . . . and abolish utterly the physiognomy of anti-Christ.'

The surrenders of the autumn of 1538 were of a dictated kind.[4] The Franciscans were made to say that wearing a grey coat with a girdle full of knots was a dumb ceremony: the Carmelites forswore the wearing of a white coat, scapular and hood, 'and they all petition for the King's licence to change their habits and to receive such livings as

---

[1] L.P., x, 804. He was Vicar of Portsmouth from 1564 to 1579.
[2] L.P., vi, 1697.
[3] L.P., xiii (2), 225. Bishop Hilsey had been a Dominican prior.
[4] L.P., xiii (2), 501 for the Franciscans; 565 for the Carmelites.

other secular priests are preferred to'. 'You promised,' wrote the Warden of the London Franciscans to Cromwell, 'if I sent the names of the brethren, to send dispensations from our papistical and slanderous apparel. It has not been rightly used for many years, and no doubt God moves the heart of princes to take it away and correct them for their sins, as He corrected the children of Israel by the Chaldeans and Babylonians. We all long for a dispensation.' Many of them, indeed, must have been of the same mind as their visitor, the Bishop of Dover. 'My friar's heart was gone two years before my habit.'[1] Early in 1539 the Bishop was congratulating himself on his progress and hoping that by Easter but few friars would be left in England. His friar's heart had gone indeed.

Quite apart from the outside pressure which Doctor Ingworth, Doctor Baskerville, and other former friars were exercising on their fellows to get them to surrender, and from the drying up of their financial resources by the decay of popular support which had undoubtedly set in, there was another reason for the comparative ease with which their surrender was effected. In the religious controversies of the day the friars were hopelessly divided. Some clung to the old ways, others flung themselves, usually in a very intemperate way, into the new. Whereas in 1537 the Prior of the Bristol Dominicans prayed God that among his audience were no privy northern hearts nor close festered stomachs among them, 'but that every man would be true to God and his prince', and that though his order was one of the oldest in England, it could avail nothing without faith, nor could a ship laden with friars' girdles or a dung-cart full of monks' cowls lead to justification, the Warden of the local Franciscans preached the opposite.[2] In Cambridge, Prior

<hr />

[1] Wright, *Suppression*, p. 197.   [2] *L.P.*, XII (1), 508.

Buckenham of the Dominicans left the realm in aid of the Bishop of Rome in 1535, while his successor, Prior Dodds, 'a man of good learning and a preacher of God's true gospel', wanted to be allowed to take away an image of Our Lady in his house to which much pilgrimage was made, later took to himself a wife, and became eventually Dean of Exeter.

In the course of the years 1534-40 a certain number of friars of conservative opinions retired oversea, amongst whom the most prominent were two Observants from Greenwich, William Peto and Henry Elston, who, from their retreat in the Netherlands, worked against the English Government, while a few more, like the Dominican prior of Newcastle-on-Tyne, crossed the border into Scotland. Their conservative martyrs included Friars Rich and Risby, involved in the Nun of Kent affair; Friar Stone, 'parboiled' at Canterbury in 1538; and Friar Forrest, burned at Smithfield in 1538; while two or three got into trouble during the Pilgrimage of Grace; and the warden and sub-warden of the Reading Franciscans were in the Tower of London with Abbot Cook in 1539: but there is no record of their coming to any further trouble, and so they were probably pardoned. In some parts of the country the friars took an active part in combating the new preachers and in upholding the old methods of devotion. 'It is more meritorious,' said Friar Arthur of Canterbury, 'to give a penny to the shrine of St. Thomas, than a noble to the poor, because one is spiritual and the other temporal', while at Stamford the Dominicans attacked a local preacher of the gospel and advocated justification by works. Works, so far as their prior, William Stafford, was concerned, consisted in taking a wife and several livings, and he ended his days in 1588 as rector of St. George in his native town. Although Doctor Stokes, prior of the Austin Friars at Norwich, was delated to Crom-well in 1537 for opposing the preaching of Matthew Parker (later to become Archbishop of Canterbury) he protested that he did detest and abhor the Bishop of Rome with all his papistical factions.[1] Persons so weak-kneed as this were not likely to cause the Government much trouble.

It was among the friars that the 'new learning' spread fastest and furthest. The fame of the foreign friars who accepted it has eclipsed that of its English votaries. The illustrious names of Martin Luther, an Austin Friar, of Oswald Geisshüssler (Myconius), a Franciscan, and of Martin Bucer, a Dominican, in Germany, or of Bernard Ochino, an Observant Franciscan, in Italy, have no equals in England. Nevertheless, there were many English friars of great learning who were involved in the new movement. Among the Austin Friars occur the names of Robert Barnes and Miles Coverdale; among the Carmelites that of John Bale; among the Dominicans that of John Hodgkin; and among the Franciscans, those of John Joseph and Guy Eton, chaplains respectively to Archbishop Cranmer and Bishop Hooper.

In Cardinal Wolsey's time there had been complaints that many Oxford friars were guilty of imbibing the new doctrines, and so long ago as 1519 Pope Leo X had given the cardinal a faculty to punish, not only the disorderly Observants, but also those who had lapsed into Lutheran-ism. One of them, Friar William Roye, gave the cardinal a vast amount of trouble. So did Friars Gardiner, Wygge and Topley of the Austin house of Stoke by Clare in Suffolk, who disseminated the doctrine of justification by faith in a wide area of East Anglia.[2] At Northampton, a little later,

---

[1] Strype's *Parker*, I, 23.   [2] *L.P.*, IV, 4218 and 4242.

Prior Goodwin, of the local house of Austin Friars, together with a Dominican called Stephen Wilson, took to holding forth in the horse-market and railing against the Blessed Sacrament. 'I was once a friar,' said the ex-prior, 'but am now at liberty, after having flattered a great while and all for money.'[1] All over the country, both before and after the suppression of their houses, were found friars or ex-friars spreading the new doctrines, causing dissensions in every parish and disgust to all who held to the old paths. It must, of course, be remembered that most of them came from the lower middle class, a class which always enjoys 'stunts', such as the friars had been accustomed to provide, and which, when it does take up new ideas, throws itself into them violently and not according to knowledge. One wonders what the rustic folk of Thorndon in Suffolk thought of the new curate whom their rector had engaged to help him in 1536. Doctor Bale had had a distinguished career at Cambridge, had joined the Carmelites, and had risen to be prior of their Ipswich house. The conservative instincts of a neighbouring squire, Sir Humphrey Wingfield, were aroused, and he wrote to the Duke of Suffolk: 'a White Friar, lately prior of the White Friars of Ipswich, preaches erroneous opinions in your manor of Thorndon. People daily resort to hear him. The consequence is that there are great quarrels among them, for they do not all accept his teaching'.[2] The Duke's bailiff was a particularly pertinacious opponent,[3] while the women prayed for the success of the rebels in the north. It is to be hoped that Doctor Bale did not use the same language in his sermons as he did in his books. Perhaps he did, for a little later he found himself under arrest. The learned antiquary, John Leyland, interested himself in his behalf and wrote to Cromwell to

---

[1] *Archaeologia*, XLVIII, p. 264.   [2] *L.P.*, XII (1), 40.   [3] *L.P.*, XII (1), 307.

urge that he was worthy of a better future, and that he ought not to remain a mere country curate. But he never got beyond an Irish bishopric.

In another country parish, that of Hampton Bishop (or Lucy) in Warwickshire, the new assistant priest, the former friar, Edward Large, this time a Franciscan,[1] was giving like trouble and Squire Lucy wrote to the bishop that the new curate (the rector was an absentee) was making himself obnoxious by speaking against things the parishioners were of long time accustomed to. If they are to be believed they were certainly hearing some strange doctrines, among others that the Ember days were named after Imber, a paramour of a certain Bishop of Rome, a charge which was probably invented by the squire's bailiff, Mr. Clopton.[2] If clergymen wanted a quiet time in parishes they did well to follow the example of old Parson Cowle of Ticehurst in Sussex, and tell the people to go on offering candles to St. Loi and St. Anthony to cure their sick cows,[3] and if the bishops would call their clergy very fools for doing so, as Bishop Sampson called this one — well, who was the worse?

But conservative squires all over the country were getting just as much frightened at the doctrines preached by crowds of ex-friars as those of the eighteenth century were at the progress of the Methodists. Their preaching gifts made them most efficacious propagandists and Cromwell used them extensively for the purpose of setting forward the King's cause. Both under Henry VIII and under Mary they furnished a considerable number of martyrs for their faith, of whom the most eminent were Doctor Barnes, formerly prior of the Cambridge Austin Friars, and Doctor

---

[1] The Franciscans of Worcester must have been deeply infected by the 'new learning'. The Warden, John Joseph, became chaplain to Archbishop Cranmer. Large had been ordained sub-deacon at Worcester as a Franciscan in 1523. He was destined to get into constant trouble for the violence of his opinions.

[2] *L.P.*, XII (2), 302 and 496.   [3] *L.P.*, XIII (1), 1199.

Cardmaker, formerly warden of the Bristol Franciscans, who perished at the stake in 1540 and 1555 respectively. Among the rank and file there were several more victims, such as John Hemsley, an Observant Friar who was burned with Anne Askew in 1546, and Anthony Parsons, another former friar, who had suffered a like fate three years before.

II

It remains to inquire into the history of the friars after the suppression of their houses. This is difficult to trace for many reasons. First, the local ties which the monks had were lacking. A study of ordination lists will show that a friar might be at one house when he was ordained acolyte, and at others when he became sub-deacon, deacon, and priest respectively. Doctor Gilbert Berkeley, the eminent Franciscan, was in 1535 ordained deacon from the Lincoln house, and priest from the Northampton house of his order, while his name appears three years later on the surrender list of the Grey Friars of York. He was then 'very loath to leave his hypocrite's coat till he was compelled by fear of punishment'.[1] However, he soon made the best of things, took a living in Norfolk and a wife, and eventually became Bishop of Bath and Wells. Secondly, the friars had no livings in their gift and so they could not, like the monks, dispose of them to their own advantage, by means of transference of the patronage before the surrender. When they did get livings it was only by luck or by the favour of individuals. Thirdly, their possessions were too small for pensions to be paid except in the case of the Trinitarian friars

---

[1] Wriothesley's *Chronicle*, p. 182.

and of a few of the heads (such as the warden of the London Franciscans), and so the reports of the various pension commissions did not concern them, unless they happened to have obtained chantries. When the chantries were suppressed under Edward VI, pensions amounting to practically the full annual value of the chantry were given to their incumbents, and a considerable number of friars were thus rewarded. Doctor Peter Brinkley, the last warden of the Grey Friars of Bury St. Edmunds, was in 1555 reported[1] as having a pension of £5 (say £150) a year; this was not from Bury, but because he had been a fellow of the lately dissolved college of Wingfield. He was at that time divorced from his wife and inhibited from performing divine service, but on Elizabeth's accession he took the opportunity of accepting a Norfolk living. Whether he took back his wife is not known.

Quite a large number of friars became bishops after the surrender. A few took the conservative side in ecclesiastical politics, such as Doctor Griffith, Bishop of Rochester (1554 — died 1558), and Doctor Hopton, Bishop of Norwich (1554 — died 1558), both of whom had been Dominicans. The greater number, however, were in favour of the new learning. These included among the Dominicans: John Scory, bishop successively of Rochester, Chichester and Hereford; John Hilsey, Bishop of Rochester (1535-38); and Richard Ingworth, Bishop of Dover (1538-44); and among the Franciscans: Gilbert Berkeley, Bishop of Bath and Wells (1559-81). The Carmelites furnished Bishop Bird of Chester and Bishop Bale of Ossory, and the Austin Friars Bishops Coverdale of Exeter and Hodgkin of Bedford. A former Dominican friar became a dean in the person of Doctor Dodds, Dean of Exeter (1560-70), while a large

---

[1] *English Historical Review*, vol. XLVIII (1933), p. 215.

number of former priors or wardens of the friars are found on cathedral staffs as prebendaries or minor canons.

On the suppression of their houses the rank and file of the friars were naturally anxious to obtain employment as soon as they could. The Crown officials were eager that they should find it, and consequently their 'capacities', or dispensations to serve as secular clergymen, were made as easy as possible for them. 'It were a charitable deed,' wrote the Bishop of Dover to Cromwell in July 1538, 'that capacities were cheaper', and a few months later he was saying that 'the bishops and curates are very hard to them without they have their capacities'.[1] Moreover, those who took the surrender were obliged to make *some* provision for them. 'Until we get their capacities we have to find them in meat and drink,' wrote Doctor London from Oxford. 'Now they be dismissed from their houses, no man will admit any of them to be curates, unless they do bring their capacities: wherefore I beseech your lordship we may have them with speed, for in the mean time the poor men be without livings.'[2] It has been pointed out that the monks had done their best to save something from the wreck for themselves. The friars did the same, only, unluckily for them, there was very little to get hold of. When their houses were suppressed there was a great deal of snatching and spoiling on the part of the mob. The friars took a hand in the business and many instances occurred of an attempted sale of plate on their part. But the poor things had normally very little to sell, as the inventories and details of sale of their possessions show. The sites and buildings were put to odd uses: many of them were begged or bought by town councils. Worcester wanted them to repair the city walls and the bridge; Reading for a Guildhall; Grimsby for a storehouse

[1] Wright, *Suppression*, p. 193.   [2] Ibid., p. 228.

for anchors and cables; Cambridge colleges for extending their premises. Thus a small proportion of the buildings were saved. In London, the great church of the Austin Friars still survives: and but for the Great Fire so would that of the Franciscans. At Norwich the nave of the Dominican church became a city hall and so remains.

It has been stated that there was a general withdrawal of the Dominicans to the Continent after the suppression of their order in England. There is no historical evidence whatever for this statement, and it is to the last degree unlikely that anything of the kind occurred. What the friars of all the orders did was to take such posts as they could get; and that whether their outlook in ecclesiastical politics was of the old or the new kind. A very good example is that of the distinguished Oxford Dominican, Doctor William Perrin, who, like many other friars, became a chantry priest at St. Paul's Cathedral. Queen Mary chose him as prior of the house of Black Friars which she founded in 1555 and which was set up in St. Bartholomew's, Smith-field, at the same time as that of the Observants at Green-wich, and where he was buried in August 1558, less than three months before the death of his patroness. His successor, Doctor Richard Hargrave, was in office as prior and provincial[1] a very short time indeed and he was one of the small minority of his order who went oversea at the accession of Queen Elizabeth. What nine out of ten of the Dominicans who surrendered in 1538 did may be seen by examining the careers of those of Gloucester. There were, at the surrender of this house, a prior and six friars. Two years later Doctor Bell, Bishop of Worcester, held a visitation of his diocese and six years after that Doctor Wakeman, Bishop of Gloucester, held another.

[1] *English Historical Review*, vol. XXXIII (1918), p. 248.

In the records of these visitations it is noted which of the clergy reported on had been once religious. We can thus trace the whole number of the friars of the Gloucester house. They were all, including the prior, serving as stipendiaries of churches in and around Gloucester.[1] Two at least of them later obtained livings. Doctor Cheyney, Bishop of Gloucester, visited his diocese in 1576, and a thorough-going scrutiny of the intellectual attainments of his clergy and of their qualifications for office was made. Of the vicar of Ashleworth, one Thomas Mekins, it was reported that he 'understandeth the Latin tongue and is seen in the scriptures but meanly'. This vicar then produced his testimonials: a certificate of his institution in October 1558 to the living of Ashleworth, and another to show that he had subscribed in August 1571 to the Thirty-nine Articles, as all clergy ordained under the old ordinal had to do under the Subscription Act of that year. He also produced a dispensation from Thomas (Cranmer), Archbishop of Canterbury, to obtain any ecclesiastical benefice to which a regular may be instituted, dated September 5th, 1538, and the royal confirmation of this document dated five days later. Why did he have to produce these particular certificates? Because, as the report goes on, 'he was formerly a religious, a friar of Gloucester'.

In July 1538 the Bishop of Dover, visitor of the friars under the Lord Privy Seal, was at Gloucester.[2] He assembled the friars of the town and, before the Mayor and aldermen, asked them 'will you continue in your houses and keep your religion and injunctions according to the same, or else give your houses into the king's hands'. Everything, according to the bishop, went smoothly. The Mayor and aldermen

[1] See *Transactions of the Bristol and Gloucestershire Archaeological Society*, vol. XLIX (1927), p. 95.
[2] Wright, *Suppression*, p. 202.

243

thought the injunctions good and reasonable; the friars said
that they were according to their rules, yet as the world was
now they were not able to keep them and live in their
houses, wherefore voluntarily they gave them into the
king's hands to the king's use. 'Mind you,' said the
bishop, 'I have no authority to suppress but only to reform
you: if you like to be reformed you may continue for all
that I care.' The friars answered that they were not able to
continue. So the visitor took their houses and gave them
letters to visit their friends . . . 'with the which they were
very well content and so departed'.

Among those who so departed was the Dominican,
Thomas Mekins. He was quite a young man, since he had
been ordained sub-deacon at Worcester only four years
before; and he had, therefore, many years of work before
him. It was, however, first necessary for him to get a dispensation to officiate as a secular clergyman and this, as
we have seen, he procured and without delay, since it was
dated only about six weeks after the surrender of his house.
He then looked out for a job and was soon successful in
finding one as curate-in-charge of Upton St. Leonards,
near by, and here he seems to have laboured for the better
part of fifteen years. Since he does not seem to have followed the example of so many of his fellow clergy in taking
a wife in Edward VI's time he would not have been
disturbed under Mary, and so could have stopped on at
Upton till his appointment to Ashleworth. He gave complete satisfaction to Bishop Hooper in the visitation of 1551,
for his answers in examination were marked *satis plus*.[1] He
could not only repeat the ten commandments, correctly,
but also the Apostles' Creed and the Lord's Prayer, which
is more than a great many of his fellow clergy could do. By

[1] *English Historical Review*, vol. LXXIII (1904), p. 106.

that time he was, of course, saying divine service in English, but he had no hesitation in returning to Latin three years later, or in making a further lapse into English five years after that. Twenty years after Bishop Cheyney's visitation he felt the infirmities of old age growing upon him, and he resigned his living. Two years later, on June 23rd 1598, he was buried in Ashleworth churchyard.

Such a career was the normal one for the friars, as anybody can gather by going into the details of their lives after the surrender. It is in country parishes, and not on the Continent, that one must look for them.

CHAPTER X

THE FATE OF THE DISPOSSESSED RELIGIOUS

I

'There is now,' wrote the French ambassador to King Francis on April 10th, 1540, 'in all England not a single monk who has not changed his habit to the robe of a secular priest.'[1] What became of these monks? This is a question which is rarely answered except in vague terms of ululation. Cardinal — then the reverend Mr. — Newman, ended his *Life of St. Bettelin*, hermit and patron of Stafford, with these words, 'and this is all, and more than all that is known of this holy man: yet nothing to what the angels know'.[2] Most writers, having neither the time nor the opportunity of going to heaven to consult the angels, have given up a search for the former monks in despair. But it is quite unnecessary to journey any farther than the Public Record Office to learn all about them. It is hardly to be imagined that the governments of Henry VIII and his successors would fail to keep strict account of the pensioners, three thousand or more in number, with whom the Ministry of Pensions — for that was one of the functions of the Court of Augmentations — was concerned: and a great mass of material, hardly any of which has found its way into print, is preserved among its records and in those of its successor, the Exchequer.

Let us see, first, what happened to the abbots and priors,

[1] *L.P.*, xv, 485.
[2] *Lives of the Saints—Hermit Saints* (1844), p. 72. The life is anonymous, but it is ascribed to Newman by Mr. W. S. Lilly in the *Dictionary of National Biography*.

and then go on with the rank and file of the religious. Every head of a house got a pension, whether his monastery was one of the smaller which disappeared as a result of the Act of 1536 or not. These pensions varied in amount according to the wealth or poverty of their former establishment, and this was in accordance with precedent. Many abbeys were burdened already with large pensions to abbots who had been deprived or who had resigned. Chester, for example, was paying the huge sum of £100 (nearly £3000) a year to ex-Abbot Birkenshaw, and Whitby £40 (about £1200) to ex-Abbot Hexham. Indeed, there are cases where more than one former head was being provided for out of the revenues of the house. All these pensions continued to be honoured by the Crown, even if the abbey had been attainted,[1] and the recipients continued to enjoy them till their deaths.

The careers of the abbots and priors whose houses fell during the final suppression differed according to whether they wished to lead an active life or whether, with *Quiescendum* for a motto, they were content to live at ease on their ample pensions. It was, of course, to the advantage of the Crown to extinguish pensions by promoting their holders to offices of greater value than the pension: and a large number of abbots became now, or subsequently, diocesan bishops. At Peterborough the abbot was the luckiest of all: for he did not even have to turn out of his house: the abbot's palace became the bishop's palace, and Doctor Chambers became bishop instead of abbot of Peterborough. Abbot Wakeman of Tewkesbury had a very short journey to make, and was soon installed in the abbot's

---

[1] e.g. one to Nicholas Sutton of Kirkstead, who was in 1554 living at Barton, Lincolnshire, on a pension of £6 13s. 4d. granted him by the abbot and convent of Kirkstead on January 14th, 1518, and confirmed by the Court of Augmentations November 10th, 1541. *P.R.O. Exchequer*, 101 76/26.

palace at Gloucester, as bishop of that newly founded see; while Abbot King of Oseney and Thame did not have to move at all when he became Bishop of Oxford, with his former abbey church as his cathedral.[1] In course of time the Gilbertine prior of Sempringham became Bishop of Lincoln, and later on, Archbishop of York; the Benedictine prior of Worcester, Bishop of Lincoln; the Carthusian prior of Sheen, Bishop of Man. It was not usual for bishops of Welsh sees in the Middle Ages to set foot inside their dioceses and some of those sees were already held by abbots or priors, or soon became so. When their houses were dissolved, the Benedictine abbots of Hyde and Eynsham were Bishops of Bangor and Llandaff respectively; the Cluniac abbot of Bermondsey, Bishop of St. Asaph; and the Augustinian prior of Bisham, Bishop of St. David's.[2]

Throughout the later Middle Ages it had been an increasing custom to confer episcopal orders on abbots and priors with a view to relieving the bishops of functions which they had no time to perform themselves, in particular the conferring of the sacraments of confirmation and orders. Some few of these, like Prior Draper of Christ Church, Twineham, Bishop of Neapolis, continued to function after the dissolution, which, of course, made no difference to their episcopal duties. The Suffragans Act of 1533 provided for a great extension of the system. The bishops who were appointed under it were nearly all former abbots and priors. Instead of holding sees with outlandish titles like Crocodilopolis from 'which they derived no more profit than heat from a glow-worm', they now assumed English names, while retaining their pensions, and holding one or more livings as well. They cannot therefore be said

[1] The abbey church of Oseney was the cathedral church of Oxford from 1541 to 1545.
[2] I do not think that any of them, except the last, ever visited Wales.

to have been in bad case. The bishoprics of Berwick, Shaftesbury, Colchester, and Thetford, were held, respectively, by the former Benedictine abbots or priors of Holy Island, Milton, Walden, and Horsham St. Faith; those of Marlborough and Shrewsbury by the Cistercian abbots of Stanley and Kimmer; those of Ipswich and Hull by the Augustinian priors of Butley and Gisburn. The ecclesiastical changes and chances of the time made no difference to the tenure of the sees of these bishops, whether diocesan or suffragan. They not only retained them right through the reigns of Henry VIII and Edward VI, and the unmarried ones through that of Mary, but even into that of Elizabeth. By that time, since most of them had been elderly men at the time of their consecration, there were few left, but the former abbot of Eynsham retained his see till his death in 1565, while the prior of Holy Island and the abbot of Kimmer were still enjoying their emoluments at the time of their deaths in 1570 and 1561 respectively.

Bishops did not venture to take wives so long as Henry VIII was alive and the Act of the Six Articles was in force, but when clerical marriage was legalized under Edward VI, 'old lecherous priests and bishops went a caterwauling', and a considerable number of bishops who had formerly been in religion were deprived by Mary for this reason, among them the Archbishop of York, the Bishops of Chester, Bristol, and Thetford. They seem to have shed their wives very easily, and were rewarded for their complaisance by being presented to Crown livings. Archbishop Holgate had the hardihood to assert that his marriage was forced on him by the Duke of Northumberland, while Bishop Bird's excuse was that of Adam, 'the woman beguiled me'. On the accession of Elizabeth such married bishops as survived returned to their functions; of the unmarried the only case of deprivation was that of Bishop Pursglove of Hull, who could not bring himself to accept the Queen's ecclesiastical settlement. He lived on in enjoyment of his pension, founded grammar schools at Tideswell in Derbyshire, his native town, and at Guisborough, where he had been prior, and was buried in the parish church of the former place in 1579. His brass, which shows him habited in the mass vestments to which he was used, is still to be seen there. He may have been 'stiff in papistry' and in 1562 was for that reason bound 'to remain at Ugthorpe in Yorkshire',[1] but he was also described as 'very wealthy'. Indeed, how otherwise could he have founded his two schools? His martyrdom was a mild one.

The number of former heads of houses who obtained deaneries was very large. The cathedrals, eight in number,[2] which had hitherto been served by regulars, were henceforth to have a staff of secular clergy. In all cases but one, the last prior of the monastic became the first dean of the secular foundation; the only exception was Canterbury. Prior Goldwell made desperate efforts to obtain this deanery, but he appears to have incurred the dislike of Cranmer, who desired the post for one of the monks, Doctor Thornden, soon to be his suffragan, as Bishop of Dover. Eventually, however, it was given to Doctor Nicholas Wotton, a distinguished ecclesiastical lawyer, sprung from a famous old Kentish family. The deaneries of all but one of the new sees created by the King were also filled by former abbots or priors. The abbots of Chester and Westminster became the first deans of those sees. At Gloucester, the abbacy was vacant at the suppression,[3]

[1] Gee, *The Elizabethan Clergy*, p. 179.
[2] Canterbury, Durham, Winchester, Worcester, Ely, Norwich, Rochester, Carlisle.
[3] Abbot Parker *alias* Malvern was dead before June 1539, when the convent wrote to Cromwell petitioning for a new election owing to their abbot's death. *L.P.*, XIV (1), 1096.

so the prior of St. Oswald's became dean, and at Peterborough, the abbot having been made bishop, the deanery was given to the Cluniac prior of St. Andrew's, Northampton. As in course of time deaneries became vacant, more of them were filled with former abbots: at Worcester, for example, the former abbot of Evesham succeeded to the deanery in 1554, and so relieved the Crown of the expense of his large pension.

Many former monks held canonries or prebends in the cathedrals, and so the Crown was relieved of part of their pensions.[1] The abbot of Buckfast became prebendary of St. Paul's; the abbot of Winchcombe, prebendary of Gloucester; the abbot of Hayles returned to his native north to become prebendary of York. The majority of the former abbots and priors held rich livings in addition to their pensions. Many of these had been in the gift of their former abbeys and were obtained by collusion with their friends and neighbours among the gentry.[2] Robert Catton, penultimate abbot of St. Alban's, had, for example, a pension of £80 and two valuable benefices,[3] all of which he retained till his death in 1552. Most of these men rarely visited their parishes, which they left in charge of curates — sometimes their former monks.

All the abbots or priors who had become deans, prebendaries or parsons, held their posts without disturbance, until their deaths, unless they had the imprudence to marry. Thus the Premonstratensian Abbot Warter of Hagnaby was deprived in 1554, not only of his wife Jane, but also of

[1] When Abbot Munslow of Winchcombe was made prebendary of Gloucester in 1546, his pension of £140 was cut down by £20, the value of the prebend.
[2] See *Essays in History Presented to R. Lane Poole*, p. 449, for how the abbot of Sherborne and his friends worked things.
[3] Campton, Bedfordshire, and Mautby, Norfolk. A visitation of the diocese of Lincoln in 1543, now in the episcopal registry at Lincoln, shows that he had a pension of £80 as well. The combined values of the two rectories was about £24, so that his total income would amount nowadays to about £3000 a year.

his Lincolnshire and Norfolk livings. When Elizabeth came to the Crown he was able to resume all three. Prior Jenyns of St. Oswald's held the deanery of Gloucester from his appointment in 1541 till his death in 1565. Had he taken a wife, however, he would have suffered the fate of Prior Salisbury of Horsham St. Faith, who lost the deanery of Norwich for this cause in 1554 and did not recover it till the accession of Elizabeth, when clergymen's wives again became the fashion. Even if they had no livings to add to their pensions, they were amply provided for. True, the parliamentary abbots lost their seats in the House of Lords. 'My Lord Pentecost has become Sir Rowland'[1] was said of the former abbot of Abingdon. That is to say he was no longer a member of the House of Lords, but a simple country clergyman. But the simple country clergyman had a fine manor house at Cumnor: he had almost as many servants as he had when he was abbot (and didn't they brawl at the parish hall of the village one Sunday with the servants of a neighbouring potentate, Sir Robert Harcourt)[2] and he had no responsibilities. 'I was never out of debt when I was abbot', said the abbot of Sawtry.[3] 'Thank God I am rid of my lewd monks', said the former abbot of Beaulieu, who, immediately before the surrender, had taken the precaution to let out a mill and other property to his sister, and after it settled in a comfortable rectory at Bentworth. The abbot of St. Alban's need no longer complain of his 'unseemly flock of brethren': nor need the abbot of Warden[4] spend his time hunting for his monks in the public houses of the neighbourhood. It is only necessary to study their wills to see how comfortably they lived. Abbot Blake of Cirencester, who died at Fairford in 1553, had a chaplain

---

[1] The first was his name in religion, the second his family name.
[2] *L.P.*, XIII (1), 736.   [3] *L.P.*, XVII, 429.   [4] Wright, *Suppression*, p. 54.

(one of his former canons), a liveried servant in the person of Thomas Liggen, gentleman, two other liveried servants, six men and three women servants out of livery, to all of whom he left money and clothes, and three shillings and fourpence to the Fairford poor box.[1] The abbot of Alnwick was able to found a county family out of the proceeds of the dissolution.[2] As to their attitude towards the ecclesiastical controversies of the day, it is natural that they should differ. The greater part of them were probably wedded to the old ways, but were ready to change their views when it was convenient. The last abbot of Missenden in Buckinghamshire made his will in August 1558. After bequests to his son and daughter, he left sets of vestments to his parish church, 'if any be occupied hereafter in the same church and so permitted'.

The number of former abbots and priors who married shows also how far many of them had drifted from their earlier profession. The last abbot of Westminster of the old foundation must have undergone a considerable change in *his* views; the two executors of his will were the two very prominent innovators, Bishop Hugh Latimer and Doctor Rowland Taylor. Had Abbot Benson survived into the reign of Queen Mary, he might well have suffered the fate of his executors. It is probable that some, at any rate, of the former abbots cherished a hope of restoration. Abbot Whitney of Dieulacres in Staffordshire had, as we have seen, done his best to make what profit he could out of the dissolution. Yet when he made his will he still apparently hoped that his abbey would be refounded, for he left a silver gilt chalice to his nephew, stipulating that if the abbey were ever restored, the chalice should be returned to it.

[1] Will in the Prerogative Court of Canterbury.
[2] See the genealogy of his descendants in *History of Northumberland*, II, 436.

The will of a Somerset clergyman in 1557 shows that there were still hopes of this kind. The rector of Hinton St. George left £2 for 'edifying the abbey of Glastonbury'.[1]

II

We now turn to the provision made for the rank and file of the religious. This must be considered under four different heads. First, there is the question of what happened to those who were attached to those cathedral churches which had hitherto been served by monks. In these cases the priors became deans, some of the senior monks prebendaries, and some of the junior monks minor canons. As to those who were not wanted; at Ely 'we assigned pensions to those whom we thought not meet to tarry . . . assigning them that tarried to take pains in choir'.[2] At Norwich, again, the prior became dean and no fewer than twenty-one monks prebendaries and minor canons. At Worcester, the new prebendaries did not even have to shift from their old houses, for the officers or obedientiaries of a large monastery like this had long ago provided themselves with separate houses. A great many of these cathedral officers were affected by the marriage question under Mary, otherwise they usually held their posts until promotion or death; as late as 1570, for example, three former monks of Norwich were still minor canons of that cathedral.

Secondly, there were the religious who at the time of the suppression of their abbeys were holding livings by dispensation from Rome or (after 1533) from Canterbury and who could not expect pensions: they had their livings instead.[3] The third class consisted of those who had elected

---

[1] *V.C.H.*, *Somerset* II, 96. [2] *L.P.*, XIV (2), 542. [3] See pp. 282, 283.

under the Act of 1536 to accept dispensations from their vows and so be qualified to hold livings.[1] Such dispensations followed medieval lines and neither then nor now were pensions given to or expected by the holders. It was their own look-out if they chose the course of going into the world instead of being transferred to still existing monasteries. If, however, they chose the latter alternative they *were* assured of a pension. When Waltham Abbey surrendered it had on its pension list besides its own canons, five from smaller Augustinian houses in Essex who had asked to remain in religion when their own houses were suppressed. Among them was a future Bishop of Rochester. Canon Edmund Freake must have found the yoke of religion far less galling than that of matrimony, for he had the misfortune to choose a shrew who was not to be tamed. Monks of attainted abbeys like Whalley were expected to go into other houses of their order. The only exceptions were those of Colchester, Glastonbury, and Reading, which, falling at a time when there were practically no monasteries left to which they could be transferred, had to be treated like those which surrendered.[2] Finally there were those who surrendered in 1538 and 1539, all of whom got pensions.

What provision, then, was available for the religious of these surrendered houses? First, they were given the bonus known as a 'reward'.[3] The Cistercian monks of Merevale, for example, got fifty shillings (say £60) apiece.[4] The Cistercians of Roche got a half-year's pension by way of reward and their 'capacity' (or dispensation) free.

The pensions themselves cannot be called small or precarious. They varied according to the revenues of the house to which the pensioner had belonged and to his

---

[1] See above, Chapter VI, p. 151.   [2] See above, Chapter VII, p. 179.
[3] See above, Chapter VI, p. 153.   [4] *L.P.*, XIII (2), 839.

length of service there. The average pension may be put at five pounds,[1] which represents about £150 nowadays. Since the law did not yet allow the holder to marry, and since modern necessities, such as tobacco, were not then even luxuries, this was really quite an adequate sum on which to live; and so the older and more decrepit of the former monks were able to do, usually in the immediate neighbourhood of their former abbeys, unless nostalgia, always very prevalent in the middle ages, drew them back to their early homes. The younger monks and canons were, however, by no means content to live in idleness and they set about getting livings as soon as they could: a detailed investigation of any surrender list will show that all but the very old pensioners were soon beneficed. Directly after the surrender of their houses they had been furnished with dispensations to do this, so that there was no question of any breach of vows. It was to the advantage of the payer of the pension, whether Crown or private individual, to extinguish these pensions by appointing the holders to livings of greater value than the pension.[1] But if any private patron chose to present a pensioner to a living this made no difference to him, and, holding a pension in addition to his stipend, he was in a better and not in a worse position than the ordinary parson.

Moreover, the former religious did not obtain these livings by good luck alone. Just before the dissolution there seems to have been, on the part of religious houses, extensive transference of patronage to individuals or trustees with the object of making subsequent provision for

---

[1] This was apparently the scale of payment for serving a cure. *L.P.*, XIII (I), 94.

[1] See *English Historical Review*, vol. XLVIII (1933), p. 203, Note 2, for the way in which the Duke of Norfolk got rid of the pensions which he had to pay the monks of Castleacre, Thetford, and Sibton, by appointing them to livings in Norfolk or Suffolk. The Crown of course, reduced its pension list in the same way.

the monks of the house in question.[1] We have already seen how Prior Munday of Bodmin and his canons were able to fend for themselves in this way. The Crown pensions were paid half-yearly by the local receiver of the Court of Augmentations. They were liable to income tax (as we should say nowadays) just as all sources of income were. The financial difficulties of successive governments some-times allowed them (in common with all annuities, clerical or lay) to fall into arrear. But on the whole they seem to have been duly paid and the receipts for them, signed by the holders, are still extant in those of the receivers' accounts which survive.[2] Many of the reports of the pension com-missioners who were now and again appointed to investi-gate cases of fraud (for, naturally, the holder's relations were not above drawing a pension after his death) are in existence, and show very clearly the then whereabouts of the pensioners and their financial resources in detail. There were certainly three commissions of this kind, namely, in 1552, 1554 and 1569 respectively.[3] Some, but by no means all, of their reports are extant. If only they had been studied more carefully we should have been spared a great many of the tears which sentimentalists have shed over the fate of the former religious.

It has been already pointed out that former monks who held livings were actually better off than their fellow parsons who had never been in religion.[4] The 1554 report on the diocese of Lincoln gives a very good instance of this. In that year the vicar of Dorrington, Lincolnshire, was one

[1] See *Essays in History Presented to R. Lane Poole*, p. 449, for details.

[2] P.R.O. Augmentation Office, Miscellanea, bundle 26, has those for Oxfordshire and neighbouring counties.

[3] The report of the 1552 Commissioners for Gloucestershire is printed in *Transactions of the Bristol and Gloucestershire Archaeological Society*, vol. XLIX (1927), pp. 98-122: that of the 1554 report from the diocese of Norwich in *English Historical Review*, vol. XLVIII (1933), pp. 209-28.

[4] See below, p. 285.

Christopher Cartwright. He had, of course, the emoluments of the benefice and a vicarage house. To these he could add his pension of £2, as former canon of the Gilbertine priory of Catley; while his wife Joan Astley was not unprovided for, since she had a pension of £2 6s. 8d. as former nun of Sempringham, also a Gilbertine house.[1] He lost his living (and probably his wife in the same year), in common with other married clergymen, but regained it at Elizabeth's accession; and perhaps he got back his wife also.

III

It is impossible to give more than a general sketch of the attitude of the former religious to the ecclesiastical controversies of the day. The majority of them were probably conservatives in religion: a minority only (and those chiefly friars) were radicals. So long as Henry VIII was alive the position of conservatives was easy enough. Their leaders, the Duke of Norfolk and Bishop Gardiner of Winchester, had just engineered the Act of the Six Articles, which effectively put a stop to all innovations. Not that these two eminent persons had much sympathy for monks. The Duke had made a great deal out of the suppression, while in all the bishop's writings there are, I think, no signs of displeasure at the suppression, except one, when, attacking the ministers of Edward VI, he says that a hundred great houses have gone down and all that was got in exchange was a building for lousy and scurvy schoolboys — hardly a polite term for Christ's Hospital. But they saw to it that the forms of religion to which they had been used were retained: and in this they had the whole-hearted support of the King.

[1] *P.R.O. Exchequer,* 101 76/26.

The leaders of the radical party, beginning with the tiresome Doctor Barnes, were incinerated. The usher who pulled down the images and defaced the beauty of Winchester College Chapel was dismissed; the little prig in Essex who bawled out texts at the back of the church and disturbed the parishioners during the 'blessed mutter of the mass' received from his father that punishment from which, as Thackeray justly observed, none but cherubs are exempt.[1] Diehard conservatives used expressions about the 'book called the Bible' like those which their successors were to use about Darwin's *Origin of Species*. If old Parson Thompson of Enfield found anybody reading the 'book of Arthur Cobler', otherwise the bible, he would try to get the offender boycotted.[2] Under these circumstances former religious who held conservative views had little difficulty in accommodating themselves to the exigencies of the time, and in serving as parsons of parishes. Doctor Feckenham, destined to be made by Queen Mary first dean of St. Paul's, then abbot of Westminster, was perhaps the most prominent of them. He must have been fitted for the role of gloomy dean if we may judge by a sermon which he preached in the last month of Henry's reign, in which he lamented that nobody dares tell his beads nowadays for fear of being laughed at.[3]

The abbot of Tower Hill was another of the old order, 'a strong stout popish prelate whom the godly men of the parish of Stepney' (otherwise the restless element headed by that typical old colonel, Edward Underhill) 'were weary of'. He again held firmly to the old paths, disturbing the preachers in his church, causing the bells to be rung when they were at sermon, and sometimes beginning to sing in

[1] See *Narratives of the Reformation* (*Camden Society*, Series I, vol. LXXVII) for these and similar tales.
[2] *L.P.*, XIV (2), 796.   [3] *L.P.*, XXI (2), 710.

the choir before the sermon was half done, and sometimes challenging the preacher in the pulpit.'[1] At Canterbury there was a regular conspiracy of the cathedral chapter — mostly consisting of former monks — against the archbishop.[2]

The death of Henry VIII made things a good deal more difficult for conservatives. The priggish boy who succeeded to the throne, fell, first into the hands of his uncle Somerset, and then into those of the more violent Northumberland; while Archbishop Cranmer, who, as was said of one of his successors, had taken a season ticket on the line of least resistance, submitted to the influence of the more strenuous Ridley, soon to displace Bonner as Bishop of London, or of former friars like Peter Martyr and John Joseph. Very early in the reign conservatism began to take alarm, as the curious incident of the arm of the late Prior Houghton shows. A London Carthusian called John Fox had, after the suppression of his house, become rector of St. Mary Mounthawe in the City of London. But his sense of vocation was too strong and in April 1547 he fled the realm and was later professed again at Louvain. He kept up correspondence with his friends in England, with a view especially of getting the arm of the late Prior Houghton — 'who had suffered death for treason in denying the King's supremacy' — conveyed to him oversea 'with other baggage that they called relics'. One of his late colleagues, Thurstan Hickman, was in the plot and associated with him was Thomas Munday, the rector of St. Leonard's, Foster Lane, formerly Prior of Bodmin in Cornwall, a clergyman whom we have already met in quite other circumstances. The consequence was that they both found themselves lodged in

---

[1] *Narratives of the Reformation, passim.*
[2] *L.P.*, XVIII (1), 546.

the Tower under a sentence of attainder.[1] But that they actually suffered execution does not seem likely. Since the former prior's will was only made four years later, it would seem probable that they escaped anything more than imprisonment. That a certain number of Carthusians besides John Fox did go oversea is shown by the fact that the Privy Council issued in 1547 an order restraining their friends from sending to them their pensions. But the remainder of the now beneficed religious remained on in their parishes, accepting, willingly or unwillingly, the liturgical changes as they came and seeing their churches lose most of their ornaments and in Archdeacon Harpsfield's phrase 'take on the aspect of synagogues'. The consequence was that the rejoicing of the people at Mary's accession was beyond description and that when the Queen rode through London the streets were full of people crying 'Jesus save her Grace', weeping tears for joy 'that the like was never seen before'.[1] The 'old use before time used' was soon restored in the churches and the clergy in general obeyed the commands of their lawful sovereign, the last supreme head of the Church of England.

Unfortunately for the peace of the Church, a sad complication had been introduced during King Edward's reign. Women had become responsible for the difficulties of a vast number of clergymen and were soon to lead to the deprivation of something like a quarter of the incumbents of England and Wales. Convocation, by a two-thirds majority had passed a resolution in favour of clerical marriage as early as December 1547; but a bill to that effect did not get through both houses of parliament till the spring of 1549. 'It were better,' said the preamble to

[1] Wriothesley's *Chronicle (Camden Society)* I, p. 184.
[2] Ibid., *Chronicle*, II, 89 and 95.

the Act 'for priests and other ministers of the church to live chaste, and without marriage: whereby they might better attend to the ministry of the gospel and be less distracted with secular cares, so that it were much to be wished that they would of themselves abstain. But great filthiness of living, with other inconveniences, had followed on the laws that compelled chastity and prohibited marriage: so that it was better they should be suffered to marry than be so restrained.' The Lateran Council of 1123 could forbid clergymen to marry and eventually to get them separated from their wives: but it could not prevent 'other inconveniences'. Zealots could maintain that in the next world clergymen's wives would be turned into black cats. But in the reeve's tale Chaucer makes the miller of Trumpington's wife to be the daughter of the vicar of the parish. 'She was fostered in a nunnery,' and by reason of her superior social station she was as proud and pert as a magpie and looked down on her husband's relations and the neighbours generally, and this though her father and mother had presumably waived a marriage ceremony in church.

A few years after Chaucer's time there seems to have been a kind of religious revival in Wales and the concubine-keeping clergymen went to Bishop de la Bere of St. David's and urged that, to avoid eternal punishment, they should have leave to dismiss their ladies. 'You shall have nothing of the kind,' said the bishop sharply. 'Why, I make about five thousand pounds a year out of the fines I levy to allow you to keep them, and the last thing I want is that you should get rid of them.'[1] Doctor Gascoigne was a spiteful Oxford don and it is, perhaps, not well to take all his stories seriously. But the later medieval records of the disciplinary

---

[1] *Loci e libro Veritatum*, p. 35.

courts of the Welsh and neighbouring dioceses show that charges of this kind were amply justified.[1] Mission preachers inveighed against the practice in vain. That it was a mortal sin to listen to the mass of a concubinary priest was the cry of one of them.

While the suppression of the religious houses was going on there was a considerable movement among the clergy in favour of turning concubines into wives. Irregular unions were exchanged for regular. Nothing, however, shocked the ordinary layman so much as the regularization of unions of this kind. 'The vicar of Mendlesham [Suffolk] my neighbour,' wrote Sir Thomas Tyrell to Cromwell, 'hath brought home his woman and children into his vicarage, openly declaring how he is married to her, and she is his lawful wife. This act by him done is in this country a monster and many do grudge at it.'[2] When John Palmes, rector of Bentworth, Hampshire, took this step, he was deprived by Bishop Gardiner. He wrote to complain to Cromwell: 'The parson of Burghfield [Berkshire] has kept a concubine these twenty years openly and has children by her, by dispensation it is said, and no man seeth black in his eye.'[3] Erasmus might throw the weight of his great authority into the scale in favour of clerical marriage, but his reasoning did not convince the King. Henry was violently opposed to the practice. He professed to fear that the clergy would gain the dominion over kings and make ecclesiastical property hereditary,[4] and would breed so fast that they would in time swamp the laity: a fear which was so far justified as to influence the theories of Malthus nearly three centuries later. 'St. Paul knew,' said Bishop Gardiner, 'that if a bishop or priest were once married, his wife must

---

[1] See *English Historical Review*, vol. XLIV (1929), p. 6.
[2] Wright, *Suppression*, p. 160.   [3] *L.P.*, XIV (I), 206.
[4] *L.P.*, XVI, 737.

pass with all her faults: and it should be too late to tell what she should be.'[1] And it was for like reasons that Queen Elizabeth, struck by the 'lack of discreet and sober behaviour in many ministers of the church, both in choosing of their wives and undiscreet living with them', ordered that 'no manner of priest or deacon shall hereafter take to his wife any manner of woman until after his examination by the bishop of the diocese and two justices of the peace'.

In respect of marriage, the former religious were, of course, under the same rules as the rest of the clergy, and directly it was safe to do so they married in shoals, as Archdeacon Harpsfield admits. That his assertion was justified is shown by the figures for one diocese alone. In that of Norwich nearly one hundred former monks canons and friars are on a list of clergy deprived for marriage by Mary's government.[2] St. Margaret's, Westminster, seems to have been almost as fashionable a church for marriages as it is to-day, and its registers show that a large number of clergy were married there during King Edward's reign, including the London Dominican friar, Doctor Aglionby.

Mary's accession was equivalent to the triumph of conservatives at a general election; and, as has been shown already, it was welcomed generally. Unluckily for the Queen, she threw herself into the arms of conservatives of the die-hard kind and further weakened her position by her fatal Spanish marriage. With most of the legislation of the last twenty years went the act allowing the clergy to marry, and wholesale deprivations were soon to be the rule. 'The parsons and curates of the City of London that were wedded were cited to appear at the Consistory in

---

[1] *Letters*, Ed. Muller, p. 305.
[2] *English Historical Review*, vol. XLVIII (1933), pp. 43-64.

Paul's before the Bishop of London's commissioners and there deprived of their benefices, and those that were and had been religious men were deprived both of their wives and benefices also.' In the following November there was a ceremony at St. Paul's which must have been worth watching. 'Five men — three priests and two temporal men — did open penance. The three priests were married, one was a canon of Elsing Spital, and one a Black Friar, and the third an Austin Friar. And this was their penance: first to come out of the vestry with sheets upon their backs, and each of them a rod in his hands with a taper light: and first came and kneeled before the high altar, and there the (Bishop) Suffragan gave them their discipline: and then went down before the Cross: and when the preacher had taken his benediction of the bishop in the midst of the church, they came down to the bishop and kneeled down in the midst of the church, and there had their discipline of him and he kissed them: and so went unto the Cross and stood there all the (sermon) time, and when he came unto the beads (bidding prayer) they turned unto the preacher and kneeled down and asked forgiveness there of him, and then he showed their opinions openly in the pulpit.' All over the country, clergymen and their wives were appearing before the bishop of the diocese or his commissary agreeing (almost invariably) to a divorce, marching round cathedrals carrying candles and receiving a whipping.

These clergy, who had of course been first deprived of their livings, were now free to take another benefice and the greater number speedily did so. Their children were legally mere bastards, and their deserted wives, left to shift for themselves, sometimes consoled themselves with new husbands. The former religious who had been deprived for marriage had, of course, their pensions to fall back on.

John Westgate alias Bower, sometime a monk of Bury St. Edmunds, was in the year following the deprivations dwelling in Bury, and it was reported of him that 'he was married and his wife died two years ago, and he is impotent and lame and hath no other promotion or living but his said pensions.'[1] The two pensions produced annually a little over £10 — say £300 nowadays — and a widower could naturally live on that. The pensions of the married religious were, however, none too secure: and if a bill which was introduced into parliament had passed, they would have been deprived of them altogether. If, however, the former religious had remained single, they were in the position of another ex-monk of Bury, Sir William Buccall, 'an honest and Catholic man, unmarried and parson of Elmswell, valued at £12, having also a pension of £6 13s. 4d.' (together nearly £500 a year). This clergyman was in no fear of disturbance and held the living continuously from 1550 to his death in 1568.

IV

There still remains to consider the case of those few religious whom Mary was able to restore to the cloister. Had the Queen got her own way there would, no doubt, have been a very extensive restoration of the religious houses. But how was she to get those who had invested in monastic lands to disgorge? It was indeed a conservative in religion, Lord Paget, who was chiefly instrumental in wrecking any chance of restoration. Even in those cases where restoration was effected, it was not possible to put

[1] *English Historical Review*, XLVIII (1933), p. 225. John Bower had a pension of £6 13s. 4d. at the surrender of Bury. The second pension of £4 was presumably from some suppressed chantry.

back the religious who had surrendered their houses to
Henry VIII. To take one example, that of Westminster.
In a list of twenty-three brethren drawn up after Mary's
restoration there are only two or three of the former monks
of Westminster.[1] The remainder, representing men in
whom the religious vocation was strong, came from all
over the country: two or three from St. Alban's and Glastonbury, and two from Ramsey can be certainly identified.
That the old foundation was not more fully represented is
easily explained. The abbot, as has been already pointed
out, had joined the innovating party; of the six monks who
became prebendaries, four were dead and the other two
had married: a course of action which seems to have been
followed by many of the minor canons and pensioned
monks, and which naturally debarred them from promotion by Mary's government. The restored house of the
Carthusians at Sheen was stocked with members of the
order from nearly all their former houses in England: and
of the fifteen brethren only three were of the old foundation.
Prior Man had become, first, Dean of Chester and then
Bishop of Man; while several of the other monks were in
enjoyment of country livings, which they saw no reason to
surrender.

With Elizabeth's accession, the fate of the restored houses
was sealed. In July 1559 'the houses of religious erected by
Queen Mary, as the monks of Westminster, the nuns and
brethren of Sion, the Black Friars of Smithfield and the
friars of Greenwich' were all suppressed. Within a year the
Carthusians were allowed to leave England in peace, to set
up Sheen Anglorum at Bruges. Since Prior Chauncy
states that they numbered twelve professed monks and three
lay brothers, the whole community must have emigrated.

[1] Pearce, *Monks of Westminster*, p. 214.

The monks of Westminster do not seem to have followed this course. Abbot Feckenham's fate was the harshest, and this learned and peace-loving prelate spent his last years in the Tower or under surveillance. There does not seem to be any record of the fate of most of the others. Stephen Bailey, one of the monks of St. Alban's, who had resigned his livings to re-enter religion, now went back to his native town; the burial is recorded in the parish register on February 1st, 1559, of 'Stephanus Bailie, *monachus*'. Of the remainder, the only other name is that of Hugh Phillips, late monk of Westminster and before that of Ramsey, who was indicted for saying mass in London in 1576.

As to the remainder of the former religious who held strict conservative views, they do not appear to have been seriously disturbed; though some of them were subjected in 1562 to surveillance of a mild kind.[1] Among the former heads there were Roger Marshall, former prior of Sempringham, whose residence was restricted to Newmarket or six miles round, and Robert Pursglove, Bishop of Hull and former Prior of Gisburn.[2] The only ordinary monks on this list were Roger Thompson, 'late a superstitious monk of Mountgrace and unlearned', who was restrained from the dioceses of York and Durham, and John Grete, a priest, late beneficed in Hampshire (formerly a monk of Hyde by Winchester), who was a prisoner in the Counter in Wood Street, London. Others, again, whom it is not so easy to trace, acted as chaplains to members of great families, who were 'evil inclined towards religion, and forbore coming to church and participating of the sacraments'. One of these was Anthony Clarke, formerly a Cistercian monk of Stratford Langthorne in Essex. After the suppression of his house he had accepted more than one

---

[1] Gee, *The Elizabethan Clergy*, p. 179.   [2] See p. 250.

living in Sussex and a prebend of Chichester Cathedral. He was deprived of these in 1560 for refusing to take the oath of supremacy, and became chaplain to Lord Montague at Cowdray, who was as loath to part with the type of worship to which he was accustomed as he was to surrender the estates (Battle among them) which his family had acquired at the suppression of the religious houses. Clarke's will shows clearly enough where his sympathies lay. 'A painted image which I had of the late virtuous queen of holy memory,' went to Doctor Langdale, another of the deprived prebendaries of Chichester, but the 'messuages in the Cathedral close', with house, stables and garden and the large amount of ready money show, first that he did not acquiesce in his deprivation, and secondly that he was quite comfortably off.[1]

The vast majority of the surviving religious, apart from those who were already in possession of bishoprics, whether diocesan or suffragan, had by now accepted the ecclesiastical changes as they came. Gilbert Berkeley, Bishop of Bath and Wells 1559-81, had been a Franciscan friar; John Scory, Bishop of Hereford 1560-65, a Dominican friar; Edmund Freake, Bishop of Rochester 1572-75 and of Norwich 1575-85, an Augustinian canon; and William Downham, Bishop of Chester 1561-77, canon of the house of Bonhommes at Ashridge; while the deans of Norwich and Exeter had been respectively a Benedictine monk and a Dominican friar. As to the rank and file of the religious they were by now absorbed into the ranks of the parochial clergy. Their pensions continued to be paid till their deaths, which had to be reported to the bishop by the churchwardens of the parish in which the holder of the pension dwelled. An additional precaution seems to have

[1] His will is in the Chichester wills, now in the registry at Winchester.

been taken by the bishops, who at their visitations caused the former religious to produce the dispensations from their vows which they had received when their monastery was dissolved. In the ordination lists of the diocese of Lincoln it is recorded that on December 21st, 1532, a certain Richard Blackwin was ordained sub-deacon at Luddington by the Bishop of Ascalon, Bishop Longland's suffragan, as a Dominican friar of Leicester. In 1576 a report which was sent by the Bishop of Lincoln to Lambeth states that the then parson of Knaptoft, Leicestershire, was Richard Blackwin, sixty-four years of age, married, ordained at Luddington by a suffragan in the time of John Longland, Bishop of Lincoln, having no letters to show because he was a religious man, ignorant in the Latin tongue and the scriptures.[1]

Such was the history of all but a small minority of the dispossessed religious, whether monks, canons or friars, and such was the way that they made the best of a bad job.

---

[1] 'State of Church' (*Lincoln Record Society*, vol. XXIII), p. 39.

EPILOGUE

EPILOGUE

HORACE WALPOLE says in one of his letters, that there were in his day freak writers on history (he might well have included himself among them) who were prepared to make a hero of James I, and to geld Charles II. He might have said the same thing to-day, when paradox is made to pass for historical evidence, and bluster for historical research. The history of the suppression of the monasteries lends itself to more misrepresentation than any other event in our annals, and gallons of ink have been wasted on it by writers, for the most part sadly ill-equipped for their task. 'Blessed are mathematics,' says Gioberti, 'for they do not attract dilettanti'; but history, and especially that of the suppression of the monasteries, does.

There are the ecclesiastical and political propagandists — Clio's worst enemies — and almost more dangerous are the smaller fry of antiquaries, who vent their whimsies with disgusting frequency in the pages of local newspapers and handbooks. To them a potsherd is of equal size to a pyramid, and they work for all that it is worth what Mr. Samuel Weller called 'this 'ere water-cart business'. 'The destructionists of the sixteenth-century,' says one of them, 'were the heralds of the great rebellion and the commonwealth, the precursors of the Revolution, and the preparers of the way for the Radicals and Communists of the present period.'[1]

Two sets of antagonists have waged war on the subject of the suppression of the English monasteries. The first may be called the scavenging party. It has had a long innings. Included in its ranks have been men of all stages

[1] F. G. Lee, *History of Thame Church*, p. 193.

of intellectual development, from Hobbes, who, very wisely, observed that 'all the changes in religion in this world are due to one and the same cause, and that is unpleasing priests', and Voltaire, who in his *Lettres sur les Anglais* urged that the prosperity of England dated from the destruction of the religious houses, to the old inhabitant who points out the underground passage which led from a monastery to a nunnery. In the course of the nineteenth century this party began to go into eclipse as a result of the general growth of toleration and sentimentalism and of a more intelligent treatment of historical material and antiquities. It has, however, recently been revived and may now, with its former crudities removed, be taken to relate the facts about the last days of the monasteries far more truly than its rival can claim to do.

The adherents of the other party are the merry Englanders, who would have us believe that persons in the Middle Ages spent their whole time in going to mass or in dancing round the maypole. Some years after the suppression a golden haze began to spread, which affected persons of very different temperaments. The scarcely orthodox Lord Herbert of Cherbury (1583-1648) admits that many people in his day felt uncomfortable about the fate of the religious houses, while the scruples of his contemporary, Sir Henry Spelman (1564-1641), went so far that he not only surrendered the tithes which accrued to him as the result of the suppression, but vainly tried to get his neighbours to follow his example. It is worth while to read his *History of Sacrilege* to see what strange arguments the subject can produce. Since the book begins in the garden of Eden, with Adam, Eve and the serpent conspiring together to deprive the Almighty of the 'priest's portion', an apple, goes on through the Old Testament and is further garnished with examples of sacrilege from the histories of Greece and Rome (for the gods of the heathen had their rights too), it is evident that Sir Henry cast his net pretty wide to find instances of the fate of those who got possession of ecclesiastical property of any kind. But his book had considerable influence, and in the eighteenth century antiquaries like Browne Willis were profoundly moved by it. That Doctor Johnson, too, should be affected by its tenets was inevitable. His prejudices were so strong that when he was in Edinburgh he only consented to visit St. Giles on the ground that it had been 'once a church', and to his remark that he hoped that John Knox had been buried in the highway ('I have been looking at his reformation') may be added that which he passed when he viewed with indignation the ruins of Oseney and Rewley near Oxford, 'I never read of a monastery, but I could fall on my knees and kiss the pavement'.

Early in the nineteenth century the movement, while retaining its antiquarian flavour, began to take on a political aspect. William Cobbett's *History of the Protestant Reformation* is one of the most amazing pieces of rubbish that was ever written, while Disraeli's *Sybil* is not much better, so far as its views of the result of the suppression and of the methods by which the new owners came by their lands are concerned. The exploitation of the monks of the sixteenth century for ecclesiastical or political purposes will doubtless go on till the day of doom. But it is sad to find in a sober set of volumes like the *Victoria County History* such statements as this: 'the lands (of Lenton Priory) have changed hands with remarkable frequency'. This is not history, but sob-stuff.

What losses, then, did the suppression of the monasteries really involve?

To contemporaries, as has been indicated already, the loss of prayers came first. This is what the Germans call a 'meta-historical' question, and far be it from me to reckon what loss did occur in this connection. Every impartial person must admit that Sir Thomas More in his *Supplication of Souls* got the better of John Frith; yet when the chantries perished ten years after the monasteries it was the conservative Bishop Gardiner who approved of their suppression. 'I understand,' wrote he in January 1546 to Sir William (soon to be Lord) Paget, 'it hath pleased the Court of Parliament to give in to the King's Majesty's hands the disposition of all hospitals, chantries and other houses, whereof I am very glad.'[1]

Then there was the loss of pilgrimages. Another meta-historical question is that of faith healing. The destruction of the shrines of the saints put a stop to that. But it would be a mistake to look upon medieval pilgrimages solely from that point of view. They were far more like modern cruises or tours. The Venetians, for example, organized trips to the Holy Land, and were the forerunners of modern travel agencies. Pilgrims did not always do credit to these expeditions, as we have seen from the case of Mrs. Smith of Walsingham. The jaundiced Langland in *Piers Plowman* went so far as to say that pilgrimages were undertaken by hermits accompanied by their wenches; and if Chaucer's pilgrims were quite respectable middle-class people, the stories which some of them told, and the unprintable words which some of them used, would cause a modern hotel manager to eject such guests from the lounge or the coffee room.

Robert Aske's claim that the monastic churches were the beauties of the land is, of course, undisputed. Nothing can be more appalling than the destruction which followed the

---

[1] *Letters*, Ed. Muller, p. 218.

suppression, and nothing can be more cynical than the often quoted description by the reverend Mr. Portinari of his doings in Lewes priory, or the letter of the reverend Mr. Crayford to the new proprietor of Titchfield abbey. 'You and Mrs. Wriothesley won't scruple to sell altars, etc. following the example of a devout Bishop of Rome.' That had happened at all former suppressions. The lead and bells went, but often the rest of the building remained almost intact, and thus in a few cases the buildings could be patched up and used again. The priory church of Bath, and that of the Cistercian abbey of Dore, were restored in the early seventeenth century, and the priory church of Brinkburn in the nineteenth. It was the eighteenth century, and not the sixteenth, which saw the ruin of the great abbey church of Eynsham, and which all but completed that of Glastonbury. However, a great many more of the buildings remain than is sometimes realized.[1] Some monastic churches were bought by the inhabitants, or by individuals of the locality, and so we still have the churches of Tewkesbury, St. Albans, Sherborne, Romsey and many more. The naves of churches in which the inhabitant had rights saved others.[2] Many of the domestic buildings were incorporated in the houses which the new proprietors were obliged to build on the site. Apart from Milton, few, if any, of the churches were left, but Ford, Lacock, Mottisfont, and many others retain nearly all the original domestic buildings, cloister, refectory, dormitory, etc.

Is it paradoxical to say that more of the medieval buildings remain in England than in the countries where the monasteries were to survive till the nineteenth or even the twentieth century? Would not the desire of the monks to

[1] A good list of these will be found in F. H. Crossley, *The English Abbey*, pp. xi to xiv.
[2] See above, Chapter II, p. 64.

277

be up to date have caused them to rebuild their houses according to the taste of the day? How many of the existing monasteries on the Continent retain medieval features? Go up into the hills to the south of the Lake of Zurich and visit the great Benedictine monastery of Einsiedeln, soon to celebrate its thousandth year of continuous existence. 'I should fear,' wrote Samuel Butler, 'that the art of heaven will be a good deal tainted with Barocco, if not with Rococo, if not with First Empire.' And so the monks of Einsiedeln seem to have thought when they rebuilt their abbey. So did those of St. Gall, of Melk, of Fulda, of the Grande Chartreuse, in fact of any continental abbey one could mention. Rarely, as at Alcobaça in Portugal, or at Jumièges in Normandy, the medieval churches were suffered to remain, but it is to be doubted if the domestic buildings ever survived in their original form.

The question of how far hospitality and almsgiving suffered by the suppression is a very difficult one and can never be satisfactorily answered. It has already been pointed out that under the Act of Suppression of 1536 the grantees of monastic lands were bound to keep 'an honest continual house and household in the same site and precinct'. Thus it was intended that inn-keeping should still be a condition of land holding. Whether it was fulfilled may be doubted. But in any case, as has been shown already, the building of inns by monasteries, and the gradual improvement of hotel accommodation everywhere, showed that individual hospitality on the grand scale was falling into disuse. When Henry VIII went to Dunstable in the summer of 1537 he preferred to put up at the White Horse inn rather than at the priory, much to the chagrin of the obsequious Prior Markham.[1] In the north,

[1] *L.P.*, xii (2), 413.

however, the result of the suppression must have been far more felt and in particular by the poorer sort of travellers.

Just as grantees of monastic lands were expected to keep up hospitality, so, apparently, were they expected to go on with the old system of doles. 'I should like you to know,' wrote a correspondent of Cromwell, early in 1539, 'what people say about what relief they have since the suppression of the religious houses. They say that they were never in so good case were it not for the unreasonable number of hounds and greyhounds which the gentlemen keep and compel their tenants to keep . . . These dogs eat up the broken meat and bread which should relieve the poor.'[1] This was the very charge which was so often levied against the monks. Apart from the unsystematic nature of almsgiving of this kind there can be no doubt that a great many of the charitable institutions were in sad want of reform. 'Please,' wrote Sir Richard Gresham, Lord Mayor of London, to the King, 'let the Lord Mayor and Corporation have the rule of St. Mary Spital, St. Bartholomew, St. Thomas, and Towerhill, which were founded in London for the aid of poor and wretched people, and not to maintain canons, priests and monks to live at pleasure.'[2] All four of these institutions still flourish and aid poor people.

When the monasteries were dissolved life interests of all kinds were respected, including those of the annuitants or corrodians. Indeed the system went on to some extent. 'Please,' wrote King Edward VI to the Dean and Chapter of Gloucester in October 1547, 'admit to the first alms room in that Cathedral after the placing of those whom we have heretofore commanded, Thomas Sanders, labourer, who was injured in my late father's time by the fall of a great piece of ordnance at Boulogne.'[3]

[1] *L.P.*, XIV (2), 810.   [2] *L.P.*, XIII (2), 492.   *S.P. Dom., Addenda*, p. 338.

On the whole it may be reckoned that though a great deal of promiscuous almsgiving disappeared as a result of the suppression, that event made no great difference to the problem of the deserving poor as a whole. Its effect has been very much exaggerated. Even so cautious a writer on the conservative side as the Abbé Constant can write 'Le paupérisme, une des plaies les plus hideuses de l'Angleterre contemporaine, date de la destruction des monastères'.[1] Was there, then, no 'paupérisme' in France in the years before the French Revolution?

So with the problem of the valiant and sturdy beggars. It was then, as now, difficult to distinguish between them and the poor and impotent, and the attempts which were made by successive governments to solve the problem extended over a period of at least one hundred and fifty years before the dissolution. One statute after another was passed against these 'abbey-lubbers',[2] a term which exceptionally ignorant sentimentalist writers have thought to refer to the religious after the dissolution. This class of rogues was scarcely affected by the suppression and continued to trouble the authorities, as much before as after that event. And it was a sensible suggestion that somebody made in 1537 that the Crown should inaugurate a great new road system and use the forced labour of valiant beggars to carry it through.[3]

The loss to learning as the result of the scattering of the contents of the monastic libraries was very great. No care seems to have been taken to preserve books and manuscripts other than those which concerned questions of property. It was only gradually that such as survived were gathered together by learned scholars, with Archbishop Matthew

---

[1] *La Réforme en Angleterre*, p. 113. There is now an English translation of this excellent book.
[2] See above, p. 32.   [3] *L.P.*, XIII (2), 1.

Parker at their head. Doctor Montague James's writings and catalogues have shown us how surprisingly large is the number of books which were thus saved. It would seem that in some cases many of the books passed into the private possession of the religious, and especially of the heads of houses, at the dissolution, either by purchase or by the simpler method of opportune borrowing. Practically the whole of the library of the Yorkshire priory of Monk Bretton was bought by the prior and monks, and twenty years after nearly a hundred of its books are found in the possession of one or other of them;[1] while the last prior of Lanthony by Gloucester seems to have removed most of the books from the library of that priory to his country house at Brockworth.

The neglect of books on the part of monks had excited the ire of Petrarch and Boccaccio, and their complaints were echoed in England by Doctor Gascoigne.[2] After the death of Thomas Walsingham at St. Alban's in about 1422 not a single monastic historian either of the first or of any other rank emerges; and how hostile the ordinary monk was to humanism, Erasmus, for one, knew only too well. Did he not find the sub-prior of Walsingham taking Greek letters for Arabic? The Observant Friar Peto told Cromwell's agent at Antwerp in 1538 that he made little of the suppression of abbeys, but thought they might be put to better use.[3] Unluckily his wish was not granted.

If Henry VIII's zeal for education had only been more powerful than his dread of an overdraft at the bank a great many of the monasteries could have been turned into seats of learning. At Oxford, the great Augustinian priory of Oseney, and the Cistercian abbey of Rewley, not to speak of the four houses of friars could have been

[1] Hunter, *South Yorkshire*, II, 274. [2] See above, p. 41. [3] *L.P.*, XIII (1), 115.

adapted for educational purposes; and at Cambridge, Barnwell Priory could have been made by the King to perform the useful function which Bishop Alcock had assigned to the nunnery of St. Radegund. And in the country the larger monasteries could have been turned into colleges or schools. Schools like Bath and St. Albans passed along with the rest of monastic property into the hands of the Crown at the dissolution, and of the few that there were, most were refounded in the time of Edward VI. The Crown in the interval does not seem, however, to have been altogether to blame. At Bath, in particular, it was the mayor and corporation who converted most of the property to their own use.[1] On the whole it may be said that the suppression did not affect more than the rich boys who were being brought up under the eye of the abbot, and who would now have to be under the care of a great nobleman, and the poor boys in the almonry or choir schools. If Mr. Leach's figure[2] of 1500 as the total number of the poor boys is correct, a considerable number of them must have lost some form of education. But by no means the whole number; for those in the choir schools of the cathedrals, old, like Canterbury and new, like Westminster, remained undisturbed, while the ushers, along with the rest of the corrodians, received pensions.

Sentimentalist writers would lead us to believe that those parishes which were served by monks or canons regular were deprived of religious ministrations as a result of the suppression, which, in fact, made no difference to them whatever. It has been pointed out that religious houses of the Premonstratensian and to a smaller extent of other orders, bestowed the best benefices in their gift on their own

---

[1] Katherine Symons, *History of Bath School*, p. 676.
[2] A. F. Leach, *Educational Charters*, p. xxxii. See above, p. 38.

canons. These men went on as incumbents of their parishes until death or marriage put an end to their tenure of the living. A canon of the Augustinian priory of Carlisle, for instance, was rector of Bewcastle from 1534 till his death in 1581. Very occasionally monks are found in charge of small parishes or chapelries. Three monks of the Cistercian abbey of Hayles were vicars of three parishes in the immediate neighbourhood. The only difference that the dissolution made to these men was that they got small pensions to supplement their stipends. All three went on till their deaths.[1]

As to small parishes where vicarages had not been ordained, chapelries, and the like, there were much the same if not more complaints of neglect on the part of the patrons to provide spiritual help before the dissolution as there were after it. 'The new prior,' complained the inhabitants of Spalding in 1518, 'has robbed us of two of our chaplains [or as we should say to-day assistant curates] and only hires unlearned ones, because he won't offer an adequate stipend. Those we have got now are both incontinent.' 'The prior of Bodmin,' complained the parishioners of that town, 'has appointed his own brother to the vicarage, who lives in London and vexes the inhabitants with citations. The prior has appointed a priest of ill living and disposition to serve the cure and finds no priest to sing in the outlying chapels.' 'The prior and convent of Lenton,' said the people of Wigston, Leicestershire, at the Bishop of Lincoln's visitation in 1518, 'are so negligent that the chancel of our church is ruinous; the rain falls in on the high altar, the ornaments rot and no distribution is made to the poor.' No doubt the squires who succeeded the monks as

[1] *Transactions of the Bristol and Gloucestershire Archaeological Society*, vol. XLIX (1927), p. 65.

patrons of churches or farmers of benefices were equally
neglectful of what was, in fact, a legal obligation; but they
were only following their predecessors' example, and it is
improbable that the suppression made any immediate
difference to the supply of clergy or the upkeep of the
churches.

That the Crown, at any rate, was mindful of its duty to
them is shown by a letter from Sir Richard Rich to the
local receiver of the Court of Augmentations in 1541. 'The
Bishop of Worcester tells me that such churches in
Gloucestershire, Worcestershire, Herefordshire, Shropshire
and Staffordshire as belong to the King (i.e. as successor to
the monks) are in such a state of decay as to need immediate repairs. You are to see what is necessary to be done
without delay.'[1] The monks of Malmesbury had a cell in
Devonshire called Pilton. They were bound to provide a
chaplain to serve the parish church there. In 1536 they
surrendered their property to the Crown. When it was
leased to Richard Duke, Esq., the Crown allowed £6 (say
£180) a year out of the rent for the maintenance of a
curate, and this charge went on for nearly 200 years.[2] All
that happened in parishes of this kind was that whereas the
curates in charge had been appointed and paid by the
monasteries they were now appointed and paid by the
farmers of the benefice. Complaints of neglect later in
the century usually arise from the fact that the supply of
clergy, as the result of the seizure of so much church property by the Crown, gradually became inadequate. And
this led the inhabitants of Durham and Northumberland to
complain to Queen Elizabeth in 1565 that 'vicars have to
serve two to five chapels each, far from the parish churches,
which have no priests unless they be vagabond Scots, who

---

[1] *L.P.*, XVI, 648.   [2] Oliver, *Monasticon dioecesis Exoniensis*, p. 245.

dare not abide in their country. They were,' they go on, 'better served when they belonged to abbeys.'[1] There was a very similar grumble from Pontefract in the time of Queen Mary.

The question as to the provision which was made for the monks has already been discussed. The total number to be provided for after the surrender of the greater houses was about 3000.[2] What a difference is this number from that which obtained in other countries in the eighteenth and early nineteenth centuries. It has been calculated that there were in France under Louis XV no fewer than 23,000 monks and 37,000 nuns. In Spain, in 1836, there were 31,000 monks and 22,000 nuns, while the Emperor Joseph II is said to have ejected 30,000 monks from their houses. How many of these received pensions? The revolutionary governments of France after 1791 and the Liberal administrations of Spain and Portugal of 1836 could not be expected to give them, while princes like Joseph II were too much imbued with the spirit of the *Aufklärung* to be eager to spend money in that way. But Charles III of Spain, a devout believer, behaved in no way more charitably, and nothing can be more pathetic than the story of the poor Jesuits, torn in 1767 from their convents, and hurried on shipboard to be wafted for months about the Mediterranean. Nothing of the kind happened in England. When the Vicar of Preston next Faversham in Kent retired from his living in 1535 he was given a pension of £5. When Faversham abbey was dissolved in 1539 one of the monks, Thomas Deve, also got a pension of £5; but he was soon able to add to it the vicarage of Selling, which he held, with his pension,

---

[1] *S.P. Dom, Addenda*, XII, p. 577.
[2] Adding about 2000 who had taken dispensations under the Act of 1536 and about 1600 friars, the total number of male religious would appear to have been just under 7000: of female, under 2000.

till his death in 1558. Which, then, was the better off, the retired vicar or the retired monk?[1]

A few words may be devoted to a somewhat similar question, that of the provision made for the servants of monasteries. The greatest possible nonsense has been written on the subject. One scribe has gone so far as to assert that 88,000 people were thrown out of work at the suppression. How he arrives at this figure he does not, of course, explain. It is obvious that the suppression could not affect the employees of the monastic estates which were leased out, as they nearly all were, while it is difficult to see how those on the demesne or home farm could suffer, since they would be wanted just as much after as before the dissolution. Therefore, the question can only concern the domestic servants, against whose swollen numbers the bishops had so often thundered.

When the large Augustinian priory of Butley in Suffolk surrendered early in 1538 the number of its 'household', beginning with the canons and ending with the dairy maids, was eighty-four.[2] Of these the twelve agricultural labourers, the five carters, the three shepherds, the two woodkeepers, the swineherd, the two wheelwrights and the keeper of the fish-house would have continued to be employed on the home farm by the Duke of Norfolk's bailiff, and then by the Frith family which bought the property six years later, and so probably would the under-steward, the surveyor, the cooper, the two keepers of the weirs, the smith, the two warreners, the two sheep reeves, the slaughtermen. The eight yeomen waiters, the three in the pantry and buttery, the barber, the gardener, the huntsman and the six women in the laundry and dairy, doubtless lost their jobs. It has, however, been pointed out that the 'rewards' which were given to the

[1] See above, p. 257.   [2] *L.P.*, XIII (1), 394.

servants of the monasteries by the Crown, or by the individual who paid the pension, represented a whole year's wages.[1] It is difficult to conceive that trustees winding-up an estate nowadays would be so generous. Moreover, this class of servant would soon be wanted in the new houses which sprang up on the site or were formed out of the domestic buildings of a suppressed house. The examples of Sir Thomas Wriothesley at Titchfield abbey and of Lord Sandys at Mottisfont priory show that the new proprietors lost no time in fitting up their new abodes, and the building trade must have flourished finely. And when the new house was finished and my Lord and my Lady installed in it, they could hardly do better than employ the laundresses and dairy maids and baker and brewer of the monks. For they knew their job and though the monastic church may have been pulled down as 'superfluous', the bakehouse, the brewhouse and the laundry were 'not superfluous' but were retained and had in use.

'The patrimony of the monks was divided between the jackals who dogged the heels of a spendthrift monarch.' This is a quotation from a popular handbook; it could hardly emanate from the works of any true servant of Clio. The best corrective to facile explanations of this kind would be to study carefully Professor Savine's table concerning the disposition of the monastic lands which is printed as an appendix to Mr. H. A. L. Fisher's *Political History of England, 1485-1547*. It shows that out of 1593 grants of monastic lands made during the reign of Henry VIII not more than one in forty were gifts; the rest were sales or exchanges. The Crown first leased most of the lands and then gradually sold them, a process which went on for at least a hundred years and which was accompanied by the

---

[1] e.g. at Waltham abbey, *V.C.H. Essex*, II. 160.

waste which invariably goes hand in hand with confiscatory methods. The few men who got the lands by gift were those who had rendered great services to the Crown, like the Dukes of Norfolk and Suffolk and the Earl of Shrewsbury, who between them had been so useful in the 'commotion times' in Lincolnshire and the North: or who, like Sir Thomas Cromwell, Sir Richard Rich and Sir Thomas Pope, had helped to create a balanced budget. They were rewarded by the nation in just the same way as was the first Duke of Marlborough when he had a grant of Blenheim (*né* Woodstock) Park, or the first Duke of Wellington when he got Stratfield Saye. As to the rest, the new owners, whether they were representatives of the founders, men high in favour of Court, or mere speculators, had to buy the lands at their true value. Whether he held religious views approximating to the new or to the old learning, made no difference to an investor. Not all of those who were granted or bought the lands were of the new way of thinking: and many of them, like the Howards and Brownes, were to suffer later on for their adherence to the old learning. And so Queen Mary found when she tried to effect restoration on a large scale.

The thorny question as to whether the new landlords were or were not harsher than the monks can probably never be solved. The affirmative statement rests chiefly on the evidence of the very violent ecclesiastical[1] and political firebrand, the ex-friar Henry Brinklow who, in his 'Complaynt of Roderyck Mors', in order to blacken the present has highly coloured the past; for most of the neglect of alms and hospitality with which he charges the new proprietors had been charged by writers like Doctor Gascoigne against the monks. It was the rapid advance in the cost of living

[1] He was an iconoclast of the most reckless kind.

which chiefly caused the rise in rents in the sixteenth century, and rents would have had to be put up in any case, whoever the landlord may have been. Does anybody seriously maintain that the colleges of Oxford and Cambridge are easier landlords than private individuals? Their bursars see to it that they are not: or of what use are they? So with the monks. They did not wish to be easy landlords. Even if they had so wished, the patrons, the high stewards and the country gentry who had so large a share in overseeing or administering their property would have seen to it that they were not.

The monasteries of the sixteenth century were not 'deformatories to which people were sent if they were too good to be practical'. Had they been what sentimentalists would have us believe, Cardinals Contarini, Caraffa, Sadoleto and Pole, together with the Archbishops of Salerno and Brindisi, would scarcely have reported that the religious orders had deteriorated to such an extent that they had become a grave scandal to seculars and did much harm by their example. They would scarcely have recommended that, provided existing interests were protected, the orders should be totally abolished: and, as a preliminary step, that they should be forbidden to receive novices, and that all unprofessed boys should be expelled from them.[1]

King Henry VIII and his visitors carried out these recommendations to the letter. First they dismissed the unprofessed boys and girls. Then they proceeded to total abolition, while carefully preserving all vested interests by grants of pensions or annuities to all who could lawfully claim them. Unluckily they did not carry out the cardinals' further recommendation that good religious should be put

---

[1] These recommendations of the year 1538 are printed in Kidd's *Documents of the Continental Reformation*, p. 314.

in to take the place of bad. The wheat and the tares perished together and over three hundred years were to pass before the religious orders, renewed and reformed, were to be seen again in England.

APPENDIX

APPENDIX TO CHAPTER X

THE careers of the religious after the suppression of the monasteries are not, as I have pointed out, by any means so difficult to trace as has been thought. In order to prove this, I will take a typical case, that of the large priory of Augustinian canons at Dunstable in Bedfordshire.

When this house surrendered on December 31st, 1539,[1] there were with the prior, twelve canons, all but two of whom were still in receipt of pensions in February 1556.[2] What had they been doing in the meantime?

1. *The Prior, Gervase Markham*, lived on at Dunstable, on his pension of £60 (say £1800), which must have been ample for his needs, especially as he did not follow the example of so many of his fellow abbots and priors and take a wife. He died in September 1561, and was buried in the parish, formerly the priory, church.

2. *The Sub-prior, Thomas Claybrooke*, had a pension of £9 (from £250 to £300 a year), and was living in 1548[3] at Hanbury in Staffordshire with William Markham, gentleman, the prior's brother. I have not been able to trace him any farther.

3. *Canon Richard Kent*, pension of £8. In 1548 he was

---

[1] *L.P.*, XIV (2), 770.

[2] In the Schedule known as Cardinal Pole's pension list (*P.R.O. Exchequer*, Misc. Books, vol. XXXI).

[3] All entries under the date 1548 are from the accounts of George Wright, Receiver for the Court of Augmentations for Bedfordshire and adjacent counties (*P.R.O. Augmentation Office*, Miscellanea bundle 26). Those of 1554 from the report of that year to the Exchequer on the pensioned religious of the diocese of Lincoln (*P.R.O. Exchequer* 101, 76/26). Those of 1543 from *Visitation of the Diocese of Lincoln*, now in the Lincoln episcopal registry. The dates of institution to livings are from episcopal registers.

'living at Pulloxhill, in the county of Bedford'. He was, in fact, vicar of Pulloxhill from 1540 until his death in 1554. Now, he did not obtain this living by chance. It had been in the gift of the prior and convent of Dunstable, who, shortly before the suppression, had given the next presentation to William Markham of Husborne Crawley, gentleman (the prior's brother), Adam Hilton of Dunstable, and Thomas Kent of Luton (Canon Kent's brother): in fact, a bargain, which was meant to, and did, secure for one of the canons a benefice then in the gift of the priory, and which was valued in the King's books at £9 10s. To this he added in 1553 the rectory of Higham Gobion, valued at £9. At the time of his death next year he was, therefore, enjoying an income from two livings and one pension which would be equivalent nowadays to nearly £800 a year.

4. *Canon George Edwards.* In 1548 he was curate of Hockliffe, near Dunstable. In 1557 he became rector of Eversholt, a living which he exchanged next year for that of Milton Bryan, in the parish church of which he was buried May 2nd, 1561. Pension £7, living nearly £12; together nowadays over £500 a year.

5. *Canon John Stalworth.* He became vicar of Husborne Crawley, Bedfordshire, early in 1546, probably as the result of a bargain like that of Canon Kent's, since the prior's brother lived in the parish and the living had formerly been in the gift of Dunstable priory. However, he resigned it after a few months and went on to become chaplain to Lord Windsor, at Princes Risborough in Buckinghamshire, a parish of which he became perpetual curate two or three years later. In 1555 Lord Windsor presented him to the rectory of Greatworth,

Northamptonshire, and there he remained till his death
in 1590. Pension £7, living £9, equivalent of nearly
£500 a year.

6. *Canon Edmund Green.* In May 1548 he was living at
Leigh, Surrey (now Kent); in November 1548 at Harrow
on the Hill. He is probably identical with Edmund
Green, rector of Edburton, Sussex (a living, like Harrow,
in the gift of the Archbishop of Canterbury), from 1551
till his death in 1557. Pension £6, living £16, between
£600 and £700 a year.

7. *Canon Peter Whyppe,* pension of £6. His name is not on
the pension list of 1556, and there is no mention of him in
the receiver's accounts of 1548, so he was, presumably,
dead by then.

8. *Canon Richard Bowstret* (or Bulsted). In 1548 he was
dwelling in Sussex with Mr. Gage. In 1555 he became
vicar of Oving and also rector of Litlington, Sussex,
both of which livings he held till his death in 1557 or
1558. Pension £7, the two livings £23; about £900 a
year.

9. *Canon Augustine Curtis.* In 1548 he was living at Framfield, Sussex. He was, in fact, vicar of Framfield from
1544 and was deprived for marriage in 1554. He must,
however, have shed his wife, because at the time of his
death in 1559 he was vicar of Eastbourne and rector of
Litlington (in which parish he had succeeded his former
colleague, Canon Bowstret). Pension £8, two livings
£38; about £1200 a year.

10. *Canon Robert Somer.* In 1548 he was dwelling at Easthampstead Latimer, Buckinghamshire. He had been

rector of this parish since 1546 and was deprived for marriage in 1554. Pension £6, living £5; over £300 a year.

11. *Canon John Nyxe.* In 1543 he was curate of Lilley in Hertfordshire, with a pension from Dunstable. In 1545 he became vicar of Offley, Hertfordshire, of which he was deprived for marriage in 1554. Pension £5 6s. 8d., living £9; over £400 a year.

12. *Canon Nicholas Claybrooke.* In 1548 he was servant to Sir Ralph Pawlett. (No name of place.) He was rector of Puttenham, Hertfordshire, from 1558 till his death in 1565. Pension £2, living £10; over £300 a year.

13. *Canon John Percyvall.* Rector of Aston Clinton, Buckinghamshire, from 1556 and buried there February 12th, 1560-61. Also rector of Easthampstead Latimer from 1558 to 1561. Pension £2, livings £28; nearly £900 a year.

With a little trouble the fate of the dispossessed religious of most of the monasteries can be ascertained in a similar way. 'The Muse of History has perhaps mercifully spared the world what would have been a picture of deep distress and misery', writes a sentimentalist. The distress and misery of the former canons of Dunstable do not seem to have been very harrowing!

NOTE. Throughout this list and in the rest of the book I have reckoned the value of money in 1536 to have been about thirty times the present value. The Reverend Dr. Salter kindly allows me to print his views on this difficult question. 'I think you are on the safe side when you multiply by thirty. I put it between thirty and thirty-five. Before the War I put it at twenty. I believe the following were roughly the amounts of wages and salaries in the Middle Ages: a poorish vicarage for an unmarried man was £5; now it could not be much less than £200. A head carpenter, head plumber, head mason, got 5d. to 6d. a day; now £4 to £6 a week; unskilled labour 1d. a day; now 5s. The supper and the dinner of college servants each cost a halfpenny, including bread, beer, meat; now probably 1s. 3d. or 1s. 6d. each meal.'

INDEX

INDEX

INDEX

INDEX

U   305

INDEX

Hereford, Earls of, 34
—— St. Guthlac's Priory, 184
    (Prior, *see* Thomas Bisley)
—— Bishops of (*see* Edward Foxe, John Scory, Thomas Spofford)
—— Cathedral of, 129
Hervey, Master, 37
Hexham Priory, 180
—— John, Abbot of Whitby, 247
Hickling Priory, 79, 81
Hickman, Thurstan, Carthusian monk, 260
Higgins, Margery, nun of Godstow, 225
Higham Priory, 101
—— Gobion, Beds, 294
Hilsey, John, Dominican, later Bishop of Rochester, 232, 233, 240
Hilton, Adam, 294
Hinton Priory, 96 *note*
Hinton St. George, Somerset, 254
Hobbes, Richard, Abbot of Woburn, 178
—— Thomas, Author of *Leviathan*, 274
Hockliffe, Beds, 294
Hodges, Mrs., 109
Hodgkin, John, Austin Friar, later Bishop of Bedford, 236, 240
Holbein, Hans, 171, 172
Holdsworth, Doctor Robert, 33
Holgate, Robert, Master of Gilbertines, later Bishop of Llandaff and Archbishop of York, 182, 249
Holland, Elizabeth, mistress of Duke of Norfolk, 162, 202
—— Sir Thomas, 202
Holme Cultram Abbey, 152
Holy Island Priory, 249
Holywell, Flint, 203
Hooper, John, Cistercian monk, later Bishop of Gloucester, 9, 205, 244
Hopton, John, Dominican, later Bishop of Norwich, 240
Horncastle, Lincs, 159, 160
Horsham St. Faith Priory, 249, 252
    (Prior, *see* John Salisbury)
Horton Monks Priory, 115 *note*
    (Prior, *see* Richard Brysley)
Hospitallers, 97
Houghton, John, Carthusian martyr, 260
Howard family, 288
—— Thomas, 3rd Duke of Norfolk, 9, 12, 16, 21, 52, 57, 115, 154, 161, 163, 164, 171, 193, 204, 256 *note*, 258, 279, 286, 288
—— Thomas, 4th Duke of, 200
—— Duchess of, Elizabeth, wife of 3rd Duke, 56, 162
—— Lord William, 200
—— Queen Katharine, 12
Hubbard, Mrs., 82
Huguenots, 42
Hull, Yorks, 52
—— suffragan bishopric of, 249, 250, 268
Hulton Abbey, 59
Humberstone Abbey, 80
Hunter, Joseph, 281 *note*
Huntingdon Priory, 75 *note*
    (Prior, *see* Hugh Oliver)
Husborne Crawley, Beds, 294
Husee, Sir John, 34
Hussey, Lord, 36, 160
Hyde Abbey, 37, 115, 248, 268

Ingworth, Richard, Dominican, later Bishop of Dover, 228, 233, 234, 240, 241, 243, 244
Injunctions, Episcopal, 74, 87, 91, 208, 212 *note*
—— Royal, 126, 132ff
Ipswich, 49, 103, 110
—— Holy Trinity Priory, 83

Ipswich, Franciscans of, 57, 230
—— Carmelites of, 237
    (Prior, *see* John Bale)
—— Suffragan bishopric of, 249
Ixworth, Thomas, monk of Wymondham, 82

Jackman, Doctor, 87, 88
James I, King, 273
—— John, 102
—— Doctor Montague, 15, 281
Jebb, Professor, 41 *note*
Jenyns, William, Prior of St. Oswald's, Gloucester, later Dean of Gloucester, 184, 252
Jervaulx Abbey, 29, 58, 137, 166, 176
    (Abbot, *see* Adam Sedbergh)
Jervis, John, 208
Jessopp, Doctor Augustus, 15
Jesuits, 11, 285
John, King, 28, 50, 121
Johnson, Doctor Samuel, 16, 54, 114, 275
Jones, Arthur, 204 *note*
Jordan, Isabel, Abbess of Wilton, 68, 211
Joseph, John, Franciscan, chaplain to Cranmer, 236, 238 *note*, 260
—— Michael, 158
—— II, Emperor, 285
Jumièges Abbey, 278

Katharine of Aragon, Queen, 13, 109, 110, 113, 178, 230
Keal, Mrs., nun of Sixhill, 223
Kendall, Lawrence, 199
Kent, Richard, canon of Dunstable, 293, 294
—— Thomas, canon of Dunstable, 294
Ketton, Rutland, 140 *note*
Kidd, Doctor Beresford, 289 *note*
Kimmer Abbey, 249
King, Robert, Abbot of Oseney and Thame, later Bishop of Oxford, 248
Kingsford, C., 227 *note*, 228 *note*
Kingsmill, Morpheta, Abbess of Wherwell, 226
—— Lady, 226
Kingswood Abbey, 140
Kirkby, Edmund, Abbot of Rievaulx, 92, 164, 165
—— Bellars Priory, 78
—— Misperton, Yorks, 165 *note*
—— Ravensworth, Yorks, 165
Kirkham Priory, 49
Kirkstead Abbey, 159, 247 *note*
    (Abbots, *see* Richard Harrison, Nicholas Sutton)
Kittel, Alice, nun of Greenfield, 214
Knaptoft, Leics, 270
Knox, John, 10, 16, 275

Lacock Abbey, 128, 196, 197, 208, 210, 213, 277
    (Abbess, *see* Joan Temmes)
Ladies, influence of, in monasteries, 32, 53, 54, 63, 66, 68, 82, 85 to 88, 91, 93, 109, 122, 125, 135
Lambeth, 118
Lamplieu, Sir John, 29
Lancaster, 167
—— Thomas, Earl of, 23, 47
—— John of Gaunt, Duke of, 446
Lanercost Priory, 50, 51, 154
Langdale, Alban, Prebendary of Chichester, 269
Langdon Abbey, 125, 141, 146
Langland, William, 276
Langley Priory, 209
—— King's, Dominicans of, 219, 224, 230, 233
Lantony Priory, 281
Large, Edward, Franciscan, 238
Lateran Council of 1123, 262
Latimer, Hugh, Bishop of Worcester, 22, 24, 29, 59, 142, 159, 171, 253
—— Lord, 163

INDEX

Missenden Abbey, 35, 87, 88, 217, 253
 (Abbot, *see* John Fox)
 (Jane, Prioress of Legbourne), 217
Monasteries:
 prayers of, 19, 276
 pilgrimages to, 22, 276
 as inns, 25, 278
 as banks, 33
 almsgiving of, 30, 278
 education in, 36ff, 282
 learning in, 41, 138, 280ff
Money values, 296, 297
Monk Bretton Priory, 281
Montalembert, Charles, Comte de, 43
Montague, Anthony, Lord (*see* Browne)
—— Henry, Lord (*see* Pole)
Monteagle, Lord, 34
Montfort, Simon de, 23
More, Sir Thomas, 109, 116, 117, 176, 276
—— William, Prior of Worcester, 42, 73, 135
Morice, Master, 37
Morland, William, monk of Louth Park, 160
Morley, Lord, 174
Morreby, Robert, monk, 150
Morris, Mr., 201
'Mors, Roderick' (*see* Henry Brinklow)
Morton, Thomas, monk of Norwich, 39
Mottisfont Priory, 227, 287
Mountgrace Priory, 117, 163, 268
 (Prior, *see* John Wilson)
Muchelney Abbey, 62
 (Abbot, *see* John Sherborne)
Muller, Professor G. A., 117 *note*, 229 *note*, 264
 note, 276 *note*
Multon, Nicholas, 158
Munday, Thomas, Prior of Bodmin, 198 to 201,
 257, 260, 261
—— Joan, 199
—— John, 199
—— Katharine, 199
Munslow, Richard, Abbot of Winchcombe, 251
 note
Musbury, Devon, 201
Myconius (*see* Oswald Geisshüssler)
Myres, J. N. L., 49 *note*

Napier, H. A., 70 *note*
Necromancy, 35, 232
Naworth Castle, Cumberland, 51
Neapolis, Bishop of (*see* John Draper)
Neath Abbey, 90, 167
Neckham, Roger, monk of Worcester, 135
Netley Abbey, 29, 150
'New learning', 138ff, 148, 159, 162, 190, 192, 217,
 220, 234ff, 253, 259ff, 286ff
Newburgh Priory, 49, 52
Newcastle, St. Bartholomew's Priory, 220
 (Prioress, *see* Agnes Lawson)
Newdigate, Sebastian, Carthusian martyr, 119
Newenham Abbey, Devon, 54, 200, 201
——. Priory, Beds, 33
Newent, Glos, 184
Newington Longeville Priory, 97, 98
Newman, Cardinal, 246
Newminster Abbey, 51
Newport, Essex, 165
Newton, John, Abbot of St. Radegund's, 93
Nichols, J. G., 197 *note*
Nicke (or Nix), Richard, Bishop of Norwich, 75
 note
Nocton Priory, 38
Norfolk, Duke of (*see* Howard, Thomas)
—— Earl of, 51
Northampton, de la Pré Abbey, 127
—— St. Andrew's Priory, 251

Northampton, Austin friars of, 232, 236, 237
 (Prior, *see* John Goodwin)
—— Dominican friars of, 237
—— Franciscan friars of, 239
Northumberland, Earl of (*see* Henry Percy)
—— Duke of (*see* John Dudley)
Norton Abbey, 151, 152, 180
Norwich Priory and Cathedral, 38, 83, 182, 183,
 192, 250 *note*, 254
—— Franciscan friars of, 57
—— Dominican friars of, 231, 242
—— Austin friars of, 236
—— Bishops of, 73, 77, 79, 80, 81, 86, 124, 139,
 208 (*see* John Hopton, Richard Nicke)
—— Dean of (*see* John Salisbury)
—— Richard, monk of, 39
Nostell, or St. Oswald's, Priory, 29, 85
 (Prior, *see* Robert Ferrar)
Nottingham, 64
Numbers of religious, estimates of, 144, 185, 205,
 227, 285
Nun of Kent (*see* Elizabeth Barton)
Nunootham Priory, 210
Nuneaton Priory, 46, 59, 209
Nunnaminster Abbey (*see* Winchester)
Nuns:
 Hospitality and almsgiving of, 205, 206
 Education by, 206
 Pensions and dispensations of, 218ff
 Marriages of, 222ff
 Queen Mary's restoration of, 219, 224
Nyxe, John, canon of Dunstable, 296

Observants, 104, 109, 118, 119, 236
Ochino, Friar Bernard, 236
Offa, King, 50
Offley, Herts, 296
Offwell, Devon, 201
Ogle, Mr., 230
Oliver, George, 31 *note*, 56 *note*, 66 *note*, 153 *note*,
 157 *note*, 189 *note*, 208 *note*, 284 *note*
—— Hugh, Prior of Leicester and later of Hun-
 tingdon, 75, 76
—— Richard, canon of Bodmin, 199
Ormerod, George, 123 *note*
Oseney Abbey, 41, 58, 248 and *note*, 275, 281
Otley, Mrs., formerly Prioress of Legbourne, 217
Oving, Sussex, 295
Oxford:
 Earls of, 48, 49, 58, 181 (*see* John de Vere)
 Maud, Countess of, 53, 66
 Religious Houses and Churches of, 40, 41, 49
 Austin friars of, 49
 Dominican friars of, 234
 Franciscan friars of, 129
 St. Bernard's College, 147
 St. Frideswide's Priory, 103, 104, 151
 St. Mary Magdalene's Church, 148 *note* (*see* also
 under Oseney and Rewley Abbeys)
 University of, 100, 101, 135, 138, 139, 281, 289
 Colleges:
 All Souls, 98
 Brasenose, 99
 Cardinal's or King's, 36, 110
 New College, 49, 97, 98, 127

Padstow, Cornwall, 199
Padua, university of, 130
Paget, Sir William (later Lord), 266, 276
Palmer, Catherine, Abbess of New Sion, 224
—— Roger, canon of Missenden, 263
Palmes, John, 263
Parker, Matthew, Archbishop of Canterbury, 25,
 236, 280, 281
—— William, Abbot of Gloucester, 183 *note*,
 250 *note*

308

INDEX

Rougham, Doctor Edmund, monk of Bury St. Edmunds, 138
Roundell, Richard, Prior of Healaugh Park, 167
Rowland, Thomas, *alias* Pentecost, Abbot of Abingdon, 252
Rowse, A. L., 55 *note*, 197 *note*
Roye, William, observant, 236
Rugge, John, prebendary of Chichester, 176
Runcorn, Cheshire, 151
Russell, John, Earl of Bedford, 220
—— Margaret, Abbess of Tarent, 220
Rutland, Earl of (*see* Thomas Manners)

Sacrilege, History of, 275
Sadoleto, Cardinal, 289
Sadyngton, John, Abbot of Leicester, 85
St. Agatha's Abbey, 31, 48, 157
St. Albans Abbey, 28, 48, 50, 64, 69, 117, 169, 251, 252, 267, 268, 277, 282
  (Abbot, *see* Robert Catton)
St. Asaph, Bishops of, 203, 216, 248 (*see* William Barlow)
St. Benet's Abbey, Norfolk, 35, 40, 82
St. Bettelin, 246
St. Bride, 23
St. Davids, Bishops of (*see* John Delabere, William Barlow)
St. Frideswide's Priory (*see* Oxford)
St. Guthlac's Priory (*see* Hereford)
St. Helen's Priory (*see* London)
St. John, Lady, 230
St. Maur, congregation of, 42
St. Neot's Priory, Hunts, 89
St. Oswald's Priory (*see* Gloucester and Nostell)
St. Osyth's Priory, 136
St. Radegund's Abbey, Kent, 93
  (Abbot, *see* John Newton)
—— Priory (*see* Cambridge)
St. Uncumber, 25
St. Ursula, 127
St. Vincent de Paul, 208
St. Winifred's Well, 203
Salerno, Archbishop of, 289
Salisbury, John, Prior of Horsham St. Faith, later Abbot of Titchfield and Dean of Norwich, 192, 252
—— Robert, Abbot of Valle Crucis, 35
—— Bishops of, 102, 103, 175 (*see* Nicholas Shaxton)
Salley Abbey, 29, 107, 149, 157, 165
  (Abbot, *see* Thomas Bolton)
Salter, Doctor H., 97 *note*, 296
Sampford, John, Abbot of Coggeshall, 181
Sampson, Richard, Bishop of Chichester, 176, 238
Sanders, Thomas, 279
Sandys, Lord, 287
—— Lady Margery, 135
Savage, George, Rector of Davenham, Cheshire, 123
Savine, Professor, 24 *note*, 30, 31, 45, 60 *note*, 287
Sawtry Abbey, 137, 252
Scory, John, Dominican, later Bishop of Rochester, 240, 269
Scott-Thomson, Miss, 178
Scrope family, 50
—— Richard, Archbishop of York, 23, 162
—— of Bolton, John, Lord, 48, 163
Sedbergh, Adam, Abbot of Jervaulx, 166
Segar, Stephen, Abbot of Hayles, 190, 191
Selborne Priory, 30, 31
Selby Abbey, 139
Selling, Kent, 285
Sempringham Priory, 248, 258, 268
  (Prior, *see* Roger Marshall)
Servants of monasteries, 61, 83, 286
Sexten, the King's fool, 27

Seymour, Jane, Queen, 171, 222
—— Sir Edward, later Duke of Somerset, 222, 260
—— Thomas (later Lord), 222
Shaftesbury Abbey, 205 to 207, 218
  (Abbess, *see* Joan Zouche)
—— suffragan bishopric of, 249
Shap Abbey, 89
  (Abbot, *see* Richard Redman)
Sharpe, Doctor Richard, 101
Shaxton, Nicholas, Bishop of Salisbury, 175
Sheen Priory, 90, 98, 267
  (Priory, *see* Henry Man)
—— Anglorum, 267
Shelley, Elizabeth, Abbess of Nunnaminster, 207, 221
Shelton, Sir John, 219
—— Gabrielle, nun of Barking, 219
Sheppey, 215
Sherborne Abbey, 62, 251 *note*, 277
—— John, Abbot of Muchelney, 62
Shere, John, Prior of Launceston, 80
Sherwood Forest, 232
Shrewsbury Abbey, 64, 170
—— suffragan bishopric of, 249
—— Earl of (*see* George Talbot)
Shulbred Priory, 47
Sibton Abbey, 256 *note*
Sion Abbey, 98, 118, 218, 224, 267
Six Articles, Act of, 127, 216, 222, 223, 249, 258
Sixhill Priory, 223
Sleigh, T., 200 *note*
Smart, John, Abbot of Wigmore and Bishop of Pavada, 73, 75
Smithfield fires, 138
Smith, William, Bishop of Lincoln, 99
—— Mrs., of Walsingham, 86, 276
Smythe, William, 160 *note*
Snow, Ellen, Prioress of Elstow, 212
'Sojourners', 106, 166, 206, 209, 231
Somer, Robert, canon of Dunstable, 295
Somerset, Duke of (*see* Sir Edward Seymour)
Southampton, 67
—— observants of, 116
Southpool, Devon, 189
Southwell, Richard, 185, 186
Spalding Priory, 35, 72, 283
Spelman, Sir Henry, 274, 275
Spenser, Doctor Miles, 124
Spofford, Thomas, Bishop of Hereford, 52
Stafford, 246
—— West, Dorset, 200
—— Edward, Duke of Buckingham, 46, 60, 115
—— William, Dominican Prior, 235
Staffordshire, 122
Stalworth, John, canon of Dunstable, 294
Stamford, Lincs, Dominicans of, 235
—— St. George's Church, 235
Stancliff, Peter, 195
Stanley Abbey, 121, 148, 150, 249
—— Walter, monk of Gloucester, 184
—— Isabel, Prioress of Derby, 212
Stapleton, Walter, Bishop of Exeter, 208
Star Chamber, 203, 204
Starkey, Thomas, 118
Stephens, Thomas, Abbot of Beaulieu, 192
Stepney, Middlesex, 259
Sterope, Edward, 102
Stewards of monasteries, 58ff, 197
Stilgo, Thomas, 42, 43
Stixwould Priory, 213
Stoke by Clare, Suffolk, Austin friars of, 236
Stokes, Doctor John, Austin friar, 235, 236
Stokesley, John, Bishop of London, 142
Stone, Friar, 235
Stoneleigh Abbey, 34

INDEX

**PHOENIX
PRESS**

GENERAL EDITORS:
SIMON SCHAMA AND ANTONIA FRASER

Phoenix Press publishes and re-publishes hundreds of the very best new and out of print books about the past. For a free colour catalogue listing more than 500 titles please

telephone: +44 (0) 1903 828 500
fax: +44 (0) 1903 828 802
e-mail: mailorder@lbsltd.co.uk
or visit our website at www.phoenixpress.co.uk

The following books might be of interest to you:

Islam

A Short History

KAREN ARMSTRONG

A vital corrective to the Western stereotype of Islam as an extreme faith. Beginning with the flight of Muhammad from Medina in the seventh century and ending with an assessment of the religion today, Karen Armstrong shows how social justice and compassion have always been central to the Islamic world-view.

Paperback £6.99   244pp + Maps   1 84212 583 4

The Church in the Dark Ages

H. DANIEL-ROPS

The distinguished French academician's history of the Catholic Church in the period 350-1050. We see the Church arising from the ashes of the Roman Empire to its flowering in the heyday of Byzantium; reeling under the onslaughts of Islam and rising again under Charlemagne.

Paperback £14.99   640pp + Maps   1 84212 465 X

The Formation of Christendom
JUDITH HERRIN

Judith Herrin's *tour de force* argues that the 'initial particularity' of Europe can be found between the fourth and the ninth centuries. Her scholarship 'is so exciting: she can convince the reader that the roots of Western distinctiveness really do lead all the way to forgotten Episcopal meetings in small towns in Asia Minor in the fourth century' Michael Ignatieff, *Observer*. 'A civilized and accomplished book' *Economist*.

Paperback £14.99   544pp + 16pp b/w + Maps   1 84212 179 0

Daily Life in Palestine at the Time of Christ
H. DANIEL-ROPS

'The wealth of information in this book about customs, language, habits, clothes, food and all the other features of everyday life will make the reading of the New Testament far more real and vivid' *The Times*.

Paperback £12.99   512pp + 24pp b/w   1 84212 509 5

Churches in the Landscape
RICHARD MORRIS

The author sets out to discover why churches occupy the sites they do, why and how these sites were selected and what this tells us about changing patterns of belief during the last 1,400 years. A radical and rewarding book.

Paperback £14.99   528pp + 16pp b/w + Maps   0 75380 117 5

The Gods of Prehistoric Man
JOHANNES MARINGER

From the ritual cannibalism and sacrificial offerings of primitive man through the Palaeolithic, Mesolithic and Neolithic periods and ending with the religions of pre-history with their cults of the spirits of the dead, this is a general introduction to pre-historic religions derived from the results of excavation.

Paperback £16.99   240pp + 48pp b/w + Line drawings   1 84212 559 1

The Ancient Gods
E.O. JAMES

The development of religion in the Middle East, Mesopotamia, Egypt, the Aegean, Greece, and Asia Minor from prehistoric times to the beginning of the Christian era.

Paperback £14.99   368pp + 48pp b/w   0 75380 810 2

The Dawn and Twilight of Zoroastrianism
RICHARD ZAEHNER

R.C. Zaehner strips away the myth behind Zoroastrianism and its prophet Zarathustra and reveals a monotheistic religion which bore remarkable similarities to Christianity. The first part describes the message of the prophet Zoroaster – his proclamation in a pagan society of one true God and all its ramifications. The second part describes how various Persian rulers attempted to absorb this inheritance into a society which was not yet ready for monotheistic religion.

Paperback £16.99   368pp + 48pp b/w + Line drawings   1 84212 165 0

Napoleon and Wellington
ANDREW ROBERTS

Award-winning historian Andrew Roberts' original and highly revisionist account of the relationship between the two giants of their age. 'Well written and well organised, his study of the relationship between the emperor and the Duke of Wellington is as entertaining as it is instructive, and is original and judicious both as military and personal history' Christopher Hibbert, *Sunday Times*

Paperback £9.99   352pp + 16pp col. b/w   1 84212 480 3

Prince of Princes
The Life of Potemkin
SIMON SEBAG MONTEFIORE

'A headlong gallop of a read' said Antony Beevor about this massive new biography of Catherine the Great's lover and co-ruler; conqueror of the Ukraine and Crimea. Exhaustively researched and beautifully written. 'Magnificent' *Independent*, 'Superb', *Daily Telegraph*, 'Splendidly written' *Sunday Telegraph*, 'This well researched and highly ambitious biography has succeeded triumphantly in re-creating the life of an extraordinary man' Antony Beevor, *Sunday Times*. Shortlisted for the Duff Cooper Memorial Prize and the Samuel Johnson Prize.

Paperback £9.99   656pp + 24pp col. b/w   1 84212 438 2

Dr Johnson's London
LIZA PICARD

The first paperback edition of this celebrated account of London from 1740-1770. With erudition and wit, Liza Picard extracts nuggets from all sorts of contemporary records to expose the substance of everyday life in the biggest city in Europe – houses and coffee-houses, climbing boys and gardens, medicine, toothpaste and gin, sex, food, manners, etiquette, crime and punishment; the practical realities of everyday life in the mid 18th century.

Paperback £9.99   384pp + 32pp col. b/w   1 84212 437 4

Empire
The British Imperial Experience From 1765 to the Present
DENIS JUDD

'Wonderfully ambitious . . . a pungent and attractive survey of the British Empire from 1765 to the present.' *London Review of Books*, 'An indispensable one-volume source.' John Keegan

Paperback £14.99   544pp + 24pp b/w + Maps   1 84212 498 6

Swords Around a Throne
Napoleon's Grande Armée
JOHN R. ELTING

'A masterpiece: quite simply the best I have ever read on this challenging subject' David Chandler, author of *Campaigns of Napoleon*. 'It is superb reading, by turns anecdotal, with narrative segments that roll like cavalry charges. Elting is a master historian' Owen Connelly, President, Society for French Historical Studies.

Paperback £15.99   784pp + 33pp b/w   0 75380 219 8

Napoleon and Josephine
An Improbable Marriage
EVANGELINE BRUCE

A compelling account of an 'improbable marriage'. 'Evangeline Bruce has quite simply given us the most illuminating addition to history to appear for many years, and the most exciting' Patrick Leigh Fermor, *Spectator*. 'Magnificent' *Daily Mail*. 'Far and away the best book that came my way in the past year . . .' Alastair Forbes, *Daily Telegraph*

Paperback £9.99   576pp + 32pp b/w   1 85799 489 2

The Rise of the Greeks
MICHAEL GRANT

The irrepressible Michael Grant takes the reader on an intriguing detective trail to understand the world of the early Greeks. With fluency and scholarship he shows how the extraordinary epoch between 1000 and 495 BC was one of the most creative in history.

Paperback £12.99   416pp + 16pp b/w + Maps   1 84212 265 7

The Classical Greeks
MICHAEL GRANT

The Golden Age of ancient Greek city-state civilization lasted from 490 to 336 BC, the period between the first wars against Persia and Carthage and the accession of Alexander the Great. Never has there been such a multiplication of talents and genius within so limited a period and Michael Grant captures this astonishing civilization at the height of its powers.

Paperback £12.99   352pp + 16pp b/w   1 84212 447 1

The Fall of the Roman Empire
MICHAEL GRANT

The fall of the western Roman empire was one of the most significant transformations throughout the whole of human history. Michael Grant explores the past with clarity and depth.

Paperback £12.99   256pp   1 85799 975 4

The Muslim Discovery of Europe
BERNARD LEWIS

A lively exploration of the sources and nature of Muslim knowledge of the West. 'No one writes about Muslim history with greater authority, or intelligence, or literary charm than Professor Bernard Lewis.' Hugh Trevor-Roper, *Sunday Times*

Paperback £14.99   352pp + 28pp b/w   1 84212 195 2

The Age of Arthur
JOHN MORRIS

A history of the British Isles from 350 to 650, 'the starting point of future British history'. 'From the resources of a mind vastly learned in the documents of the Arthurian age, John Morris has created more than the most devoted of Arthurian enthusiasts could have hoped for . . . Winston Churchill would have loved this book.' *TLS*

Paperback £14.99   684pp + Maps   1 84212 477 3

Londinium
JOHN MORRIS

The authoritative account of earliest London from pre-Roman Britain to the Age of Arthur, examining subjects as diverse as food, religion, politics and sport.

Paperback £14.99   400pp + 8pp b/w   0 75380 660 6

The Birth of the Modern
World Society 1815-1830
PAUL JOHNSON

An examination of how the matrix of the modern world was formed. 'A work of this kind stands or falls . . . on the richness of its material, the scope of its coverage, the intelligence of its arguments, and on all these counts this book not merely stands, but towers above any other history of the period.' *Sunday Telegraph*

Paperback £11.99   1120pp   1 85799 366 7

Collision of Empires
Britain in Three World Wars 1793-1945
A.D. HARVEY

'Delightfully opinionated, well-documented insights into the three wars which constituted the rise, stagger and fall of the British Empire.' Andrew Roberts, *The Times*

Paperback £14.99   800pp   1 85799 125 7

History of the Dutch-Speaking Peoples 1555-1648
PIETER GEYL

An unforgettable portrait of Dutch life during the sixteenth and seventeenth centuries, this new paperback edition combines the two volumes *The Revolt of the Netherlands 1555-1609* and *The Netherlands in the Seventeenth Century 1609-1648* of Pieter Geyl's magnificent History.

Paperback £16.99   640pp + Maps   1 84212 225 8

The European Powers 1900-1945
MARTIN GILBERT

Martin Gilbert analyses the dramatic changes that altered the face of Europe from the strong and prosperous European Empires of 1900 to a new order reeling from the effect of two wasteful wars with influence transferred to the United States and the Soviet Union.

Paperback £12.99   316pp + 16pp b/w + Maps   1 84212 216 9

The Discoverers
A History of Man's Search to Know the World and Himself
DANIEL J. BOORSTIN

This Pulitzer Prize-winning saga of human discovery, the first in the trilogy, is the story of countless Columbuses. 'A new and fascinating approach to history . . . rich in unknowns and surprises' Barbara Tuchman. 'A ravishing book . . . [with] a verve, an audacity and a grasp of every sort of knowledge that is outrageous and wonderful . . . I can't think of any other living writer who could have attempted, let alone accomplished it.' Alistair Cooke, 'An adventure story . . . great good fun to read.' *New York Times*

Paperback £16.99   768pp   1 84212 227 4

The Creators
A History of Heroes of the Imagination
DANIEL J. BOORSTIN

A panoramic yet minutely detailed history of the arts from Homer
and Giotto to Picasso and Virginia Woolf encompassing 3,000 years
of academic and intellectual invention. 'He combines lively opinion
and a distinguished historian's erudition, with a first-class journalist's
clarity and eye for the revealing anecdote . . . Irresistible.' *USA Today*

Paperback £16.99   832pp   1 84212 229 0

The Seekers
The Story of Man's Continuing Quest to Understand his World
DANIEL J. BOORSTIN

The final volume in the trilogy looks at the great men in history who
sought meaning and purpose in our existence from Moses, Plato and
Socrates through to Marx, Toynbee, Carlyle and Einstein. 'This
completion of the trilogy on humanity's quest for understanding
confirms Boorstin's rank as one of the giants of 20th century
American scholarship.' George F. Will

Paperback £12.99   320pp   1 84212 228 2